THE BRAND FASCINATION SYSTEM

ADVANTAGE + TACTIC = **YOUR MESSAGE**

 In / Pa
BOLD,
ARTISTIC,
UNORTHODOX

 In / Po
PIONEERING,
IRREVERENT,
ENTREPRENEURIAL

 In / Pr
ELITE,
CUTTING-EDGE,
PROGRESSIVE

 In
FLEXIBL
DELIBER
THOUGHT

 Pa / In
SOCIAL,
ENERGIZING,
OUT OF THE BOX

 Pa / Po
DYNAMIC,
INCLUSIVE,
ENGAGING

 Pa / Pr
STYLISH,
EXPRESSIVE,
EMO. INTELLIGENT

 Pa / Tr
LOYAL,
SINCERE,
NURTURING

 Pa / My
DISCERNING,
PERCEPTIVE,
CONSIDERATE

 Pa / AI
ATTENTIVE,
DEDICATED,
EFFICIENT

 Po / In
INVENTIVE,
UNTRADITIONAL,
SELF-PROPELLED

 Po / Pa
SPIRITED,
MOTIVATING,
COMPELLING

 Po / Pr
AMBITIOUS,
FOCUSED,
CONFIDENT

 Po / Tr
PROMINENT,
GENUINE,
SURE-FOOTED

 Po / My
INTENSE,
METHODICAL,
SELF-RELIANT

 Po / AI
PROACTIVE,
CAUTIONARY,
STRONG WILLED

 Pr / In
ORIGINAL,
ENTERPRISING,
FWD-THINKING

 Pr / Pa
INSIGHTFUL,
DISTINGUISHED,
IN THE KNOW

 Pr / Po
RESPECTED,
COMPETITIVE,
RESULTS ORIENTED

 Pr / Tr
CLASSIC,
ESTABLISHED,
BEST IN CLASS

 Pr / My
SKILLFUL,
RESTRAINED,
POLISHED

 Pr / AI
DISCIPLINED,
SYSTEMATIC,
INTELLECTUAL

 Tr / In
CURIOUS,
ADAPTABLE,
OPEN-MINDED

 Tr / Pa
DEPENDABLE,
TRUSTWORTHY,
APPROACHABLE

 Tr / Po
STABLE,
DIGNIFIED,
HARDWORKING

 Tr / Pr
SUBTLE,
CAPABLE,
LEVELHEADED

 Tr / My
ANALYTICAL,
PROTECTIVE,
PURPOSEFUL

 Tr / AI
PREPARED,
PRINCIPLED,
CONSCIENTIOUS

 My / In
NIMBLE,
UNASSUMING,
INDEPENDENT

 My / Pa
TACTFUL,
MINDFUL,
SELF-SUFFICIENT

 My / Po
REALISTIC,
INTENTIONAL,
TO THE POINT

 My / Pr
ASTUTE,
ELEGANT,
DISCREET

 My / Tr
ASSURED,
UNRUFFLED,
OBSERVANT

 My / AI
ON TARGET,
REASONED,
PRAGMATIC

 AI / In
JUDICIOUS,
STRATEGIC,
FINE-TUNED

 AI / Pa
PRACTICAL,
ORGANIZED,
CONSTRUCTIVE,

 AI / Po
DECISIVE,
TIRELESS,
FORTHRIGHT

 AI / Pr
SKILLED,
DETAILED,
PRODUCTIVE

 AI / Tr
STEADFAST,
COMPOSED,
STRUCTURED

 AI / My
ACCURATE,
CLEAR-CUT,
METICULOUS

Created by **Sally Hogshead**.   Discover more at **BrandFascination.com**.   email: **hello@HowToFascinate.com**.

FASCINATE
REVISED *and* UPDATED

FASCINATE
REVISED *and* UPDATED

How to Make Your Brand
Impossible to Resist

SALLY HOGSHEAD

HARPER
BUSINESS

An Imprint of HarperCollins*Publishers*

HarperCollins books may be purchased for educational, business, or sales promotional use. For information, please e-mail the Special Markets Department at SPsales@harpercollins.com.

Originally published as *Fascinate* in a different form in 2010 by Harper Business, an imprint of HarperCollins Publishers.

REVISED EDITION

Art by Emily Johnson and Rosemary Miller

Endpaper illustration by Prescott Perez-Fox

Library of Congress Cataloging-in-Publication Data has been applied for.

ISBN 978-0-06-220648-0

16 17 18 19 20   OV/RRD   10 9 8 7 6 5 4 3 2

In my research, I learned that 96% of parents find their own children fascinating. I'm no exception. This book is dedicated to our eight children: Ian, Gunnar, Max, Lura, Karli, Isabelle, Quinton, and Asher. You are 110% fascinating.

Contents

PART II: THE SEVEN FASCINATION ADVANTAGES
How to Make Your Brand Impossible to Resist

PART III: TACTICS
A Practical System to Customize Your Message

Introducing This Revised and Updated Edition

The Black Magic of Branding

I entered the lobby of TBWA advertising agency on Madison Avenue wearing my new $19.95 white vinyl pumps, my unruly hair gelled back into a bow. It was the summer of 1991, two weeks after my college graduation.

TBWA had recently debuted the iconic Absolut Vodka campaign and was now polishing its fame to blinding perfection. Entering the all-white lobby made most people feel suddenly self-conscious, acutely aware of some otherwise irrelevant detail, such as the fact that the dry cleaner's seamstress had recently resewn a button with a slightly off-color thread.

Yet on the first day of my unpaid summer internship, walking into that lobby, I felt no intimidation whatsoever. Not because I possessed that same unattainable cool, but quite the opposite. I was too clueless even to have a clue of how clueless I was.

My first week at my internship, I heard a rumor that the creative department's staff locked their file drawers at night. Why? So no one could steal their ideas. This intrigued me greatly. What kind of intellectual bullion could possibly fill those files? These same employees casually left personal valuables such as watches and cameras on their desks at night, yet neurotically locked their file drawers? Whatever lay inside those OfficeMax treasure chests, I wanted some of it.

At that early stage of my career, the creative process seemed supernatural to me. How could anyone possibly distill the intricacies of a company, then hone them into an idea sharp enough to cut through people's natural resistance, into their hearts and their brains, ultimately connecting with the magical decision-making hot button that decides which toothpaste or hotel room or politician to choose? I had no idea how a plain, dull fact could metamorphose into a message with the power to change behaviors and beliefs. It seemed like black magic. The alchemy of golden ideas.

Over the course of the summer, I learned (while fetching coffee) why writers and art directors kept their ideas under lock and key. Those scribbles and words could perform witchcraft. Even crumpled cocktail napkins might contain exactly the right doodle to transform struggling companies into market champions. Fascinating ideas could generate hundreds of millions of dollars for the client, realign entire product categories, and become a pop culture phenomenon—not to mention skyrocketing the careers of those behind them.

I longed to write something so valuable that it had to be locked away at night. But I didn't know how.

After my internship, I was hired as a junior copywriter at the legendary agency Wieden + Kennedy. It was a dream job, and I felt the way a young programmer might feel to be hired at the headquarters of Google. I couldn't wait to finally see for myself how to perform this witchcraft I'd witnessed in my internship. With stars in my eyes and a skip in my step, I moved to their new office in Philadelphia, ready to create ads for brands such as Nike.

My first day of this new job, still walking on air, I returned to the office after a cheese steak lunch. Entering the lobby, I saw the entire staff standing in a circle. "Wow," I trilled to myself, "agency life is so social!" Turns out, this wasn't a social event. It was a layoff. The office was closing after the loss of a key client.

Well, it'd been a great three hours.

I moved back home, still wondering how to create million-dollar ideas.

Marshall McLuhan wrote, "Historians and archaeologists will one day discover that the ads of our time are the richest and most faithful daily reflections any society ever made of its whole range of activities." But how were these ads created, exactly? While searching for my next job, at night I studied books about advertising. I pored over famous ads, trying to decode the thinking process behind them, hoping to one day wave a wand and make ideas appear.

My favorite advertising copywriter was Luke Sullivan, in Minneapolis. His saber-toothed wit and strategic elegance impressed me greatly. One day my phone rang and my jaw dropped. "Sally, this is Luke Sullivan. Come work at my agency." Off I moved, eager to learn this mysterious thing called branding.*

While it snowed outside, I thrived inside the agency, learning from some of the most award-winning professionals in the field. Each department within an agency specializes in a different type of thought process, from research and strategy to media and design. I adored them all. By the time those cryogenic pumpkins emerged from the melting ice in April, still smiling, my training was well under way.

In my mid-twenties, I became one of the most award-winning copywriters in the United States. My career accelerated from copywriter to creative director, from New York to Los Angeles, from small assignments to global campaigns.

If you watch *Mad Men*, you know that ad agencies can seem like sexy, tempestuous workplaces, filled with adrenaline and

---

* The move to Minneapolis was easy, because as a Florida native, I didn't even own a winter coat. Within days of my arrival, a blizzard hit, bringing a -60 wind chill. This was just before Halloween, so for months, hundreds of pumpkins remained frozen in a bizarre orange-spotted Ice Age.

Ping-Pong tables. Traditional agencies can deliver amazingly customized service and handholding, and any type of marketing you can think of. On the downside, they're extremely expensive for clients (for a single color copy, a client might be billed thirty dollars), and brutally intense for the staff. I've seen employees bring a couch into their office for all-nighters.

I wanted something different. At age twenty-seven, I opened my own ad agency in L.A. It was a dizzying time to be in advertising, right at the cusp of the dot-com bubble. Entrepreneurs who had never turned a profit had money to burn.

Instead of buying into the hype, my agency cofounder and I wanted to create a new breed of advertising, less traditional and more unexpected. Unlike the fabled agencies I'd worked in before, which had impressive lobbies and catered lunches, we wanted to be a true start-up. Yet what we lacked in marble washrooms, we made up for in audacity.

Apple Computers famously began as a start-up in a garage. Our building was also a garage—a converted mechanic's garage on Electric Avenue in Venice Beach, California. We opened our doors in 1997 (or should I say, "rolled up our doors"). It was a notoriously sketchy area, and occasionally during conference calls, clients might ask if that was gunfire they had heard on speakerphone. The neighborhood ice cream truck driver didn't coast merrily along; he floored it to avoid getting caught.* Every day was an adventure, and we loved every minute.

We attracted a certain breed of client, those who wanted edgy, provocative ways to get people buzzing. Many of these clients didn't have huge budgets, and that was fine by me. Layers of bureauracracy suffocate creativity.

---

* Instead of ignoring this polarizing location, we showcased it. To introduce ourselves to prospective clients, we mailed out bright yellow rearview mirror hang-tags that said, *"Please don't slash my tires. I'm visiting the agency."* Controversial? Yes. Effective? Absolutely. This simple piece of direct mail brought many of our first clients.

Don't get me wrong—who doesn't love meetings that begin with ahi tuna or a frothy cappuccino? Yet all that expense often comes at the cost of big ideas.

You can't stand out if you're trying to blend in.

Hogsworth, Hogsbreath, Hogshead

It's probably not a coincidence that I gravitated to polarizing ideas. I was born with a polarizing last name. I learned the value of standing out. Even today, when I check into hotels, clerks sometimes think it is a stage name.

A few years after surviving the 'hood of Venice Beach, I went on to open a consultancy, which I named 62 Gallons.* Soon I was working with Nikon, BMW, Rolex, Jaguar, Mike's Hard Lemonade, and Target. I often worked under an NDA (a non-disclosure agreement) so that the client wouldn't know that the idea hadn't come from within the agency's walls. It was a carousel of brainstorming and rainmaking.

On Monday morning I might be in Manhattan creating the name for a new top-secret Pepsi product. Monday afternoon I'd take a car over to the Cole Haan offices to create print ads for a new shoe line. I'd jump on a plane to Aflac headquarters in Columbus, Georgia, to update the duck's image. Before returning home, I might stop in Detroit to work with Ford on next year's campaign, or help develop ideas on a pitch for Johnson & Johnson. I was crafting a strategic brief for American Express one day, and writing taglines for Godiva the next.

Mental Cross-Training

That variety might sound confusing, but for me, it was an era of insight. Each agency has its own form of black magic. Each guards

---

* A "hogshead" is a wooden barrel that holds 62 gallons of liquid. When people refuse to believe that this is my real name, I hand them my business card. In small type, it says: *"A hogshead is a barrel that holds 62 gallons. So what's your last name, smartass?"*

its secrets jealously. And each has perfected a different type of specialty.

Imagine being a chef, and having the opportunity to tour the kitchens of five-star restaurants, studying the local ingredients and unique recipes of each. Or imagine an automotive engineer working at a different car manufacturer each week, from Toyota to Tesla, learning how each car is precisely engineered to optimize gas mileage or technology. It was like being a clothing designer with insider access to the top fashion houses, learning how each one crafts its creations, from sketching and sewing, from couture to catwalks.

By working in and among and between world-class teams, I could combine different methodologies for new combinations. I didn't have to adhere to a fixed set of rules, and handpicked the best of each. Along the way I found ways to bypass the usual steps, jumping straight to the end game.

Speed is a terrific competitive advantage. Everyone needs better ideas, faster. By solving problems in a matter of hours, in my thirties, I was one of the most highly paid brand experts in the country.

Weirdly, I didn't really know my own creative process. It was like a party trick, an odd but convenient intuition. Some people can instantly count cards during a poker game, others can solve a Rubik's Cube puzzle in under a minute. My party trick was branding.

An Algorithm for Branding

At the start of my career, I had to fumble a lot of bad ideas to arrive at a decent one. Yet my cross-training showed me an algorithm.

An "algorithm" is a formula to solve a problem with predictable steps. Computers use algorithms to run elaborate programs. People use algorithms to decipher encrypted military codes. Algorithms improve your odds of getting the "right" answer.

Without a system, creating a good idea is a hit-or-miss process. Blank pieces of paper become evil things. They seem so innocent at first, a virginal white canvas. As the pressure to create an idea builds, that blank piece of paper will stare you in the face, smirking, taunting you to write something brilliant. What will you say? How will you say it? What words will you use? I'll show you what to say, and how to say it. Instead of feeling paralyzed, you will quickly get in your groove and let the ideas flow. Soon, that blank piece of paper won't be so blank anymore.

If you have a template for good ideas, then creativity becomes a democracy. Anyone can have access to smart communication, even without a marketing department or years of training.

Democratic Design

Ikea's business model is as quirky as its furniture. The company believes that good design shouldn't be reserved for the elite; instead, it markets good design for the masses. Each piece of furniture is a collaboration between the company and the consumer. In exchange for assembling the furniture yourself, you get better design at a lower price. Ikea calls this "democratic design."

A replicable process for ideas makes it possible to have "democratic branding." Anyone can develop good ideas. I want to bring branding out of the ivory tower and into the trenches.

Most businesses have limited time or money, but that doesn't mean they can't create effective and engaging messages. Just as you no longer need a travel agent to book your cruise, or a trip to the doctor to learn the symptoms of a common cold, you no longer need a marketer to do marketing.

Marketing for Non-Marketers

If it were easy to create a brand message, then anyone could do it.

And if anyone could build a brand, then branding experts would be out of business.

Here's why: If a process is confusing and terribly difficult, only a few exquisitely talented minds do it. That's why many agencies cultivate an intimidating image, hotbeds of new and exciting trends. Brand development usually requires months of research, development, and testing. The process is not for the faint of heart or the low of budget.

Someone coached me that when presenting ideas to a client, it should be just one idea, so that it would be one of a kind. Like a precious jewel sitting atop a black velvet cushion. By doing so, it would feel more rare and unreplicable.

I believe that's backward. Brands live inside communities, not corporations. Your brand lives inside conversations and aspirations. A brand lives in workplaces and schools. Inside homes and dinner table conversations. Brands aren't static; they are living, breathing things that organically change and evolve as new people join the conversation.

Your brand won't shatter like your grandmother's brittle china doll. Don't keep your brand high on the shelf, out of reach. Hold your brand, push it, stretch it, and see how far it can go. A brand shouldn't live under lock and key, hidden away at night. Quite the opposite. It should unite people, giving them a shared sense of ownership. Don't just give consumers a better option to purchase . . . give them a better perspective on themselves and their world.

How the World Sees You (and Your Brand)

If you're a brand, it doesn't matter how you see your consumers; it matters how your consumers see *you*.

Corporations don't create brands. People do.

The people inside your company are also the keepers of your brand. An outside party won't know the culture and spirit and nuances like your team. You might not have a dedicated marketing department, and that's okay.

But what if the branding process could be open source, accessible to anyone?

Nobody knows your brand like *you*. You just need a template to follow. Or a hack.

Branding Hacks

You've probably heard of "life hacks"—clever shortcuts that allow you to save time, money, or hassle. Life hacks might reveal how to sneak more green vegetables into your kids' meals, or how to relax more quickly to fall asleep. A productivity hack might show you how to speed-read. And the author Tim Ferriss once described a "sport hack," in which he supposedly hacked the national Chinese kickboxing championship by winning with only a few weeks of training. Josh Linkner, venture capitalist and entrepreneur, describes hacking this way: "Putting motives aside, the act of hacking requires tremendous creativity. A hack is an innovative and unorthodox way to crack big problems."

So what about marketing? Can we "hack" that process?

What if branding could be open source, accessible to anyone?

It can be. It should be. You can do this. You can build your brand. You *should* build your brand. In fact, if you want to compete in a crowded and competitive marketplace, you must.

And you don't need an ad agency.

Life Beyond the Ad Agency

I loved being in advertising. Yet ad agency life is not one that mixes well with motherhood.* I left the jet-setting world of advertising to be closer to my family, as an author.

---

* In ad agencies, you might hear one account executive say to another, "Relax, it's not brain surgery." Yet when publications list the most stressful jobs, advertising executive and brain surgeon top the list. What polar opposites! I once heard this: one surgeon says to another, "Relax, it's not advertising."

The Original *Fascinate*

My book *Fascinate* was published in 2010, and in that book I explored how our brains become captivated by certain people and ideas. I outlined the seven ways in which brands fascinate us. I gave the *why*, but not the *how*. The truth is, I didn't yet know all the steps.

Now, here we are with the revised edition of *Fascinate*. Inside these pages, you might recognize a few of my favorite stories. This is not a small revision; as my editors can attest, it's a major overhaul. More major, in fact, than I think any of us realized. We ripped the entire book apart and rebuilt it to be a fascinatingly practical guide.*

While the original *Fascinate* hinted what my branding algorithm woud one day become, the actual process was fuzzy and intuitive. Now I've spelled it out.

This Book in Your Hands

- *New stories and action steps*: Over 60% of the content is completely new, with fresh case studies and examples.
- *Brand Fascination Profile*: We built an algorithm (literally) so that you can measure your own product or service, to measure your advantages. Get your brand profile at <u>BrandFascination.com</u>.
- *TurboBranding*: My favorite difference in this new edition is the step-by-step process in parts III and IV, which give you a blazingly fast way to create brand messages in about an hour. I believe it's your fastest, easiest way to create a fascinating brand message.

---

* This revised version of *Fascinate* took longer to write than the original book itself: three (very, very long) years.

Is This Book for You?

You might be a small business owner without an in-house marketing person. You might be a midsized business, looking for a faster, more efficient system. Or an entrepreneur, looking for a way to differentiate in the marketplace. This book is for you.

You might work inside an ad agency, PR firm, or other type of communication company. You might feel stuck on an assignment, and need a burst of inspiration. You might work within a marketing department of a global corporation, and want a better way to position your products.

You might be a coach or adviser, wanting to apply the exact steps in this book for a working session with your team or clients. You might be a nonprofit looking for ways to get a message across without spending dollars. In fact, you might have no experience with branding, or even zero confidence in your creativity. No problem.

You just may be curious to find new ways to fascinate people in daily life. Great. Welcome. You're in the right place.

A sneak peek at what's coming up in the next pages:

Part I explores how and why your brain becomes fascinated.
Part II reveals the seven Advantages, and how they create
    a state of intense focus.
Part III gives a practical system to customize any message,
    with tactics.
Part IV shows the five-step action plan for you and your
    team to get started right away.

Yes, branding *is* mysterious. It *is* fascinating. It *is* a form of witchcraft.

Yet there are patterns to the process. Once you have the patterns, you can bring it to life.

I'll do the black magic.

Then, I'll hand you the wand.

FASCINATE
REVISED *and* UPDATED

The Origin of Fascination Witchcraft

A look inside your brain: neurology, biology, history,
and a two-thousand-year-old word that reveals why
you can't market the same way you did yesterday.

Little-Known Secrets of Marketing Black Magic

More weight!" cried the old man, begging to be crushed more quickly. "More weight!" It was the summer of 1692, in Salem Village, Massachusetts. The old man's ribs snapped one by one, in sickening succession, each audible to the hundreds of townsfolk encircling his execution. But his pleas were answered instead with the same painfully slow addition of stones upon his chest.

His crime? Giles Corey had been accused of "fascination." Under his spell, the townspeople were said to have became hostage to his thoughts, losing the ability to think rationally or to protest.

Yet Corey refused to confess to being a warlock. For two days, six burly men lifted heavy stones and set them onto his chest and stomach. Still he said nothing, asking only for more weight to speed his death. The sheriff stood over him, impatiently waiting for a confession and occasionally using his cane to push the old man's tongue back inside his mouth. Then at last, Corey was silenced by the final stone dropping upon his breast.*

The concept of fascination didn't begin with Giles Corey in Salem Village. Throughout cultures, across continents, since the birth of civilization itself, people have studied the ways in which fascination spellbinds us, hypnotizes us, captivates us with black magic.

The word "fascinate" comes from the Latin *fascinare*, "to bewitch or hold captive so others are powerless to resist."

The word "fascination" comes from the ancient Latin *fascinare*, "to bewitch." All around the world, ancient cultures were fascinated with fascination. The Romans believed it was an evil curse, and for protection worshipped one of the earliest Latin divinities: Fascinus, the god of fascination. Fascinus was worshipped by "vestal virgins" (young girls selected to remain virgins for thirty years or else be buried alive), and Roman children wore phallic-shaped amulet necklaces to symbolize him.

In Mesopotamia, Persians believed fascination could cause deadly maladies. In Istanbul, citizens painted passages from the Koran upon their houses to defend their families from the spell of fascination's evil eye. Fortunately, by 280 B.C., Greece's first pastoral poet, Theocritus, seemed to have found a safeguard: an old woman's spit. During the Renaissance, the bookshelves of Europe were filled with weighty tomes on the subject. *De Fascino* defined fascination as "an open covenant with Satan . . . witchcraft of the eyes, or words . . . to so compel men that they are no longer free, nor of sane understanding."

Years later, *Tractatus de Fascinatione* warned against lounging in bed too late in the morning wearing nightcaps (yes, nightcaps), or

---

* Good news: Massachusetts no longer issues death sentences on charges of fascination.

breaking a religious fast on green peas (yes, green peas). How to prevent and cure? In many cases, the remedy seems almost worse than the disease: the skin of a hyena's forehead, dust in which a mule had rolled, and a broth stewed from the ashes of a hangman's rope. Not exactly goods you could pick up on an afternoon Costco run. In the absence of hyena forehead skin, it seems one could also lick the skin of a child's forehead.

If all that sounds like quackery, let's consult a doctor with whom you might be more familiar: Sigmund Freud. In 1921, Freud labeled the relationship between a therapist and a patient as "fascination," a form of hypnosis. He went on to describe romantic love as a state in which an individual becomes so submissively engrossed in his object of "fascination" that he becomes hypnotized, losing his critical faculties, in "bondage of love."

Freud, apparently, wasn't the only one comparing fascination with hypnosis. The 1911 edition of the *Encyclopaedia Britannica* describes fascination as a "hypnotic condition, marked by muscular contraction, but with consciousness and power of remembrance." Even our modern *Webster's Dictionary* sounds a bit sinister in comparing fascination to witchcraft: "bewitching, or enchanting . . . the exercise of a powerful or irresistible influence on the affections or passions; unseen, inexplicable influence."

Yet as we'll see, the ability to fascinate isn't witchcraft or hypnotism. And it doesn't come from wearing nightcaps or eating green peas. It is a tool. Rather than something to be feared, it is a discipline to be mastered.

The Most Fascinating Option Wins

Until now, the act of fascinating others has been an unpredictable occurrence, a product of luck or timing or mysticism, rather than an ability to be directed at will. But in the pages of this book, using both art and science, we'll clear up the mystery. Along the way, we'll uncover what fascinates people, and why it fascinates them. We'll hear from leading experts in psychology, evolutionary biology, neurology, and other -ologies, all shaken and served with a slice of pop culture. We'll point to marketing, but this book isn't just for marketers. Marketing is just a metaphor for the modern world.

Every day, in every relationship, you're "marketing" your ideas to be heard. You want clients to hire you, or customers to recommend you. You want your dad to visit, or your dog to fetch. Your influence will be measured by your ability to fascinate.

Now that we've established that fascination must precede action, the question becomes how to harness this instinctive force. If you master the forces that influence human behavior, you win. You can win bigger budgets, more time, better relationships, greater admiration, deeper trust.

But if you fail to attract and spellbind people, you will lose the battle. It's that simple. As a business, if you can't persuade customers to act, you might as well donate your entire marketing budget to charity.

Is your message provoking strong and immediate emotional reactions? Is it creating advocates and inciting conversation? Are you forcing competitors to realign? If so, you're already flirting with marketing's darker arts. The ancient Romans understood the fearsome force of fascination. But they didn't know how to strategically and methodically use it to their advantage.

In fact, fascination is a positive force of attraction that allows you to make sure your message is heard and remembered. By the end of this book, you'll know how to bewitch a roomful of skeptical sales managers. You'll turn ordinary parts of your business into irresistible hooks to capture your ideal customers. Your words will become more memorable, your conversations more persuasive, your customers more engaged, and your sales more numerous. And you, my friend, can apply these same principles to attract and spellbind the people around you. Let's start by understanding what exactly "fascination" means, in the truest sense.

You won't even need any vestal virgins.

The Boy and the Chandeliers

Watching the boy, you might assume he was either daydreaming or bored. But actually the opposite was true. He was coming alive. Pulse accelerating, pupils dilating, sweat trickling, he stared at the iron chandeliers overhead. Suspended by chains from the ceiling, these chandeliers swung in graceful arcs after their wax candles were lit. The boy watched, hypnotized. He realized something: the chandeliers took an equal number of heartbeats to complete each arc, every single time, whether that arc was big or small. This boy wasn't merely "interested" in the swaying chandeliers. He wasn't just "paying attention" to them. He was *fascinated* by them, and their movement. They swung back and forth. Back and forth. Like a pendulum.

It was during this moment of fascination in the Pisa Cathedral that the seventeen-year-old Galileo Galilei unlocked the most basic rhythm in the universe: isochronism, a conceptual leap in physics that soon led to his invention of the pendulum clock, which led to modern timekeeping.

Even if you haven't invented timekeeping, you've experienced this spellbinding focus. It's when you become lost in a moment, losing track of time and the world around you, completely focused on a person or a message. When you fascinate other people, not only do they focus on you and your message, but they're also more likely to believe, care about, and retell your message.

Will the Real Fascination Please Stand Up?

The word "fascination" gets tossed around so often in conversation that it's lost its former magnificence. We say that something is "fascinating" when we more often mean "interesting" or "attention getting," using the same hyperbole as when describing a tennis match as "awesome" or a matinee movie as "incredible." In these latter examples, we don't actually mean that the tennis game inspired awe or that the movie was difficult to believe. Similarly, "fascination" is far more intense than its paler cousins "interest" or "attention." Paying attention is disciplined, rational, and voluntary—an entirely self-directed act—whereas fascination is consuming, urgent, uncivilized . . . overall, a state of affairs that makes "attention" look rather prudish by comparison, a schoolmarm loudly whacking the ruler upon her desk for control.

The Kelton Study of Fascination

To understand why we become fascinated, and how we fascinate others, we'll delve into the results from the first in-depth national marketing survey of fascination. Developed and executed specifically for this book, the Kelton Study of Fascination examined more than a thousand people around the United States from a broad range of ages, industries, and professional levels. Our research found that people want to *be fascinated*, and even more so, that they want to *be fascinating*.

> Two ways this applies to your branding:
> • How can you help customers feel more *fascinating* to others? Rather than putting all your focus on fascinating your customers . . . help them feel more fascinating. People are willing to pay almost a week's salary to be the most fascinating person in any situation. (A big opportunity if your brand can help them feel more confident and engaging in conversation.)
> • People want to feel fascinated by a product or experience, and will often pay far more for a brand that fascinates them than one that does not. (A big opportunity if your brand can *fascinate*.)

Companies will add more value, and compete more effectively, by identifying and applying the way in which they persuade.

(You'll learn how in Part II.) Those who don't will be pushed aside or, worse, forgotten. Messages that fail to fascinate will become irrelevant. It's that simple. This might not be fair. But as Salem Villager Giles Corey can attest, fascination doesn't always play nice.

In a distracted and overwhelmed world, everything, including you, your communication, and your relationships, must fight tooth and nail to get noticed. Without fascination we can't sell products off shelves, persuade shareholders to invest, teach students to read, or convince spouses to vacation in Bora-Bora next February. Yet with fascination on your side, your ideas will become impossible to resist.

Spellbinding

We all have certain behaviors that don't exactly make sense, even to ourselves. We make certain choices, and take certain actions, without understanding exactly *why*. Here's why: In a state of fascination, we don't think and act quite logically. We do things we don't understand, we believe messages we don't agree with, and we buy things we don't even want. At its most extreme, fascination short-circuits the logical evaluation process. Rather than coolly analyzing a decision, we're gripped by involuntary responses. We might think we're in control of our own choices, but much of the time, we're not. Remember the original Latin meaning of "fascinate": "To bewitch or hold captive so others are powerless to resist."

Fascination explains why people join suicidal cults, or develop fetishes, or willingly obey tyrannical dictators. More commonly (but just as irrationally), they buy sports cars they can't afford, procrastinate in the face of major deadlines, or fall in love with the "wrong" person. Yet once you understand how to influence decisions, these actions begin to make sense.

You'll see why your behavior is influenced by this force of intense focus, too. Whether you realize it or not, your preferences are often driven by deep primal forces. You often don't *choose* to be fascinated any more than you *choose* to feel thirsty or fall asleep.

Yet once you understand why people pay attention to certain messages, it's easier and faster to create messages that influence behavior. You do have a choice. You can turn weak into wicked.

Languages

Growing up in Jacksonville, Florida, everyone I knew spoke the same language (and that language was Southern, y'all!). Our community was not diverse. While we could buy pickled pigs' feet at any convenience store, there was only one Japanese restaurant on the outskirts of town.

This was the early '80s, and from a pop culture perspective, it was not our finest moment. Almost everyone I knew went to the same Ruby Tuesday and TGI Friday's restaurants, shopped in the same Gap and Limited stores at the mall, attended the same school, and listened to the same top forty songs. If one of my friends said, "Ohmygod, I, like, totally looooove the new Madonna song," we all nodded in enthusiastic agreement.

Then, in the summer of 1983, I spent a few months in Japan. I spoke only a few words of Japanese. Communication was difficult. I lacked not only the actual words, but also the context and behavioral clues to interpret what was being said. I struggled with even simple questions, let alone conversation. It was draining.*

After a month or so, however, I had picked up a few more words ("Which way to McDonald's?") and learned my host family's body language and nuances. My sense of connection with others grew

---

* It didn't help that in 1983, my teeth were wrapped in gleaming orthodontic braces, something most Japanese people had not seen, so from their perspective I had massive steel fangs.

as I could understand more, and be understood. I even became a sushi fan (kinda). I learned a basic principle of communication: even when two people speak the same words, they're not necessarily saying the same thing.

Even if two people both speak English, and use the same words, they're not necessarily understanding each other. For example, let's say you're managing a project with tight deadlines. You need information from your coworker. When you inquire about the status of the project, if they say, "It's almost done," you might be confused. Is it truly about to be finished? Will they finish on time? Are they procrastinating? Do they need guidance? To understand what's really going on, you need to understand the meaning behind the words.

Similarly, you may be speaking a different "language" than your audience. You may be using all the right words, yet still not being heard. When I use the word "language," I don't mean that you're marketing to Brazil versus Bangkok. Your "language" is how your brand speaks, acts, and engages. It's how you're heard by others.

Introducing the Seven Fascination Advantages
Over the past decade, in my most recent research, I identified seven modes of communication. Each one triggers a hardwired response from your audience.

I created the Fascinate system to give you a practical way to explain what makes your products and services different, and why your audience should care.

Anytime you have a branding challenge, come back to this book. By combining your top Advantage with tactics, you'll have a simple process for marketing messages. Once you no longer have to stress over your messages, you and your team will experience less conflict, waste fewer marketing dollars, and have more momentum in the marketplace.

THE SEVEN LANGUAGES OF FASCINATION

INNOVATION	THE LANGUAGE OF CREATIVITY
PASSION	THE LANGUAGE OF RELATIONSHIP
POWER	THE LANGUAGE OF CONFIDENCE
PRESTIGE	THE LANGUAGE OF EXCELLENCE
TRUST	THE LANGUAGE OF STABILITY
MYSTIQUE	THE LANGUAGE OF LISTENING
ALERT	THE LANGUAGE OF DETAILS

PART I

Fascinate or Fail

Will you fascinate? Or will you fail?

The Science of Fascination

The Most Popular Brand That Nobody Likes

The bitter, sweetly harsh taste is unmistakable. Some say it tastes like Robitussin. Others say it reminds them of black licorice. I think that's putting it kindly. I'd compare it to a shot of battery acid laced with kerosene.

So let me ask you. Have you ever had a shot of Jägermeister? Did you like the taste?

If you didn't like the taste, that's okay. Few people do. Very, very few. And yet the brand has grown exponentially. Jägermeister is one of the top-selling spirits in the world. So how is that possible?

If you're reading this book (and I happen to know you are), the odds are quite good that you've done a shot of Jägermeister. If I may, allow me to make a prediction about your experience of it at some point.

It was past midnight on a Friday or Saturday night. You were with a group, standing at the bar. Somebody in your group—the troublemaker, perhaps—suggested with a sly smile, "Hey, let's do a shot of Jäger."

Your first thought was to decline. You already knew the shot would corrode your throat, and you knew you'd make a face of disgust as soon as you managed to down the whole thing. But the mere suggestion of a shot of Jäger hit a hidden crazy button inside your brain. A chance to find out exactly what was beyond your wildest imagination.

As the bartender poured the liqueur, it seemed heavy enough to plop into the shot glass—*glub glub glub*—and concentrated enough to make permanent stains on an asphalt highway. When your shot arrived, you hesitated imperceptibly, jaw clenched.

What was going on in that moment? You were playing a mind game with yourself. Psyching yourself up and bracing yourself at the same time, like an extreme skier dropping down the face of a double-black-diamond run. The shot was cold, but not cold enough to kill the pain.

Afterward, you looked to your friends and smiled with a mixture of victory and relief. Your empty shot glass became a medal of valor.

So what just happened?

You didn't do the Jäger shot *despite* the unpleasant taste. You did that shot *because* of it.

A History of Liquid Fascination

The year was 1878. Wintertime stag hunting was a popular pastime in Germany. Hunting parties braved the cold, and a shot of liqueur helped take the edge off the chill. A hunter named Curt Mast developed a drink for his stag-hunting excursions. What were his ingredients? Only a handful of people knew. It was a secret mixture of fifty-six herbs, spices, and blooms.

Mast named his drink Jägermeister, which translates to "Master Hunter." The greatest hunter of them all.

Because Mast didn't want a bottle to shatter while hunting, he tested various designs while on his horse, dropping different bottles while galloping at full speed, until he discovered the specific squared shape that was the least likely to shatter. This led to the iconic squared dark-green bottle we know today.

Mast adorned his shatterproof green bottle with imagery of mystical hunting legends. For instance, a Christian cross glowed eerily between the curved antlers of a stag. This cross was in homage to Saint Hubertus, the patron saint of hunting. Legend has it that Hubertus converted to Christianity when he saw a vision of a stag with a glowing crucifix between its antlers. Images of the saint, born in 656, still hang in churches around the world.

In 1935, Jäger was commercially released in Germany, marketed as an after-dinner digestif. While it had originally helped hunters brave the chill, now it helped the digestive system brave the bratwurst.

The green bottle later served in the fields of World War II as an anesthetic for wounded soldiers. In the 1980s, however, it made the leap from painkiller to hangover creator.

In 1985, an American marketer and entrepreneur, Sidney Frank, bought the rights to import the drink into the United States from Germany. This wasn't an obvious move at the time. The drink was only a very modest seller, barely worth the license. Up to that point, the digestif was a nostalgic drink for traditional blue-collar German immigrants who remembered it from the homeland.

But then everything changed. Frank came across a short article in the *Baton Rouge Advocate*. It described his digestif as a cult drink, hopped up with opium, Quaaludes, and aphrodisiacs.

A conventional marketer would have suppressed the article, worrying about reputation damage. Frank did quite the opposite. He made hundreds of copies of the newspaper article, and plastered them in college bars all around the country. So it began.

College students visiting New Orleans swarmed to the bars, clutching bottles of the mysterious brown elixir, bringing them back to campus and secretively sharing them with friends. Hurry up, get your bottle soon, because surely an imported drink with opium will be illegal at any moment.

And what about that stag pictured on the label? Rumors spread that the drink contained deer's blood. What about the cross? People researched the religious symbolism. And how about that mysterious poem in the design? What was it saying about God and man and beasts?

It seemed everyone (including the authorities) wanted to know: What exactly floated inside that potion?*

Thus spread the cult, student to student, school to school, a wildfire lit with the taste of kerosene.

These students were not merely buying a drink. They were not even buying flavor. They were buying a flirtation with forbidden ingredients. If their hard-won Jäger bottle tasted delicious, it wouldn't be nearly as compelling. In fact, the more horrific the drink tasted, the more convincing the rumors. With such a repellent flavor, surely an aphrodisiac or two must be lurking in there somewhere.

The Brand Promise of a Toxic Experience

In 1975, the two reigning soda brands, Coca-Cola and Pepsi, waged a war over which cola tasted better. Heard of it? The Pepsi Challenge? It became nearly as competitive as a scene out of *Game of Thrones*. In a spontaneous blind taste test, consumers were asked to take a sip from two unmarked cups of soda (one with Coke, the other Pepsi), and name which one tasted better. Pepsi claimed to be more delicious than Coke, and vice versa, on and on, for years.

The whole mammoth marketing campaign hinged on one factor: taste. Virtually every drink on the market sells itself on the basis of taste. With good reason. Taste is a perfectly rational

---

* Jägermeister has never confirmed any of the fifty-six ingredients. It doesn't have to. The beverage is imported, and the headquarters in Germany refuses to reveal its secrets. You're welcome to believe whatever you want.

reason to buy one soda rather than another. So how can Jäger sell despite the taste?

Think this through. Can you imagine doing a blind taste test challenge for Jäger, like the Pepsi Challenge? Um, no. Imagine people's facial expressions the first time they did a shot.*

Yet what if you're a marketer trying to sell a drink, and that drink's taste is (in the eyes of many) your main disadvantage? Sidney Frank actively touted the unappealing flavor: a poster showed a man who had just finished consuming a shot with a grimace on his face.

This approach took the barrier head-on, turning the shot into a rallying cry. It elevated the product beyond rational benefits, adding to its growing mythology. With this drink, bad flavor isn't a barrier to trying it; it's a reason for it. An overall toxic experience is part of the brand's promise. Customers can dislike your product but still love its message, if they love what your brand says about them.

Many brands are faced with the difficult task of selling a product that people don't necessarily want to buy. Nobody gets excited about buying headache medication, car mufflers, or burial plots. The beauty of Jäger's marketing is that it sells an extraordinary volume—at a premium price point, no less—of a product that people don't even want and, more to the point, actively dislike.

So how does the brand manage to sell almost as much as Absolut, when the taste puts hair on the tongue?

Under the Spell of Fascination

Think about your own purchase decisions. Why do you buy certain brands and not others? Why do you remember certain messages, but forget the rest?

---

* If the company did conduct a blind taste test, what drink would it even compete against? Kahlúa? Not really. Peppermint schnapps? Hmm. Formaldehyde? Yeah, maybe.

More often than you realize, you aren't just buying a product. You're buying the emotions, connotations, values, and priorities of the brand. Brands give us a shorthand. In a distracted and confusing world, these shortcuts help consumers make sense of all the options. And if you're trying to stand out, finding shortcuts is critical.

For instance, I'll describe a man to you. I won't tell you how old he is, what he does for a living, or what kind of personality he has. Instead, I'll just describe the brands he buys. What do you envision with the following examples?

1. He's wearing a Tommy Bahama shirt, driving a Jeep.
2. He's wearing a Tommy Hilfiger shirt, driving a Volvo.
3. He's wearing Diesel jeans and driving a BMW coupe.
4. He's wearing an oversized Tag Heuer watch and driving a Hummer.

You probably have different mental images for each of these men, based on the brands they choose.

Just as a Tommy Bahama shirt sends a message that the wearer is laid back, the dark-brown liquid of Jägermeister sends a message as well. When you order a Jäger, you're telling anyone who witnesses it that you're willing to stick your toe over the line, if not hurl your body across it. You refuse to drink from the mainstream.

The shot is not *better* than other spirits, but it is decidedly *different.**

When people buy a shot of Jäger, they aren't buying a *drink*. They're buying an *experience*. By holding the shot glass, they're announcing that they have officially turned up the volume on the evening ahead. This explains why Jäger is so popular among groups at bars. It's a team-building exercise. Can you imagine someone at

---

* As one bartender described it, "There's drunk . . . and then there's Jägermeister drunk."

home alone on a Tuesday, pouring a Jäger bomb? It makes about as much sense as sitting on your own lap. Even the logo has become shorthand for stepping it up a notch. Once someone suggests a round of Jäger, mental bells start ringing inside the minds of the group, signaling that it's one of "those nights."

That's a very specific brand promise, one that's unlikely to be confused with that of any chardonnay.

All this doesn't make sense, of course, on a rational level. It doesn't have to. The brand is not selling a rational benefit (such as better gas mileage or longer-lasting paint), but an emotional experience. When you see the hidden patterns in how fascination casts a spell on people, seemingly irrational behaviors become clear.

The good news is that, without even realizing it, you already have intensely fascinating qualities built right into your brand. And once you build your communication around those qualities, you can compete against bigger companies, bigger marketing budgets, and even better products. I call these qualities your "orange tickets."

Do You Want the Orange Ticket, or the Green?

Let's go on a ride.

The Mission Space ride at the Epcot theme park in Orlando, Florida, is based on the conceit that the rider is training to be an astronaut, practicing to save planet Earth while hurling through the atmosphere inside a capsule. When you enter this ride, you get a choice: Do you want the orange ticket, or the green ticket? I was curious. Why two tickets? What's the difference? Which should I choose?

I looked back and forth, from the orange-ticket line to the green-ticket line and back again. They had separate entrances. The orange-ticket line was long, with a forty-five-minute wait. The line for the less intense green-ticket ride, on the other hand, was short. Which ride would you choose? A less intense ride, with a brief wait? Or a more intense ride, with a long wait? As I weighed my options, I overheard someone say, "The green ticket is for little kids and old people."

I chose the orange ticket. Of course.

The attendant handed me a large orange plastic ticket, and I saw others nervously making their choice. Entering the orange gateway, I glanced behind my shoulder to the green entrance. Little kids and old people streamed in. I felt good about my decision.

As I joined the long line, I glanced at my orange ticket. Skimming the bulleted list of disclaimers, I could tell this would not be your average ride. The ticket was filled with warnings. Dire warnings. With a surge of adrenaline, I read everything that could potentially go wrong, from nausea to back injury. I questioned my bravado.

I wasn't the only person who felt that jolt of adrenaline. Ahead of me, the single-file line buzzed with excitement and anticipation. People whooped and woo-hooed, congratulating each other, as though we'd just embarked on an episode of *Amazing Race*. We were pumped, making knowing glances at each other, affirming our decision, congratulating ourselves, chests puffed. We hadn't wimped out. We were Team Orange.

Yet as the line crawled along, more dire warnings flashed on either side of us. An Orwellian voice announced that it was *not too late* to exit the orange ride.

"It's not too late," I told myself. I could still escape what now appeared to be near-certain death. I wouldn't be the only one to give up. A couple in matching Nebraska T-shirts held hands to reassure each other while quietly exiting the line, eyes downcast to avoid eye contact with their former ridemates. I could exit behind that Nebraska couple, and downgrade to green. No shame.

Yet like most people in that line, I felt a strange sense of commitment. I'd dialed in for this half an hour ago, and by golly, I wasn't going to quit now. Within minutes, our parade of strangers had bonded into a team. People took selfies with their orange ticket, proudly posting them on Facebook. There was tweeting and retweeting. It was a marketer's dream.

Our team of tourists continued through the tunnel, the air thick with anticipation for what lay ahead. Our collective mood alternated between swagger and curiosity. Was this a ride, or an extreme sport?

At last, the wait was over. The ride lay immediately ahead. It was go time. Inside the capsule, barf bags waited expectantly.

As the ride began, someone exclaimed that *this* was the best ride she had been on all day—and that she couldn't wait to go back and do the ride again. My last thought, as I sat down and clutched my barf bag, was that it was remarkable to have repeat customers for a ride that hadn't technically started yet. That's the last thing I remember before my life flashed in front of my eyes.

So, was this ride good? Yes. And yes, it was intense. But even better than the ride was the emotional experience. We did it! As we slowed down to a stop, I congratulated myself. Sure, I might be a little dizzy, but that barf bag was clearly empty. (And yay, I am not paralyzed!)

I wasn't the only one who felt giddy with accomplishment. All around me, riders high-fived as they exited the ride. People emerged from the ride thrilled and flushed, beaming with a collective sense of accomplishment. From the looks on people's faces, you'd have thought we had just completed the Iditarod. We hadn't just *chosen* orange . . . we'd *earned* it.

I watched a pack of teenagers run back to the start to get new orange tickets and do it all over again. More high-fives. More tweets. More congratulations. They were already repeat customers, recruiting others, building loyalty and talk value on social media.

The marketer inside me wanted to know what exactly the difference was between the orange-ticket ride and the green. Why all the fuss?

I walked back to the start to the same attendant, chose the green ticket, and entered. The lined moved quickly. There was no buzz, no nervous anticipation, and no chest-thumping. Nobody took a selfie and posted it to Facebook to show off his green ticket. No repeat customers who finished the ride and immediately ran back to the start. People exited and left, looking underwhelmed. As soon as it started, we were done. Pfffffft.

But guess what?

(Suspenseful pause . . .)

It was mostly the same ride.

The green ride is the same story line, about a capsule going into space. It's the same structural format, same graphic design, same uniform on the attendants. The difference is that it doesn't spin as fast as the orange ride.

Yet the green version doesn't just lack intensity—it lacks emotion. It lacks energy and engagement.

Why is the orange-ticket experience fascinating, while the green is forgettable? These rides might appear to be the same, but small details turn an average process into an unforgettable one. A few smart tweaks transform even a boring brand into an intensely desirable winner. It might be as simple as changing a name.

The Little Town with a Fascinating Name

Centuries ago, a little town in Wales struggled with a common branding problem: how to attract more tourists and residents, without building new attractions, expensive marketing, or a lengthy makeover?

In 1850, a humble cobbler came up with a big idea . . . create the world's longest name. And thus was born Llanfairpwllgwyngyllgogerychwyrndrobwllllantysiliogogogoch. This fascinating name attracted attention, and with it, tourism dollars. The name change became an orange ticket.

Today, people visit from around the globe, growing its population and economy. Jimmy Kimmel and staff members of the *Huffington Post* have competed in the annual contest to find the most "interesting" way to pronounce the name.*

How about your brand? How could you turn your green-ticket experiences into orange tickets? How could you turn your customer service into an orange ticket? How about your talent recruitment, or your company celebrations? The rewards are huge. My research shows that with a few strategic changes, people will wait in line for your services, post online about your products, refer prospects to your website, and compete to show you off to their friends.

While these two rides looked very similar, and appeared to be interchangeable, they delivered completely different experiences. One was fascinating, while the other was just another ride. Using the same fascination that impels people to pay more for a luxury brand of sunglasses than the same pair without a logo, your brand can focus on just a few traits and make them spellbinding.

Different Is Orange

Your customers *want* the orange ticket. They want to be engaged and fascinated. Remember: different is better than better. And different is orange. Give people the orange ticket, and you can leverage a distinct attitude, mind-set, and point of view.

I'm sure you get this—but this story isn't about an amusement park ride. It's about your product, and brand, and you, and whether or not you will win the battle for attention. Every time you market, you are offering either the orange ticket, or the green. You're either captivating, or a commodity. You're fascinating, or forgotten.

---

* Afraid to pronounce this town's long name? You might just have hippopotomonstrosesquipedaliaphobia: the fear of long words.

What is your orange ticket? The answer lies in your brand's main Advantage. Once you identify your brand's key mode of communication, you can heighten these points of difference, and turn them into something unforgettable.

Fascination Turns Green into Orange

At the end of our journey together, you'll understand why people buy luxury goods without an appreciable difference in quality, rave about favorite companies without being paid endorsers, or research products without any intention to actually buy them. In your "Action Plan for Teams," your team will have a road map to apply these principles. Together, you'll take something that's relatively meaningless (e.g., a swoosh symbol) and give it meaning (e.g., the Nike logo).

I'll point out examples from marketing, culture, fashion, music, food, hobbies, holidays, and even boring stuff like dust bunnies. Any product, and any company, can perform marketing witchcraft to captivate customers.

Buying vs. Paying

In one of my favorite nuggets of marketing research, I asked women how much they'd be willing to pay for a pair of sunglasses—one pair with a Chanel logo, and one with no logo. The two pairs of sunglasses themselves had the same functionality, yet each had a very different perceived value. In fact, the logo was worth more than the sunglasses themselves. The learning: When women buy Chanel sunglasses, they're *buying* sunglasses, but *paying* for the brand. In this experiment, Chanel was not *better*, but it was *different*.

Often, when people *buy* a product, they are actually *paying* for an intangible benefit. When buying Chanel sunglasses, women are paying for the logo. When college graduates (and their parents) *buy* an Ivy League education, they're often paying for the brand name of the college.

When people buy your product, what are they paying for? The

experience? The cachet? The assurance of quality? Just as a pair of sunglasses with a Chanel logo can be worth exponentially more than the same pair without a logo, how can you elevate your point of difference above similar products?

This is the heart of differentiation. It's tough to be better. But far easier to be different.

When a Choice Is Not Really a Choice

We all have certain behaviors that don't exactly make sense, even to ourselves. We make certain choices and take certain actions without understanding exactly why. In a state of fascination, you are more likely to buy certain brands, remember certain speeches, or hire certain people. In those moments, your brain bypasses the usual decision-making processes.

Within these seemingly irrational behaviors, clear patterns emerge. For instance, when you communicate passionately, people tend to see you as approachable and human. When you communicate powerfully, they perceive you as confident. When you spark curiosity, they want to learn more.

The next time you find yourself engrossed in a game of golf, or craving a specific food, or focusing like mad to meet a deadline at work, ask yourself: What's actually going on here? Earlier, we talked about the seven Advantages and how they persuade and influence behavior. Underneath the surface, which of the seven Advantages is causing this rapt state? Once you understand how fascination works, you might realize that your behavior is being driven by something far different from what you think. It might be the Advantages at work. The Advantages may seem surprising at first, but they're the brain's hardwired response to messages.

On a First Date? Measure His Elbows

The idea that symmetry equals beauty has been rattling around pop culture for a few years, based on research from the

evolutionary biologists Steven Gangestad and Randy Thornhill. Their study began by measuring seven body points, such as
elbows, and ended with the theory that symmetry translates not
only to better DNA, and better treatment from parents, but also
to better sex.

Men with symmetrical elbow bones are simply more fascinating: they have more fun in the bedroom, more frequently,
with more-beautiful partners. Evolutionary biologists have predicted not only sexual prowess on the basis of body symmetry
measurements, but also the levels of physical dominance, emotional stability, and day-to-day health, and even the likelihood
of fidelity.

Measuring elbows seems like running one of those free Internet background checks: fast, free, with more information than you
needed or wanted. But what if there are no overt cues, such as
elbows, to measure? Can you be fascinated by beauty, even if you
can't actually *see* the person?

Are Beautiful People Still More Attractive with the Lights Off?

Buried deeper in Gangestad and Thornhill's research is an even
kookier finding: the beauty bias still applies in the dark. Attractive
people, a study found, literally smell different. Or more specifically, better. Even when everything is hidden from view, women
will still choose symmetrical males.

A final blow to nonsymmetrical guys everywhere: with highly
symmetrical partners, women were found to be more than twice
as likely to climax during intercourse (which offers a biological advantage, by funneling sperm into the uterus to promote
conception).

For the less symmetrical among us, take heart. While you'll
never be able to control certain fascination influences, other influences are more malleable. Attracting potential mates might be as
simple as pulling your T-shirt out of the laundry hamper.

The Laboratory Known as a Strip Club

Multiple studies have confirmed that women are more fascinating to their mates while ovulating. When women are especially fertile, their male partners become more attentive, are more vigilant, and engage in "mate-guarding" behavior to keep other men away. To find out more, researchers from the University of New Mexico "examined ovulatory cycle effects on tip earnings by professional lap dancers working in gentlemen's clubs." In other words, they wanted to know how this dynamic played out in the sex laboratory known as a strip club.* The researchers found that the strippers' tips fluctuated depending on their menstrual cycle. While ovulating, fertile strippers earned almost 30% more in tips than they did during other times of the month. However, dancers on birth control pills saw no such boost in tips. Birth control essentially wiped out these dancers' prime earning days. Over the course of a year, using the pill could potentially mean thousands of dollars in lost income.† If your genes can be responsible for attraction, and the birth control pill can reverse that attraction, what other fascinations are driving your behavior without your knowledge? The answers often lie in how your brain becomes captivated by communication.

On our journey through flirtation, we've seen how our personal notion of attractiveness is rooted deep within us. We might be irresistibly, magnetically drawn to a certain person without having any idea that our desire is not a conscious choice. It doesn't end with physical attraction—it only starts there. Brands fascinate in similar deeply rooted ways.

---

* Imagine the conversation between a researcher and a stripper: "Hello there, Kandi, you look very nice this afternoon. Those six-inch Lucite heels make you really, ah, tall. Anyway, in order to get reimbursed by the university for this study, can I please get a receipt for any dollar bills I tip you?"

† A stripper's income rises and falls with the ability to fascinate, and guess what: they're not the only ones. We all use involuntary signals to persuade clients.

The Biology of Fascination

WHY YOUR BRAIN WAS DESIGNED TO BE FASCINATED

Why We Were Born Knowing Exactly How to Persuade

A million generations after our reptilian brains retreated to the base of our brain stems, fascination continues to be our most basic form of attention. Why? Because fascination, at some level, is based on survival. The most fascinating option wins. Everything else goes extinct.

The same instincts that allowed our evolutionary forefathers to hunt woolly mammoths for dinner are still very much in place today, even as we order a double Whopper through the speaker of the Burger King drive-through. These instincts were perfectly suited for our cave-dwelling existence, but make less sense today. When communicating with any of your fellow *Homo sapiens*, remember that you're not just dealing with the person you see before you, you're also dealing with advantages that went undiscovered for millions of years. These leftover survival instincts clash with our modern environment, and much of our behavior lives in the far less rational areas of our brain.

The Ultimate Fascination Machine

We're constantly reading the facial cues of those around us, searching for signals: smiles, wide eyes, scowls, tears. By looking at just two eyes, a nose, and a smile, we can decipher and predict an extraordinary range of emotions, personality traits, and intentions. Faces are so key to our survival, in fact, that we're born to be fascinated by them.

In the early 1960s, a developmental psychologist named Robert Fantz set out to discover whether we're born with an innate ability to perceive certain forms; specifically, faces. Without the aid of today's sophisticated magnetic resonance imaging (MRI) brain scans, Fantz set up his own low-tech, simple experiment. Over his infant subjects, he cleverly set a display board with two pictures: a high-contrast bull's-eye on the left, and next to it, a simple sketch of a face. Behind the display board, Fantz then watched the babies through a peephole. What he saw changed developmental psychology.

A Baby's Very First Party Trick

Although newborns' eyes appear to wander aimlessly or stare with glazed indifference, Fantz learned that the opposite is true. Newborns focus on certain shapes far more than on others, with a decided preference for the human face. He found that by two months of age, babies will stare at a drawing of the human face twice as often, and twice as long, as they will at a bull's-eye. No coincidence, then, that the range at which babies can most clearly see objects is twelve inches, roughly the same number of inches as the distance to view a mother's face while nursing.

Fantz's findings startled the developmental community, proving that a fascination with faces is more "nature" than "nurture." His experiments proved that even at birth, we arrive prepackaged with survival mechanisms to help us connect with others and form close relationships.

Facial fascination is such a critical skill that our brain has a region specifically for recognizing, interpreting, and responding to human faces: the fusiform face area, or FFA. Located deep within the temporal lobe, on the underside of the brain, the FFA drives the high-level visual processing needed to distinguish and interpret faces and expressions. Building on Fantz's findings, neuroscientists have recently discovered that they can pinpoint the hardwiring in the brain through the use of brain imaging. Researchers can analyze whether you prefer, say, bean burritos over chicken chimichangas. Our hardwired preferences allow marketers to access our instant, and involuntary, perceptions of the world. The auto manufacturer DaimlerChrysler used MRI technology to study how young men responded to three different car body styles: sports cars, sedans, and small cars. Sports cars, by far, created the highest levels of brain activity. ("What? Young men excited by Ferraris? You don't say!")

While this initial finding isn't a shocker, the news wasn't that the activity occurred, but rather exactly *where* the activity occurred. It took place in the nucleus accumbens, a deep and primal area linked to intense physical reward. Previously, scientists had thought this area responded only to immediate physical rewards, such as chocolate and cocaine. But now for the first time, researchers watched as abstract man-made objects stimulated these mental explosions.

More startling was what happened next. Still reading the brain patterning, researchers then asked the young men which specific brands were most attractive. While the young men appraised which models were their favorites, activity fired off in their brains once again. But to the researchers' astonishment, this time, the fireworks centered in the FFA region—the region that identifies *faces*.

Advertising frequently manipulates this response. Michelin tires plunks a couple of animated eyes and a smile onto a charmless stack of tires, and presto, those tires have a sparkling personality.

Same with Scrubbing Bubbles, and many other brands developed in the '70s and '80s.*

Mona Lisa, and the 83% Happy Smile

One certain face has, for centuries, fascinated us: that of the *Mona Lisa*. We're unable to pinpoint the precise emotions behind Leonardo da Vinci's famously enigmatic subject, and therefore continue to be fascinated by it. The *Mona Lisa* was recently analyzed by cutting-edge software developed to recognize facial emotion. *Mona Lisa*'s smile, according to the program, is 83% happy, 9% disgusted, 6% fearful, and 2% angry. Over the past few hundred years, that smile has become a cottage industry; thousands of families make the trek to Paris each year to get an up-close-and-personal look.

Of all the facial fascination cues that we give off, our smile might be the most important. Yet from an evolutionary perspective, the human smile puzzled scientists for years. Throughout the animal kingdom, retracting the mouth's corners and baring the teeth is a sign of aggression, like a snarl, intended to display dominant intentions or even imminent attack. Yet in humans, this same retraction of the mouth's corners and baring of the teeth signals appeasement, deference, and submission. You smile to put others at ease as a bonding cue. But this makes no sense.

Why, Exactly, Do Humans Smile?

The smile enigma stumped anthropologists for hundreds of years. Finally, John J. Ohala, a professor from the Department of Linguistics at the University of California, Berkeley, revealed his answer. We smile, he discovered, not for the visual cues. We smile because of the way it sounds. Or more specifically, because of the way it makes *our voice* sound.

---

* Considering the research on faces, perhaps we should bring this technique back. The Cisco Cowboy? The 3M Three Musketeers?

To understand the smile enigma, we must first understand why we respond differently to low voices and high voices. Bigger animals have deeper voices, at a lower pitch, and a louder sound. Think of a dog growl's deep, imposing, aggressive vibration. Among animals, a deep, low pitch sends a threatening signal. A higher voice and a smaller size, conversely, are signs of appeasement or timidity. When a dog lowers itself downward on its front paws, in the classic "let's play!" pose, it's making itself seem smaller and less threatening.

We see this "high pitch versus low pitch" phenomenon in the human world as well. A higher voice is seen as more polite and deferential. When we coo to babies in baby talk, we raise our voices *and* our eyebrows. ("Oooh, loooook at the baaaaby!!") But can you imagine using this same voice with your boss or employees? ("Ooooh, such a gooood little TPS report!") When we want to appear authoritative or dominant, we change both our voice and our face, lowering our voices and eyebrows.*

In China, where a high, sweet falsetto is preferred, some women entering the job market believe that a syrupy-sugary voice will help them land a better job. The cosmetic surgery market now offers "voice beauty operations" to burn away a portion of the vocal cord, thus scarring the cord and raising the pitch. This questionable procedure creates a more "polite" voice by mimicking the vocal pitch of a little girl.

Now back to smiles. In 1980, at the one hundredth meeting of the Acoustical Society of America, John J. Ohala stunned the audience with his findings. In his paper "The Acoustic Origin of

---

* There's a wired connection between pitch of voice and facial expression, and David Huron, a professor of music and the head of the Cognitive and Systematic Musicology Laboratory in the School of Music at Ohio State University, offers a simple experiment you can do right now to prove this. Sing a note at a comfortable pitch, with your mouth in an "O." As you're doing this, note your facial expression. Now sing the *highest* note that you're capable of; notice how you raise your chin and eyebrows. Finally, sing the *lowest* note you can; your chin and eyebrows lower, into a more aggressive expression.

the Smile," he revealed that the smile didn't begin as a visual cue, as had always been assumed, but something else entirely. "High vocal tract resonances may also enhance the infantile character of the vocalization by seeming to originate from a shorter vocal tract. Higher resonances can be achieved by a trumpet-like flaring of the tract and/or by retracting the corners of the mouth." In other words, when we smile, we pull the cheek flesh back against our teeth, we make our mouth cavity smaller—and our voice higher, politer, and friendlier. The smile started as a way to *sound less threatening*, and evolved into a way to *look more approachable*. Not a visual cue, but an aural cue.

From a social-interaction perspective, then, smiles aren't window dressing. We're fascinated with smiles because they communicate friendly intentions and a desire to bond. From an evolutionary perspective, that's important.

Why Girls Fall for the Funny Guy

A sense of humor, like a smile, is also fascinating for evolutionary reasons. Recent studies show that women are more attracted to funny men, because humor broadcasts a rich surplus of intellect and health to a potential mate. Just as a peacock's tail and a lion's mane attract a mate by demonstrating a wealth of survival resources, so does humor impress a female. (If you're sick and starving, you're probably not cracking jokes.) Funny guys, biologically speaking, have a higher likelihood of providing for their offspring.

A Smile Was the Original Social Media

So far, several experts have shown us that we rely on specific visual cues to make first impressions. So what happens during a phone call? When you can't actually see someone, what role does your smile play? During a call, the person at the other end can't see you, but he or she can hear your aural cues.

Remember, from an anthropological perspective, you're not smiling in order to *look* friendly. On a phone call, use your smile for its original, intended purpose: to *sound* friendlier. When you create a certain type of impression in your viewer or listener, you attract them to you and your message.

Just as we're constantly using cues to form an opinion about other people, we're also forming opinions about objects, ideas, and brands. Some will fascinate us. Most won't.

Fascinate the Goldfish

WHY YOUR OLD TRICKS WON'T WORK IN A WORLD WITH A NINE-SECOND ATTENTION SPAN

The Birth of Marketing and the Death of the Attention Span

Egyptians were the original advertisers, using papyrus to create sales messages and posters. (One might imagine putting ads on the sides of chariots rather than city buses.) Then, for about the next five thousand years, the development of new marketing media and outlets kept a veritable snail's pace with the times' slow technological advancements.

In the second half of the twentieth century, the a cappella radio commercial and characters such as Tony the Tiger and the Pillsbury Doughboy entered the advertising scene. But still, even with the arrival of the three-martini lunch, there were still only three television networks to distract you and compete for your attention. In this relatively simplistic marketing environment, advertising excelled largely by virtue of one persistent tactic: repetition. And to illustrate why the repetition method worked so well, join me on a tour of three-hundred-year-old English landscaping.

The Old Model of Attention

The maze at Hampton Court in London is one of the most famous hedge mazes in the world. It lies on a grassy expanse behind a palace once inhabited by Henry VIII, a half mile of hedges twisted into a complex labyrinth. The maze, which looks like something directly out of *Alice in Wonderland*, also happens to be the perfect place for a study about memory.

Researchers took a chronic amnesiac to the maze, and asked him if he'd ever been there. No, he replied, he had not. They gave him a whistle, and had him wind his way through the hedges. Upon reaching the center, he blew his whistle. Researchers recorded the time. The next day, they did the same thing. They asked the amnesiac if he'd ever been to the maze, to which his reply was no. Off they sent him again with the whistle, and again they timed the speed with which he reached the center.

Day after day, same thing. Again they asked if he'd ever been to the maze, again the reply was no. Again they timed how long it took him to reach the center.

Though the patient had no recollection of his time in the maze, something strange happened. Each time the patient made his way through the maze, he did it differently. Specifically, he did it faster. Without actively remembering the maze, he was subconsciously learning. Over time, he built up a mental schema of the labyrinth.

Memory, the scientists learned, works whether we realize it or not. All day, we passively take in messages from the world around us, even if we're not conscious of those messages. Enough messages, drilled in over decades, will eventually shape our actions. It's inefficient, but for several decades in the twentieth century, it's how advertising worked. Like the amnesiac in the maze, consumers have passively absorbed brand messages, cumulatively, over the course of years, without realizing it.

Sound a little crazy? It's why you remember jingles from your childhood, and why you gravitate toward the brands you remember fondly from your youth.

What happened since then? Why is it no longer good enough to jingle your audience to death?

The Modern Marketing Maze

Today, the maze changes every day, making a marketer's job far more difficult than it was in the good old days. Unless you have the biggest budget of all your competitors, it no longer works to repeatedly drill in messages. You must fascinate.

Here's a prime example: In 2010, a new product was introduced into the market, and, upon release, it received some resoundingly harsh criticism. A year later, the *New York Times* recapped the public flogging:

> *"An utter disappointment and abysmal failure."*
> —ORANGE COUNTY WEB DESIGN BLOG

> *"Consumers seem genuinely baffled by why they might need it."*
> —*BUSINESSWEEK*

> *"Insanely great it is not."*
> —*MARKETWATCH*

> *"My god, am I underwhelmed."*
> —*GIZMODO*

Wow! That's a tough set of reviews. What kind of lemon was this product, exactly? Well, it was Apple's iPad. The fastest-selling gadget in the history of electronics. How could an "utter and abysmal failure" colossally break sales records? That type of success simply isn't rational. It can't be predicted and plotted on a graph.

No, that's marketing witchcraft at its finest. Apple found a way to position the iPad not as another rather cold, utilitarian piece of technology but rather something with which one could have both a physical and also an emotional connection.

Sigmund Freud once described intense emotional attachment as fascination. Romantic love is a state in which an individual becomes so submissively engrossed in his object of fascination that he becomes hypnotized. People found themselves hypnotized by the iPad, turning it from a rational purchase into a fascination. (Who would have guessed that Sigmund Freud and Steve Jobs understood fascination in the same way?)

As we've said before, fascination goes beyond rational thinking. It transforms customers into fanatics, and your brand's products into must-have purchases.

You probably don't have millions in ad budget dollars, or world-class R&D. That's okay. You can stand out, and sell more without spending more, as long as you understand your brand's Advantage, and apply smart tactics. (You'll learn about tactics, and how to do this, in parts II and III.)

The goal here is not to spend more money on marketing. It's actually to spend *less* money by marketing more effectively. Spend less but see better results. Outthink instead of outspend. If you don't have the biggest budget, then be the most fascinating.

Fascinate the Goldfish

Back in the days of the Salem Witch Trials, the average attention span was about twenty minutes long. (An estimated one minute for each year of age, up until age twenty.)

But later a little thing called "the Internet" happened. And then Wi-Fi and the explosion of the smartphone, a distraction we can take with us wherever we go. Now we have messages coming at us from every direction: voicemails and videos, emails and apps, updates and upgrades, tweets and retweets.

So how do our brains respond to all this stimulation? Turns out, we're learning to process information differently. We think more quickly, change direction more often, and get distracted more easily. The BBC has described the effect of technology on the human brain as follows: "The addictive nature of web browsing can leave you with an attention span of nine seconds—the same as a goldfish."

In fact, the attention span might not even be nine seconds these days. It might be eight seconds, or seven, or six. A recent Microsoft study says the attention span is now eight seconds. But for now, let's go with nine, in the spirit of positive thinking.

If you get only a few seconds to capture your customer's attention before it turns toward a new topic, you'd better act quickly. In this distracted environment, you have only an instant to communicate, convince, and convert.

You've surely watched the goldfish swim away, right in front of your eyes. It's when you're in the middle of a conversation, and someone whips out an iPhone and begins checking emails. It's when you're making a presentation, and you can see people having a side conversation in the back of the room. It's when you find out through the grapevine that your loyal client is now working with someone else.

In my national market research, I learned that if a brand earns a customer's interest during this critical nine seconds (in other words, if it can fascinate them quickly), the customer will be more likely to respond to the marketing. However, if customers become distracted or confused, they will simply "swim away" like goldfish.

If you communicate with a slew of haphazard and conflicting messages, it's difficult to develop a clearly established route. You'll seem confused, or inauthentic, and the audience will be less likely to understand what you stand for.

In other words, you must learn how to fascinate the goldfish.

Attention Is More Valuable Than Money or Time

Until recently, information was scarce, and attention was plentiful. If you could inform or entertain a consumer, your information had power. Wars were won with cracked codes and information systems.

When information was scarce and attention was plentiful, traditional marketing made sense. That's why we were all raised with classic schoolmarm marketing principles such as "reach" and "frequency."

But now the opposite is true. Information is plentiful, and attention is scarce. Search engines have turned information into a commodity. At the same time, attention has became more and more limited, and consumers have become overwhelmed with options. Your influence is determined by your ability to get people to take action.

Yet it's not easy to break through and be heard. Every time you communicate, you face three deadly threats.

The Three Deadly Threats to Communication

Some companies have large marketing departments staffed with experienced and talented writers, designers, and strategists. They draw from dream budgets and produce high-quality materials. Yet often even all of those resources aren't enough. Why? What gets in the way of a strong marketing message?

Today, every piece of your communication faces three enemies: distraction, competition, and commoditization. In my book *How the World Sees You*, I define these three deadly threats to all your communications—from team meetings to personal introductions to buying Google AdWords.

These same threats apply to brands:

Distraction: Your audience won't pay attention.

In our chaotic world, our minds and our lives have become so cluttered that we rarely focus on just one thing at any given time.

We've thrown open the doors to the short-attention-span theater, and now the show parades around us at a rate of five thousand marketing messages per day, faster than FedEx, louder than a pop star, bigger than Disney World.

Attention spans are shrinking at a rate inverse to the growing number of distractions. Our brains are becoming trained and rewarded to be distracted. For a brand, the only defense is to get and hold customers' attention by fascinating them.

Competition: Other brands are catching up, and surpassing you.

Most of us grew up believing that, to compete, we need to be better than the competition. We need better skills, better players, better résumés. But what happens when your best is no longer good enough? What happens when that amazing software application you just spent beaucoup bucks developing is blindsided by an even better program? One that's less expensive, to boot?

Better is fragile. It can be trampled in a nanosecond. Attempting to be better puts companies on a hamster wheel, running faster and faster—and in the same direction as everyone else—to keep up. Better is weak.

Different is king. When you can differentiate yourself in the market, you step off the hamster wheel, never to return. You only look back to witness the frenzy your brand is causing in the hamster cage you left behind.

Here's your choice: Spend a lot of time and money in pursuit of *better*. Or find what makes you *different*, and then do it on purpose.

Commoditization: People assume you're just like everyone else in your category, without any distinguishing qualities.

What's your specialty? Hmm, don't have one? You might be becoming a commodity. If that's the case, you're in trouble. You'll have to lower prices, because people won't see any reason to pay more for you. You'll have to spend more on marketing, because nobody will be buzzing about you or advocating for you. You'll become watered down to mush, the lowest common denominator, struggling to get noticed in a world that quickly forgets me-too brands.

The Schoolmarm
and the Sorcerer

WHY MARKETING IS LOSING ITS POWERS OF PERSUASION

The Prudish Schoolmarm

Traditional marketing is the schoolmarm of the communication world. She's cranky and slow, intent on following the rules and calculating the safest route. But we're not in Kansas anymore, Toto. The old rules do not apply.

The schoolmarm can't keep up in a distracted, competitive, commoditized market. She's too expensive. Too nervous. She's scared to take risks. She just wants to keep doing it the same way it's always been done.

Schoolmarm marketing focuses on speaking to the maximum number of people the maximum number of times, drilling in the same message. (Buy! Buy! Buy!) This leads to wasted dollars, and can actually damage your brand, because it makes people less likely to want to connect with you in the future.

Adding Value vs. Taking Up Space

Harsh reality: Not only will spending money on weak advertising *not help* your brand, it will actually damage it. When you force a

captive audience to watch your messages, or when you serve irrelevant messages, people avoid you, delete you, or put you in their
mental spam folder. You know the guy at the mixer who talks only
about himself? Yeah. Don't be that guy in your marketing. You
might not think of your marketing as spam, but if nobody gets
value out of it . . . sorry, you're spam.

If you're not adding value, you're just taking up space.

The schoolmarm's marketing process is costly, lengthy, and
labor intensive. For big brands, it usually goes something like this:
Fly around the country doing weeks of research. Fly home to have
a meeting. Fly for more research. Meet again. Write a strategic
brief. Create ads. Fly to test those ads. Buy media for the ads. Buy
more media. And more media. Hit your audience over the head
until they buy your product. Repeat.

This formula used to work quite efficiently. But not now. Today,
you need to find a slightly unfair advantage.

> You can go through these intricate steps to differentiate your brand.
>
> Or you can get in the express lane.
>
> Which do you want? Schoolmarm or shortcut?

Let's put down the prissy pointer stick, and pick up a sorcerer's
wand. We're about to perform marketing witchcraft.

Fascination is a fearsome force of influence, one that is not to
be taken lightly. It spellbinds your listeners. It pulls them toward
you, binding them to you, hypnotizing them. Ancient Romans
understood this. So did the witches in Salem. So should you.*

Fascination doesn't have to scream in people's faces, repeat the
same tired message, or stick out its hand and lamely ask for attention with a cold-fish handshake and a business card. Rather than

---

* Any force that has the ability to persuade others should be treated with respect and care.
Use it for good, not evil.

pushing yourself on people, pull them toward you. You're crafting messages that people actually want. Instead of barging in on
tightly protected attention spans, you're enticing the right people
to become more deeply involved with you.

One More Lesson from the Most Popular Brand Nobody Likes

Your company can't always be better than the competition. But
you can be *different*.

And if you follow the example of Jägermeister, you can transform even seemingly ordinary (or even foul-tasting!) products into
orange tickets.

Here's an example of how I applied this myself (in a somewhat
ironic way).

I first shared the story of Jägermeister in the original edition
of *Fascinate*. Shortly after the book was published in 2010, I gave a
keynote speech for thousands of marketers in Toronto at an event
named the Art of Marketing. I was nervous. Not only was I a relatively new speaker, but I was slotted to speak immediately after
someone I admired tremendously: Seth Godin. I'd followed his
writing and thinking for years.

Now, if you've never given a speech immediately after someone
who is a hero to the audience, well, it's pretty nerve-racking. To
make matters worse, minutes before I went onstage, I went on
Twitter and saw hundreds of glowing tweets of praise about his
speech. The audience was swooning over him. Tweet after tweet,
the superlatives flowed into my Twitter stream. Oh, did I mention
I was the next speaker?

How could I follow one of the marketing greats and still stand
out in my own way? I couldn't necessarily be *better* than Seth
Godin. I couldn't out-Seth Seth. But I could be *different*. And different is better than better.

I'd planned to describe Jäger as a case study in my speech, and
I carried a bottle in my bag as a visual aid. As I walked onto that

enormous stage, Jumbotron-style live video screens captured my every move. I reminded myself that I couldn't make just another speech, and I didn't have to.

I asked the audience a single question: "Who has never tasted Jägermeister?"

Hands went up. I went into the audience, explaining that the green bottle held one of the top-selling spirits in the world. Surely it must be delicious, right? Then I started serving shots.

That's when things got interesting.

As I walked down the aisle, I motioned for the cameraman to follow me. He quickly got the idea, capturing the facial expressions of the blissfully ignorant audience members about to do their very first shot of the brown liquid. The giant screen showed close-ups of their priceless expressions ("Yuck!" . . . "Ewww!" . . . "Ughhh!"). They were Jäger virgins no more. The audience went wild.

As the audience witnessed, a brand can be simultaneously popular and disliked.

Despite possibly breaking a few laws for serving alcohol in the building, this "reverse product demonstration" created such a Twitter frenzy that Jägermeister became one of the top trending topics in Canada during the speech.*

Within an hour of the speech's finale, my cell phone rang. It was Jägermeister's marketing director. I froze, seized by a fear that I was in some kind of trouble.

That was not the case. They'd seen the activity on Twitter, and traced it back to my speech in Toronto. The marketing director said, "We don't know what you're doing, but it's working. Come to New York and talk with us."

---

* My clients sometimes request that I repeat this interaction at my events. On the upside, I've made a couple of TSA folks very happy when they discover what they get to confiscate from inside my carry-on baggage.

For much of 2010 and 2011, I worked closely with the Jäger team and many talented folks, leading new research and creative development. Together, we created all kinds of new ways to fascinate consumers. The next year, Jägermeister was named one of the ten most innovative brands in the world by *Advertising Age* magazine.

Are you starting to see why different is better than better?

Turning Murder into Business

For most business owners, an arrest by undercover police officers at your establishment would be cause for major damage control. Especially when that arrest captures a most-wanted criminal by the FBI . . . the first-ever FBI-documented female serial killer . . . who just happened to be a regular . . . who just happened to seek out and kill the very types of men who are your best customers.

Ice-Cold Beer and Killer Women

Introducing the Last Resort bar in Daytona Beach, Florida.

In 1991, Aileen Carol Wuornos went on a male-only killing spree until her arrest at a raid at the Last Resort. Instead of suppressing its relationship to a mass murderer and going into damage-control mode, the Last Resort turned it into an orange ticket.

The 1991 arrest still draws visitors from as far away as Australia, who share in the dark Wuornos allure. Visiting Daytona Beach for a family vacation with the kids? Be sure to stop by for a Wuornos-themed birthday party (which includes her bug-eyed photo in the cake frosting). Pick up a few bottles of the bar's "Crazed Killer Hot Sauce," with a label featuring a photo of Aileen Wuornos on her execution date (October 9, 2002, 9:47 a.m.).

Just as Jägermeister's importer, Sidney Frank, turned negative

PR into a bonus for the brand, so did the Last Resort pivot from damage control to media gold mine.*

When you identify orange tickets within your own brand, you will win more customers, more engagement, more relationships, more conversation, and more referrals, without really changing your product itself.

> Identify what your brand is already doing right—and then do more of it.

There's never been a time when it's more important to understand how your brand should communicate, and how to apply that insight to add distinct value. There has never been a greater opportunity to stand out and win.

If you believe that your brand matters—that your message matters—then you have a responsibility to deliver that message in a way that gets people to sit up and take notice. That's true whether you are writing a brochure or delivering a church sermon. Having an important message means nothing if nobody listens and takes action.

You will not win by being quiet. You will win by being heard.

---

* On a blazingly hot summer day, my family drove along US 1, and stopped at the Daytona Beach Flea Market. This cacophonous tent is a bazaar meets yard sale. Customers can sort through a selection of brass knuckles and disco cassettes, used cookware and heirloom paintings. I found a ventriloquist doll that looked like W. C. Fields (creepy yet cool). The vendors accept only cash, so I walked to the bar next door to use the ATM. And that, my friends, is how I discovered the Last Resort bar. The bar's tagline: "Home of Ice-Cold Beer and Killer Women."

A Million Years of
Personal Branding

HOW ALL BRANDING, INCLUDING PERSONAL BRANDING, DATES BACK TO OUR HAIRIER ANCESTORS

The Branding of You

Do you have a fascinating personal brand?

I'm not asking if you're charismatic, sexy, extroverted, or any of the other qualities that have become associated with the notion of being fascinating. In fact, the most fascinating people are often not charismatic or outgoing. Like the most fascinating brands, they understand how to position themselves to impress and influence their audience. They know how to be heard and remembered.

To become more fascinating, you don't have to *change* who you are. You have to become *more* of who you are.

To make a difference, you must become a celebrity of sorts, in your own way—someone who fascinates a specific audience.

Whether you're in the role of a CEO earning the respect of your board of directors, or a Little League coach teaching six-year-olds how to slide into home plate, fascination helps you earn the currency of attention, and you can cash in that attention to accomplish any type of communication goal.

In my book *How the World Sees You*, I identify exactly which traits are most likely to be your most fascinating. I describe how you can more meaningfully connect with the people around you who matter most. Your most fascinating traits help you close deals, earn traffic on your blog, win votes in an election, or accomplish any other endeavor that demands connection.

Ancient cultures realized that fascination holds people captive, making them powerless to resist. They protected their children from this evil force with amulets and ceremonies. Clearly, they knew something that we have since forgotten.

Propaganda: Marketing's Evil Cousin

For a moment, let's see just how evil fascination can become when it falls into the wrong hands.

Imagine a group of people in a locked room.

Those people hear a single message, repeatedly and consistently. Same message, over and over, with few deviations and little conflicting information. When there's no conflicting input, even a false message will be trusted. Pretty soon, that roomful of people will begin to believe the message, no matter how irrational or wrong it is.

However, if these people hear a variety of viewpoints, they're more likely to start questioning the message, forming opinions, and making their own decisions.

If you're a propagandist, you don't want opposing viewpoints—especially if your message must violate and transform an audience's beliefs in order to succeed. If you want to brainwash a group, it is not enough to repeat a message. You must squelch dissenters. Then, followers are forced to trust what you say, because it's all they know.*

Now that we've reviewed why people submit to propaganda, let's apply those same principles to understand our own behavior. Why do you follow certain people but not others?

Let's turn to the world of cult leaders (and what you can learn from them beyond the fashion recommendations of shaved heads and orange robes).

Beyond the Cult of Personality

Celebrities are almost a socially sanctioned form of cult leaders. From Miley Cyrus to Kim Kardashian to all six degrees of Kevin Bacon, we're fascinated by famous people—sometimes merely because they're famous.

For most fans of celebrities, according to experts, star-watching is a captivating diversion. In the extreme, however, fans become more than captivated. They're actually captive.

A study in the *British Journal of Psychology* found that 20% of us are at risk of replacing emotional connection in our real lives with a full-blown celebrity obsession. The fascination displayed by this 20% goes beyond downloading songs or imitating a hairstyle. Members of this group become disengaged from their real lives, abandoning rational priorities, becoming consumed the way cult members are: blindly following a charismatic alpha leader, mimicking behavior, conforming to a certain way of dressing, talking, and living.

How do cults systematically leverage the darkest powers of fascination? How do they push beyond fascination, to obsession?

---

* In the extreme, the abuse of fascination leads to the ugliest outcomes. In his autobiography *Mein Kampf*, Adolf Hitler describes the "art of propaganda" as a type of marketing. "What, for example, would we say about a poster that was supposed to advertise a new soap and that described other soaps as 'good'? We would only shake our heads. Exactly the same applies to political advertising."

Cult leaders brainwash their followers, turning otherwise logical people into programmed recruits who lose their ability to think for themselves in their quest to follow the leader.

Celebrity worship draws on the same hardwired drive to follow the leader. When people become fascinated by celebrities, they are literally spellbound, hypnotized, which often leads them to irrational behavior that closely resembles that of a cult member. They reject family and friends, and create a false universe that revolves around an event, a person, or even a brand.

Take a Sip of Kool-Aid and Read On

We all experience at least a fleeting interest with movie stars, professional athletes, or even celebrity CEOs such as Warren Buffett. At what point does that interest cross the line from fan to fanatical? At what point does a personal passion cross into an obsession? When do enthusiasts become cult members?

In the same way cult members sacrifice their personal lives for a group, one might say the same occurs with other individuals and groups that aren't normally considered "cults." One man's cult is another man's brand.

Like cults, fascinating brands don't try to speak to everyone. They narrowly target and recruit a specific type of person and mind-set, even to the point of polarizing outsiders. Is this so different from being a fervid devotee of a certain brand?

At my alma mater, Duke University, students would camp out in tents for a week in order to snag seats at Final Four basketball games. Is that a cult?

How about iPhone buyers waiting in line for the next release?

What about NFL sports fans during the playoffs, or Brazilian soccer fans during the World Cup?

What about NASCAR fans' devotion to certain drivers?

Phish fans and Deadheads?

Ironman triathletes who train seven days a week?

What can you learn from all this in order to lead people in an inspiring direction?

Flirtation and Fascination

The darkened cocktail lounge of the Saint Paul airport Marriott is a social petri dish, commingling business travelers from otherwise unrelated companies, cities, and professions. The lounge's ferns-and-brass ambiance offers these road warriors a comforting mixture of familiarity and anonymity.

In between serving Sam Adamses and glasses of Kendall-Jackson chardonnay, bartenders witness the nightly routine of strangers engaged in flirtation, a timeworn ritual that often progresses from suggestive glances to the elevator banks in two hours or less. Had these bartenders studied Irenäus Eibl-Eibesfeldt's research in evolutionary anthropology, they'd realize that they're front and center at a nightly performance of the flirtation tango, a series of dance steps choreographed over the millennia by the Martha Graham of mating dances, Mother Nature herself.

Whether a woman regularly quotes Carrie Bradshaw from *Sex and the City* or belongs to a society with no written language, she'll flirt using almost exactly the same nonverbal signals as other women across continents, cultures, and geographies. Eibl-Eibesfeldt discovered that women from around the globe, from craggy, remote islands to metropolitan centers, use the same repertoire of gestures when determining whether a potential mate is available and interested. Flirting, like all fascinations, is innate.

The Canoodling Tango

In her aptly named book *Sex*, Joann Ellison Rodgers describes Eibl-Eibesfeldt's discovery of just how all women flirt. A female begins fascinating a male by smiling at him, raising her brows to make her eyes appear wider and more childlike, then quickly lowering her lids while tucking her chin slightly down, in an effort to bring him closer. After averting her gaze to the side, she will, within moments and almost without exception, put her hands on or near her mouth and giggle, lick her lips, or thrust out her chest while gazing at the object of her intended affection. And it's consistent, regardless of language, socioeconomic status, or religious upbringing. For men, says Rodgers, the fascination ritual is less submissive but no less standardized. A man will puff out his chest, jut his chin, arch his back, gesture with his hands and arms, and swagger in dominant motions to draw attention to his power (not unlike the way a male pigeon puffs his chest, or a male gorilla struts). Like a woman's flirtation, his motions advertise critical cues about his reproductive fitness.

Fascination. Flirtation.

Just as we're born to be fascinated by specific signals from potential mates, we're also born knowing how to fascinate potential mates as well. Flirtation is the most elemental of all fascinations, one of a handful of instinctive cues on which all life depends. No flirtation, no mating. No mating, no offspring. No offspring, no family, no passing of the genes, no species.

Fascination Is a Force of Attraction

This force of attraction heightens intellectual, emotional, and physical focus. Couples in the Saint Paul airport Marriott fall into this captivated grip, and you experience it, too. When you impulsively decide to see a certain movie, when you crave your favorite chocolate almond ice cream, or when you hit repeat on your iPad to hear that song one more time, you're experiencing a similar, if less intense, attraction.

Attraction doesn't have to make sense. In most cases, attraction is highly irrational. We generally don't decide to be fascinated any more than we decide to be attracted to a certain person, because the root causes of our fascinations are hardwired into us long before we have any say in the matter.

Fascination takes many forms, but all tap into instinctive triggers, such as the need to hunt, to control, to feel secure, to nurture, and to be nurtured. Some fascinations last only a heartbeat, while others last beyond a sixty-first wedding anniversary. No matter how long it lasts or what behavior it motivates, or which trigger inspires it, every fascination binds with a singularly intense connection. We are, if only for a moment, utterly spellbound. Herein lies the power of fascination: it strips away our usual rational barriers, exposing our minds, leaving us vulnerable to influence, naked to persuasion.

Speaking of naked, let's check back in with our couples flirting in the Saint Paul airport Marriott lounge.

At the bar, a paralegal is progressing nicely through her flirtation with the service engineer from Sacramento. They're performing their steps in the mating dance with predictable precision. Yes, it's all a bit crazy. But if the notion that you're not in control of your flirtation seems crazy, take heart: you're not as crazy as you will be once you're infatuated.

The Mental Disorder Known as Infatuation

As things progress during flirtation, our neurochemistry rewards us with "infatuation." Fascination and infatuation both originate in the limbic area of the brain, the part that houses rage, ecstasy, sadness, sexual arousal, and the fight-or-flight response.

In his book *Love Sick: Love as a Mental Illness*, Frank Tallis writes that if we take the symptoms of falling in love and "check them against accepted diagnostic criteria for mental illness, we find that most 'lovers' qualify for diagnoses of obsession illness, depression or manic depression." Other symptoms include insomnia, hyperactivity, and loss of appetite. Ah, ain't love grand? Eli Finkel, a Northwestern University psychologist, describes how falling in love can make "otherwise normal people do very wild things. They'll stalk, hack into e-mail, eavesdrop and do other things they'd never do in a rational frame of mind." Helen Fisher, an evolutionary anthropologist, explains that the elevated dopamine levels experienced during the rush of falling in love can drive us to take risks that might otherwise seem unthinkable. So love really does conquer all, and not always in a good way.

Why would our brains throw us into a temporary insanity? What's the evolutionary purpose? Fisher says that our brains are literally "built to fall in love" because it's in our evolutionary best interest *not* to think clearly during the two-year time period it takes to meet, court, and produce a child, or else we might come to our senses and avoid the inconvenience of child rearing altogether.

By leveraging these same principles, you can captivate your customers, so they fall head over heels in love with your brand.

First Comes Love, Then Comes Marriage,
Then Comes Branding in a Baby Carriage

Most elements of fascination work at the subconscious level. Unlike the act of paying attention, which is rational, being fascinated has more in common with the less logical behaviors of passion. We don't even realize it's happening any more than we realize that we're flirting for reasons that have less to do with hearts and flowers and more to do with our biological urge to procreate. Whether you realize it or not, you experience fascination's irrational grip. You might do a shot of Jägermeister without actually liking the taste, because it takes like forbidden fruit. Or a shot of whiskey.

Why Prohibition Was Prohibited

Smart organizations recognize a business opportunity when they see it. So when Prohibition began in the United States on January 17, 1920, the Mafia expanded beyond gambling and thievery, and into the far more profitable pursuit of bootlegging. Overnight, the manufacture, sale, and distribution of alcoholic beverages became illegal in the United States. As the black market for hard liquor flourished, the mob became wealthier than ever, growing so pervasive and powerful from alcohol profits that the Chicago mob boss Al Capone earned more than $100 million a year. The Mafia held a national convention in 1928 to formalize its reign, even discussing a nationwide crime syndicate.

The "Noble Experiment," as Prohibition was called, didn't dampen drinking. Drinking moved underground into speakeasy clubs, and beating Prohibition became a hobby enjoyed by millions of Americans. John D. Rockefeller, a onetime proponent, later admitted its failure, writing that "drinking has generally increased; the speakeasy has replaced the saloon; a vast army of lawbreakers has appeared; many of our best citizens have openly ignored Prohibition; respect for the law has been greatly lessened; and crime has increased to a level never seen before." Thanks to Prohibition, alcohol became fermented forbidden fruit. Americans were thirstier than ever, until 1933 when Prohibition was repealed. When something is forbidden, it becomes fascinating. Even if that something is illegal.

Fascination shapes behavior in many ways. The ancient cultures knew that. Now it's time for you to harness and control it.

Your Brand's Advantage

HOW TO IDENTIFY WHAT MAKES YOUR BRAND FASCINATING

Identifying Your Brand's Advantage

When your brand speaks clearly in the right Advantage to the right customers, wonderful things happen. Phones ring. Products fly off shelves. Revenue increases. Marketing gets much, much easier. It all begins with pinpointing what makes you different.

Different is better than better.

In a distracted, competitive, commoditized environment, even slight differences give you a competitive edge. Once you identify your brand's Advantage, you'll have clear steps to follow to spellbind your ideal customers and top talent. You will consistently communicate directly with your ideal target audience. Instead of being all things to all people, you'll become intensely valuable.

National Study of Fascination

In the national Kelton Study of Fascination, we measured the return on investment (ROI) for brands that fascinate customers. In a state of fascination, people will pay higher prices. In some cases, they'll pay up to 400% more.

Each of the seven Advantages has a different mind-set, attitude, and way of attracting attention. Each casts a specialized spell.

Finished that Red Bull yet? Moving on to ice cream.

Are You Pistachio? Or Vanilla?

Vanilla ice cream is a crowd-pleaser. Most people like it, and almost everyone will eat it. It's easy, comfortable, and safe. The Gap khakis of ice cream. Yet vanilla has a competitive disadvantage: it's an obvious choice, and it can be inherently less fascinating.

Far fewer people, on the other hand, like pistachio ice cream. Pistachio is a distinct and polarizing choice. Yet the people who like pistachio usually love it. *Reeeally* love it. Crazy love it. Although fewer people buy pistachio, the flavor has a competitive advantage: rather than dumbing down its taste to appeal to the majority, the producer can focus on serving a tightly defined core with a distinct point of difference.

There's nothing wrong with vanilla, of course. I keep vanilla in my freezer when my goal is to appeal to the maximum number of people with the minimum amount of whining. Yet while vanilla might be an easy choice for the masses, it's not necessarily the right choice for *you*. Beware vanilla (unless you have the biggest marketing budget).

The goal of pistachio isn't to please everyone. It's to engage a few people really, really well.

The Underdog's Unfair Advantage

If you have the biggest marketing budget in your category, vanilla is probably a smart place to focus on. You want the lowest common denominator. Your goal should be to avoid polarizing a substantial segment of the market, especially if your brand has an established, trusted presence among customers. Vanilla brands, such as Walmart and Kellogg, fascinate with the repetition and familiarity of the Trust Advantage, often expanding their market share through mass media (for instance, a Super Bowl spot rather than targeted social media ads).

But let's say you don't have the biggest budget. Let's assume you need to compete fiercely without vast resources, or even without an established market presence. That's where pistachio comes in.

The smaller base of pistachio-loving customers has the potential to become intensely dedicated—even fanatical.

You can either be the *vanilla* of your category, or the *pistachio*.

As long as you have the biggest budget in your category, you can afford to be boring, because you can simply repeat your message over and over to create awareness. Along those same lines, if you are the most famous in your category, you can be boring, if you can continue to generate that awareness.

But what if don't have the biggest budget? Or if you aren't the most famous? What then? Then, my friend, you must be the most fascinating. Let me explain.

Pistachio Is an Orange Ticket

In this case, my friends, you must highlight what makes you different. And that's where pistachio comes in. Instead of trying to outdo your competition, focus on what makes you different. The goal is to find where you and your product diverge from standard expectations.

Most brands want to cluster smack-dab in the middle of the bell curve, where vanilla and chocolate and strawberry live. In the comfort zone. But when you create fascinating experiences that elicit a strong and immediate response, you push out to the fringe.

If not pistachio flavor, perhaps cast a spell with Jägermeister flavor?

The Seven Forms of Witchcraft

We're about to embark on a journey winding through these seven forms of persuasion: Innovation, Passion, Power, Prestige, Trust, Mystique, and Alert. Each is a world unto itself, a set of strategies to create marketing magic.

PART II

The Seven Fascination Advantages: How to Make Your Brand Impossible to Resist

Meet your new arsenal: Innovation, Passion, Power, Prestige, Trust, Mystique, and Alert.

The System behind
the Spellbinding

So far, we've explored Sigmund Freud, the Salem Witch Trials, and other examples of bewitching communication. Now it's your turn to see the system behind how fascination works, and how you can apply it, too.

This part of the book is your guide to the seven forms of fascination: Innovation, Passion, Power, Prestige, Trust, Mystique, and Alert. Each casts a different spell. With Passion, people are more likely to fall in love with your brand. Power makes them likely to follow you. Prestige earns their respect. Alert protects the details, so they feel safe.

Most of us have remarkably little understanding of why we ourselves become fascinated, and even less understanding of how to fascinate our customers and clients. The ability to fascinate is not commonly thought of as something that can be measured and created at will. Yet this is not the case. Fascination can be measured, and you'll measure your brand's profile soon, with the Fascination Advantage for Brands.

Whether you're competing in a product category or a political party, a sports team or a dating circle, you must become fluent in fascination. You must know how to systematically create it, then measure it.

How do certain brands fascinate you? How can your brand fascinate others? To succeed in an attention-starved world, you must understand how fascination applies to your job, your company, your family, and your relationships. And finally, you must understand the implications of living in a fascination-driven world, one in which the ordinary dies a slow death.

You already possess much of what you need to become more fascinating, and in today's environment, you have no choice but to use it. Intelligently applied, fascination will give you a tool more influential than branding, more persuasive than propaganda, more lasting than brainwashing.

Make Your Brand Impossible to Resist

Fascinations cover the gamut of human behavior, from sublime to straightlaced, from frivolous to world-changing, yet all can be categorized as one of seven different modes of communication: Innovation, Passion, Power, Prestige, Trust, Mystique, and Alert. Each of these has a different attitude and style, a different voice and vocabulary.

Rather than be confused by the options, we'll go step-by-step through the process. We'll align all your communication with one main point, like a North Star. Instead of randomly stumbling on ideas, or reinventing the wheel each time you write an ad, you'll now have a step-by-step plan. Whether you are an analytical thinker or a creative fireball, you'll find it much easier to develop and execute marketing plans when they follow a system.

As you read the descriptions of each Advantage in the chapters that follow, pay close attention to the lists of five adjectives. You can literally use these words to describe your brand to your ideal customer. They can become the starting point for your marketing copy.

For instance, Innovation brands are *forward-thinking, entrepreneurial, bold, surprising,* and *visionary.* A brand whose primary Advantage is Innovation might use these words to describe itself:

"a *forward-thinking visionary* company that offers *surprisingly bold* ideas to *entrepreneurial* leaders." Incorporating these adjectives helps the brand speak the language of creativity.

A brand with the Alert Advantage would look to these adjectives: *organized, detailed, efficient, precise,* and *methodical.* An Alert brand's marketing copy should sound very different from that of an Innovation brand. "We guarantee *organized* and *detailed* delivery of every order." Or, "our agents are the most *efficient* and *precise* in the industry." These adjectives steer the communication to speak the language of details.

Branding for All

"Branding" is often seen as marketing's fancier cousin. Many small businesses believe, mistakenly, that only those with large budgets can do branding. This is understandable, since usually only organizations with impressive experience or budgets can afford a brand campaign.

I have a different point of view. I believe that everyone should be able to create a great brand, without a big budget or extensive expertise.

The purpose of the Fascinate System is to give you a simple, practical process for establishing the overall voice of your brand. By getting clear on how you describe yourself to your prospects and customers, you can streamline your creative process. This will also help you and your team keep all messaging on track, so you can unify your efforts.

It's time to perform a little marketing witchcraft of your own, and spellbind your audience. Don't worry, there's a clear system. You're about to understand your marketing in a new way, and realize how your ideal customer sees you at your best. The process is almost like alchemy, transforming ordinary products into gold.

Our first Advantage is Innovation, the language of creativity. How could you captivate with Innovation? Let's find out.

Innovation

THE LANGUAGE OF CREATIVITY

The World's Most Expensive Dinosaur Food

Recently, while browsing in a gift shop, I saw a small package of Dinosaur Food on the counter. The label showed terrified little kids running from a T-rex, mouths open in fear. It included a candy that looked like worms and I knew my kids would love it.

As I paid my $3.99, the sales clerk remarked how often this popular gift sold out of stock.

The kids opened the little cellophane bag, their eyes growing wide to be eating REAL Dinosaur Food. I was a hero, victoriously returning from a prehistoric era rather than a store down the street. I peered more closely at my $3.99 purchase. Inside the bag was . . . five gummy worms. Five. Slightly smooshed. I'd paid $3.99 for five generic gummy worms, which actually cost about three cents. At least the worms could have had tiny widemouthed screams of sheer terror.

Yet I have to applaud this product. Simply calling it "Dinosaur Food" elevates its perceived value by 1,000%.

This little example demonstrates a very, very big principle of fascination. When you speak the language of creativity, you can transform a dull commodity into something magical. Rather than charging just for the generic value of the product, you can charge for the experience.

This, my friends, is black magic in action.

The packaging didn't cost more than that of regular candy. The candy itself didn't cost more than regular candy. All it cost was an idea. Even if you're selling an ordinary product, when you cast a spell of fascination, you can transform a staple into a story line.

Here's another example of turning a commodity product into a fascinating experience.

Expensive Whiskey, Meet Expensive Granite

When drinking a glass of whiskey, you might notice how melting ice dilutes the complex flavor. How to chill the whiskey without the melting ice? Well, you could either drink it very quickly—or you could toss in a few chilled whiskey stones. These aren't just *any* stones, mind you. Or . . . maybe they are? The stones themselves are usually made of granite, which is a plentiful and relatively inexpensive material. Yet simply marketing the granite with a new application and fascinating packaging elevates the price of nine small rocks to about twenty bucks.

Your brand can turn vanilla into pistachio. You can turn a green ticket into an orange one. And by applying Innovation, you can even serve Dinosaur Food.

What Is "Innovation"?

Innovation is the most creative of all the seven Advantages. It imagines. It tweaks. It invents. It surprises. It introduces new options, new behaviors, and new ways of thinking. It isn't afraid to kick up some dust. It refuses to play follow the leader.

If your brand's Advantage is Innovation, make sure you consistently defy the ordinary. Take nothing for granted. Refuse to drink from the mainstream. Make bureaucrats nervous. Never live by default.

If it ain't broke . . . break it.

> ## INNOVATION:
> ### THE LANGUAGE OF CREATIVITY
> Innovation changes the game with a new approach. It challenges assumptions, pushing people to think in new ways.

Five Adjectives to Differentiate Your Innovation Brand

Will Innovation be your brand's primary Advantage? If so, you can revolutionize a product, a client, or an entire industry. When your brand speaks the language of creativity, your communication will be forward-thinking, entrepreneurial, bold, surprising, and visionary.

FIVE ADJECTIVES TO DIFFERENTIATE
YOUR INNOVATION BRAND

FORWARD-THINKING

Innovation companies consciously avoid falling into ruts. If a service is usually sold one way, they find ways to sell it another way.

ENTREPRENEURIAL

Instead of plodding along behind others, they bring a hungry mindset and feisty attitude.

BOLD

Other brands might be bigger, but none are bolder.

SURPRISING

They push us to think ahead of the curve.

VISIONARY

Rather than see the world as it is, Innovation brands show us what the world can become.

How Innovation Fascinates

We're rarely fascinated by the ordinary. Surprises, however, interrupt our expectation of how the world looks and behaves. When man bites dog, or when snow falls in August, that's worth a second look.

Innovation brands open our eyes. They change our expectations, and even the way we make assumptions. They give people an opportunity to see the world from a new perspective. It's the tiny fashion house inventing trends a year ahead of the mainstream. It's how Amazon disrupts the traditional publishing model by allowing authors to self-publish and distribute through its website.

If you speak the language of creativity, you challenge us to break old habits—or at the very least, to consider new possibilities. You force competitors to realign. You're not afraid to try something new.*

In stagnant and saturated categories (such as mortgage sales or health care), Innovation players have a competitive edge over bigger, more established companies. If your marketing budget is limited, or you're new to the market, creativity offers a strong competitive edge over more-established brands.

What seemed startling a decade ago now seems hardly worth a second glance to increasingly jaded and bored audiences. Brands become irrelevant unless they can tweak their game. They have to work harder to get the same result.

To help you get started with Innovation, here's a sample of how an Innovation brand could describe itself to potential customers.

How Brands Use Innovation in Their Marketing
Innovation follows certain patterns. Consciously measure your communication against these four pillars:
- Invent surprising solutions.
- Turn something old into something new.
- Do the opposite.
- Infuse a dose of vice.

---

*A man owned both a bar and a Harley. During his life, he collected several large Harley tattoos on his back and shoulders. When he died, his son had the tattoos removed, tanned, and framed, and hung them in the bar. I'm uncertain if this is a positive for patrons at the bar; however, it is good proof that Harley fascinates.

Develop messages that consistently deliver at least three of these four pillars of Innovation. Before you send that email, or publish that ad, check back with these four pillars. If not, push your ideas further in order to speak the language of creativity.

Invent Surprising Solutions

It's easy to follow what everyone else is doing. It might take more effort, but you can also attract interest by inventing unexpected solutions.

Don't expect to surprise your audience with the same trick repeatedly. You can either use the same surprise with new people, or new surprises with the same people. Either reinvent your audience, or reinvent your material. Jack-in-the-boxes fail to surprise after a few times.

What if you're a restaurant, and you also want to encourage the use of sign language? How could you apply creativity, and communicate with customers who don't know sign language? At Signs, a restaurant in Toronto, patrons must order in sign language. Icons next to the menu items make it easy for those who haven't a clue how to say "French toast and coffee" using their hands. Most diners enter a completely different world when they sit down for a meal at Signs, and get an experience they can't help talking about.

Turn Something Old into Something New

Are your sales falling? Is your niche becoming obsolete? When it's time to discover creative solutions, look to Innovation.

Who Says a Household Cleaner Can't Be a Toy?

Before World War II, most US homes were heated by coal. The thick coal smoke left black soot marks on nearby wallpaper. How to clean the soot? Noah and Joseph McVicker developed and sold a doughlike cleaning product to be rubbed on the coal stain.

Years later, sales of soot cleaner fell sharply when coal was replaced by natural gas. The brand was on the verge of demise. How to boost sales of an obsolete household cleaner? This brand went in the exact opposite direction, and positioned the soot cleaner as a children's toy. It become one of one of the world's most popular and creative toys: Play-Doh.

Play-Doh has inspired over seven hundred million pounds of creativity among children everywhere. Ironically, what once was a cleaner is now the bane of parents everywhere when that brightly colored dough gets smooshed into the carpet. Where's the carpet cleaner for this former wallpaper cleaner?

If your product is becoming outdated or irrelevant, you always have the option to creatively reinvent the old into something entirely new.*

Do the Opposite

Brands tend to mimic each other, watching to see what everyone else is doing before taking action. For instance, car dealerships have big vinyl signs outside. Pet stores have a dog or cat or bird in the logo. Pharmaceutical companies use the "Rx" symbol. Yes, these are easy shorthands, but they also make you look like everyone else. How could you stand out? What if you did the exact opposite of what people expect from your brand or category?

A Tropical Island on the Freezing Hudson River

Against the freezing winter wind, I pulled my coat's woolen collar up around my neck, stomping my feet to feel them inside my boots. A hundred feet in front of me, a tanned couple in bathing suits played volleyball on a tropical island.

---

* Remember Play-Doh's oddly distinctive smell? It was also in the original product, added to mask the underlying chemical smell of the cleaning agent.

What were we doing? We were staging a PR stunt so surprising that it would fascinate the media. For weeks before this morning, we'd been secretly building a small island in New York City's Hudson River. This tropical island was complete with tons of sand, palm trees, a thatched-roof hut with hammock and hot tub, and a life jacket–wearing dog.

Before the big reveal, we'd towed the island into place under the black of night. As the sun rose, the press caught on. As I watched the island, my hair blew in all directions from the CNN news choppers churning the air overhead. Dozens of TV reporters filmed live segments and streamed early-morning updates to their stations. The CBS morning show called it New York's "sixth borough."

Blowing warm breath into my cupped palms, I watched as the couple took a break from playing volleyball to relax in the hot tub. They reached for their margaritas topped off with tiny paper umbrellas. We sent messages to the couple with a trained carrier pigeon.

My client, Scripps Networks (the company behind HGTV and the Food Network), wanted the world to know that it was all about creating extraordinary life experiences. This untraditional piece of marketing was nothing short of extraordinary. Knowing this, I'd given my team a challenge: create something so audacious, so newsworthy, that it would be impossible for the media to ignore. The annual advertising budget was $3 million. As the advertising director, I asked my client to put aside 10% of the overall budget to develop one idea that was risky yet promising.

In twenty-four hours, this $300,000 investment earned an estimated $30 million in free media exposure: one hundred times the original investment.

Infuse a Dose of Vice

That devil sitting on your shoulder, whispering in your ear? He's whispering vice.

Rules are rarely fascinating, but bending them, very much so. When you push a boundary, or reinvent an expectation, you fascinate with creativity. You're stepping your toe over the line, flirting with the unexpected.

If you want to tap into one of the oldest forms of persuasion, have a dance with the bad girl. The word "vice" comes from the Latin *vitium*, meaning "failing or defect," because vice reveals our delight with bad behavior or mischievousness. (You might have a vice for *The Real Housewives of Beverly Hills*, or late-night karaoke, or McDonald's Sausage McGriddles. No judgments on my end.)

Let's see how a boring product can apply a zing of vice, and turn a commodity into a fascinating experience. Let's travel to Las Vegas, where we'll speak the language of creativity to serve a different type of candy.

Hard Rock Hotel: Advanced Partying

Peter Morton, the heir to the Morton's steakhouse fortune, had a dazzling jewel in the crown of coolness: the Hard Rock Hotel in Las Vegas. At the time, the Hard Rock Hotel was the epitome of everything young/cool/beautiful.

The Hard Rock Hotel was not just a hotel. It was more of a commitment. Only once you'd mastered beginner skills were you ready for this experience. Everything from the exclusively dark lobby to the "Rehab" pool party every Sunday challenged guests, even goaded them, to step it up a notch. (Tequila shots? Been there. Beer bongs? Done that.)

Yet the hotel also faced its own challenge: how to advertise to this jaded audience, without looking like the brand was trying too hard. And from a budgetary standpoint, how to reach people in LA, without buying mass media? The answer: infuse a dose of vice.

Together, my partner Mark DiMassimo and I created "The Guide to Advanced Partying." At the seductively lit welcome desk, guests were greeted with a room key tucked inside a delicious little guidebook. This guide answered questions that "advanced partiers" might encounter during their stay. A few headlines:

All-nighters and the how-tos of annulment: There's a reason we don't have a wedding chapel here. If you and your new spouse aren't blood relatives or under the age of sixteen, annulment is tough to come by. But look on the bright side: you can show your grandkids the bar tab from your first date.

Does waking up with singles tucked in your undies make you slutty? Or entrepreneurial?: While a shake of your groove thang on the bar can certainly offset your trip's expenses, we'd like to introduce a more lucrative source of income: our poker tables. You won't even have to make a career change for the night.

To help these twentysomethings recover from their Vegas weekend, guests received "rest prescriptions." The prescription said, "Please be advised that my patient must be confined to bed for the next forty-eight hours and will be unable to work."

By infusing a drop of vice, a brand can attract a difficult-to-reach clientele through word of mouth.*

---

* In the first edition of *Fascinate*, I described Innovation as "Vice." Ever been tempted to eat something you shouldn't, buy something you can't afford, or rebel against a strict rule? That's Vice. Vice comes from Innovation, but Innovation isn't always Vice. Brands use Vice to entice you to into a new way of doing things. I revised the term Vice to "Innovation," which better reflects the myriad ways in which you can encourage people to change behavior and be different.

THE LANGUAGE OF CREATIVITY

INNOVATION

AT A GLANCE

Change the game.

DEVELOP MESSAGES THAT ARE:

Forward-Thinking • Entrepreneurial • Bold • Surprising • Visionary

PILLARS OF INNOVATION BRANDS:

➤ Invent surprising solutions.

➤ Turn something old into something new.

➤ Do the opposite.

➤ Add a dose of vice.

Does your brand fascinate with Innovation? Get your Brand Profile at BrandFascination.com.

Next, on to the Passion Advantage.

Does your brand speak the language of relationship? If so, you attract us, drawing us in, making us feel emotionally connected with your brand. (Hugs all around!)

Passion

THE PASSION ADVANTAGE

EXPRESSIVE • OPTIMISTIC • SENSORY • WARM • SOCIAL

The Bubble Parade

A few years ago, I had a magical experience. In a hospital, of all places.

My little girl had recurring ear infections, and she needed minor surgery to put tubes in her ears. When the big day came, we entered the hospital, and she didn't seem afraid. Yet as we took the elevator up to the pre-op room, I could tell she was becoming increasingly nervous as the floors ticked by.

Over the next two hours, the nurses prepped her for surgery, giving her IV fluids and a swallow of medicine. I was by her side the whole time.

Finally it was time to go into the operating room, and the nurse came to wheel her away from me. My heart tightened.

To ease her fears, the pediatric nurses gathered around her and created a "bubble parade," blowing little soap bubbles as they went into the operating room. To create this fairy-tale experience, they used a wand. Specifically, a bubble wand. All the worry and fear melted from my daughter's face as she was captivated by the magical moment.

As a parent, I felt a great deal of gratitude for this small but meaningful touch. As a marketer, I was awed. I'd just witnessed my daughter's customer experience switch from anxiety to anticipation in less than ten seconds. The magical bubble parade interaction was simple to execute, immediately beneficial, virtually free, replicable, and rewarding for both the customer and the employee.

When you speak to people in the language of relationship by giving them an emotional experience, they will remember the feeling. The language of relationship can even turn a sterile service into a vibrantly heartwarming memory. As Maya Angelou said, "I've learned that people will forget what you said, people will forget what you did, but people will never forget how you made them feel."

What Is "Passion"?

Passion makes our hearts swell, our pulses race, and our emotions rise.

It excites and encourages. It cheerleads and plays. It inspires and intoxicates. It flirts and coaxes. When you communicate with Passion, you make people feel like they can do more, be more, and become more.

Passion doesn't rely on rational information, or stem from wise and reasonable decision making, which can be easy to ignore, especially if we don't feel like analyzing something. (Whether we *should* crave cheesy Taco Bell nachos rarely determines whether we actually *do* crave them.) Passion comes from the heart and from the gut. As a result, this form of communication is especially useful in heightening connection and desire.

When you effectively speak the language of relationship, on some level, we'll fall in love with you.

PASSION:
THE LANGUAGE OF RELATIONSHIP

Engaging, heartwarming, and inspirational, Passion elevates emotions and connects us to something bigger than ourselves.

Five Adjectives to Differentiate Your Passion Brand

Does your brand inspire and motivate others to connect with you? If so, you speak the language of relationship. Build your messaging around the following five qualities:

FIVE ADJECTIVES TO DIFFERENTIATE
YOUR PASSION BRAND

EXPRESSIVE

Passion brands use vivid words, colors and images.

OPTIMISTIC

These are the "life is good" brands. They bring out our best by showing us how good things can be, making us want to jump in with both feet.

SENSORY

This form of communication engages our senses.

WARM

Passion brands wrap us up in a warm blanket and serve us mental chocolate chip cookies.

SOCIAL

These brands make us want to share and participate in the conversation.

How Passion Fascinates

When thirsty, we might crave an orange Slurpee from 7-Eleven. When hungry, we might crave fresh oysters in Saint Augustine. When tired, we might seek the retreat of a tub of bubbles. These are all Passion cues. When you understand the hardwired attraction behind these cues, your brand can build a stronger attachment with its customers.

Every time you communicate, you are either drawing people closer, or pushing them away. Whether you realize it or not, every single aspect of your brand—from your logo, to your call center, to your tagline—is either pulling people in, or turning them off. Every single action and message develops an emotional connection (or not). Your colors. Your photos. Your attitude.

The Passion mode of communication taps into a decision-making process outside reason and logic. Because Passion focuses on emotion, it can increase the perceived attraction of impulsive purchases.

Passion influences us by creating irresistible messages that overcome rational resistance. It never overwhelms with numbers and graphs, and instead offers an evocative experience. Adding more data to the instruction manual won't increase Passion.

If you're selling something that is not explicitly addressing a practical need or requirement, this Advantage can tip things over the line, turning "I really shouldn't" into "I really shouldn't—but I will anyway."

Of all the seven Advantages, Passion is the fastest way to build an emotional connection.

How Brands Use Passion in Their Marketing

To speak the language of relationship, every time you communicate with your customers, consider the following:

- Woo with wow.
- Use the five senses.
- Put lust before logic.
- Create a strong and immediate emotional response.

Your goal is to attract rabid fans, and pull your audience closer. Get ready to pick up your magic wand and perform marketing witchcraft. We're about to turn basic transactions into magical and spellbinding experiences.

Woo with Wow

Many Italian restaurants have cliché "When the moon hits your eye like a big pizza pie"–type songs playing in the background. To woo with wow, a standard experience won't cut it. You have to provoke an emotional response that captivates your customer.

The quirky Italian restaurant chain Buca di Beppo plays Italian lessons in the restroom. Also, instead of lovely but somewhat banal imagery of Tuscan countrysides lining the wall, customers are greeted by a statue that pees into the fountain. Woo? Maybe. Wow? Definitely.

Use the Five Senses

Sight, sound, taste, smell, and touch—these senses are practically built for black magic. If you speak the language of relationship, use them whenever you can. Stimulating the five senses heightens the brand experience, making it more intensely fascinating.

Scent is an underrated marketing tool. Rather than exploring all five senses, let's see what your nose knows.

The Sweet Smell of Success

As any Realtor can tell you, a house sells more quickly when buyers walk through the front door to homey scents of baking bread and hot coffee. Applying the language of relationship, you might invoke a similarly positive response from clients walking into your office with the scent of coffee brewing near the front door.

Hanging in the window of Jimmy John's sandwich shops, a neon sign advertises "Free Smells." While this sign promises the enticing experience of baking bread, it also reinforces freshness. A small-town hardware store might point out its traditional scent of freshly cut wood, to emphasize its customized service.

New Car Smell and Old Ashtrays

If corporate perfume isn't your thing, how about a nice ashtray air freshener?

The archetypical English pub has a distinctive smoke-tinged scent. Whether patrons realize it or not, that scent is a big part of the classic pub experience. On some level, we expect how an English pub should smell. The Trust Advantage (see page 121) also comes into play here, because we expect this scent to be consistently part of the classic pub atmosphere.

When smoking was banned in public spaces, pubs grappled with the question of how to retain their immediately identifiable smell. Would a pub by any other scent smell as sweet?

"Many pub patrons don't feel the same in a smoke-free environment," says Frank Knight, the founder of the air fragrance company Dale Air. Not to worry. The company's new air freshener offers an unusual scent: ashtray. "From what I have heard, it's because of the awful smells the tobacco used to veil, such as body odor and vomit," Knight says. (Alrighty then!)

Back in New York City, scent also plays a fascinating role. Half a block away from Artisanal Bistro, the scent of exotic cheeses billows down the street like a pennant. Inside, it's an olfactory immersion. Artisanal Bistro offers 250 of the world's top cheeses.*

This shop doesn't just sell cheeses; it sells the experience of cheese. Scent is core to the brand experience.

Lingerie, Saliva, and Other Sensual Brand Connections

The *Journal of Consumer Research* reports that merely holding a lacy bra will make a man more likely to seek immediate rewards such as

---

* One cheese that Artisanal Bistro thankfully does not offer: Casu marzu, a Sardinian cheese with live maggots. The maggots can jump up to five inches out of cheese while you're eating it, so it's a good idea to shield it with your hand to stop them jumping into your eyes.

an indulgent dessert, or to spend a greater amount of money. Just the hint of Passion causes a "greater urgency to consume anything rewarding." The two appetites become intertwined in the brain. As the brain opens to possibilities, the wallet opens as well.

Sometimes a company wants to create an un-Passionate experience for strategic reasons. Shopping malls contain an intentionally unfascinating environment in the middle, so that customers are more likely to flock to the stores. That's also why you won't see a clock in a mall (so you lose track of time and stay there longer). And it's also why the acoustics are bad in malls, so that stores seem like a comforting alternative.

Sensory experiences fascinate us. It's why we splurge on spa appointments and music concerts. For products that seem irrational on the surface, consider Passion. Why else would someone order a Hardee's Monster Thickburger (1,420 calories and 107 grams of fat), or a Baskin-Robbins large Heath Bar Shake (2,310 calories and 108 grams of fat)?

Passion bypasses scrutiny and cynicism. It's rarely lukewarm, or "take it or leave it." Passion can be overcome with willpower, but it's unlikely to be forgotten or ignored. Passion is not about utility or function.

When you create emotional bonds, people are more likely to act on your message. One way to do this? Forgo logic, and build lust.

Put Lust before Logic

An eternally favorite deadly sin, lust fascinates through experience: our appetites and passions of sight, sound, taste, touch, and scent. We anticipate what it might be like to fulfill a craving, and that anticipation pulls us closer. As early as the sixth century AD, lust emerged as public enemy number one for Christians. And not without reason. Overcoming desire is no easy task. Buddhism presents the overcoming of desire as an ideal. The five senses shape our behavior in many ways, like a temptress holding a skeleton key to fit any chastity belt.*

The Wet Voice

Her voice has been described as "cotton candy, smoke, wind, lollipops and velvet"; "champagne lava"; "the slow folding and unfolding of a pink cashmere sweater."

David Huron from Ohio State University uses a different word to describe Marilyn Monroe's famous voice: "wet."

"When we see something we want to eat, when we receive praise, and even when we hug our children, our mouths literally water," says Huron. In any type of pleasure state, our mouths produce more saliva. Our tongue moves more fluidly within the mucous membranes of our mouth, creating what Huron calls "oral wetness cues." Oral wetness is a subtle and involuntary reflex; however, it broadcasts our emotional state.

Your mouth also waters when you experience positive emotions. When you hug someone you love, or listen to a favorite song. Even when you hear good news. It's an unconscious response to positive emotions.

Marilyn Monroe's wet voice communicated openness. Her voice was also "aspirated," says Huron, meaning that she increased the amount of air through her vocal cords when speaking, almost like whispering. We all aspirate our voices when we're murmuring to a person right next to us. Yet Marilyn manipulated her wetness cues as part of her brand image. She communicated with a "pillow talk" effect even while onstage, speaking as though physically intimate with each person in the audience. (Cue your mental replay of her aural masterpiece, "Happy Birthday, Mr. President.")

---

* In the original edition of this book, Passion was named "Lust." Lust, however, is only a part (albeit a juicy one) of the bigger package of captivating strategies within the umbrella of the Passion Advantage. As we rolled out the Fascination Advantage system in 2012, we broadened this category to reflect the diversity of Passion.

Passion communication doesn't necessarily involve pink cashmere and pillows, but it does rely on neurological cues of attachment and proximity.

Create a Strong and Immediate Emotional Response

Want to fascinate with Passion? You already have biology on your side.

Our mouths create not only more saliva in anticipation of pleasure, but in some cases, a different type of saliva. *Motor Trend* magazine once described a Maserati as inspiring "visceral, carnal automotive lust." One UK study suggests that this description is literally quite accurate.

Researchers assessed the levels of arousal in a group of women, measuring the amount of testosterone present in their saliva. First, they tested the women's saliva. Then they tested it again, after the women had listened to the sound of Italian sports cars such as Ferraris, Lamborghinis, and Maseratis.

The result? One hundred percent of the women demonstrated a significant jump in testosterone levels after listening to the growl of Italian sports car engines. But it's not just any car engine that turns women on. When the women listened to a comparatively weak engine, their testosterone levels plummeted below normal. Smaller engines, it seems, trigger less immediate response. In other words, a brand can also make people feel *disconnected*.

Great design frequently uses Passion, especially when that design brings a human touch to an object or makes its functionality more experiential. For example, like the nurses who staged the bubble parade I mentioned before, an industrial designer at GE has created colorful pediatric MRI machines that look like pirate ships and submarines for the kids.

Even if your product itself seems off-putting or cold, or even boring, you can still make it fascinating by applying Passion. Inspire strong emotions, and don't be lukewarm.

Could you add human elements that create a strong and immediate emotional reaction to your brand? How about your product design? Your stores? Your website? Instead of sending emails to customers from a generic email address, could you send an email from an actual person?

THE LANGUAGE OF RELATIONSHIP

PASSION

AT A GLANCE

Connect with emotion.

DEVELOP MESSAGES THAT ARE:

Expressive • Optimistic • Sensory • Warm • Social

PILLARS OF PASSION BRANDS:

> Woo with wow.

> Use the five senses.

> Put lust before logic.

> Create a strong and immediate emotional response.

Does your brand fascinate with Passion?
Get your Brand Profile at BrandFascination.com.

We've experienced the warmth and emotion of Passion. Now we'll move into the strength and authority of Power, the language of confidence.

Power

THE POWER ADVANTAGE

ASSERTIVE • GOAL ORIENTED • DECISIVE • PURPOSEFUL • OPINIONATED

Trust the Chef

You may remember the Soup Nazi from *Seinfeld*. But are you familiar with the Sushi Dictators? These guys aren't actors, and the clientele is real. Each dictator has his own irritable quirks, and in many cases, their patrons aren't even allowed to order, because the chef selects the meal. If you look up Sushi Nozawa in LA, it's one of the highest-rated restaurants in terms of the food. The *Zagat* description, however, clearly calls out its infamous reputation: "Makes the Soup Nazi look polite." A *Wall Street Journal* article by reporter Katy McLaughlin described its *omakase* tradition, which means "trust the chef," explaining that some consumers go because they think they're getting an authentic meal. But as the psychologist David Stewart explains in the article, "people value praise more when it comes from people who don't give it out easily." People go to these restaurants in search of both "modest risk" and "approbation," Stewart says, "perhaps in the form of an uni handroll."

When I lived in LA, one of my favorite restaurants was Sushi Sasabune. More a fluorescent-lit, dingy greasy spoon than a sushi mecca, it has yellowed handwritten signs on the walls that say threateningly, "No California roll. No bowl of rice." (These are typical favorites of sushi newbies.) Instead of having a name tag, every waiter's shirt simply says, "Trust me." This was an order, not a request. Chefs occasionally yell at customers for making poor choices, and they kick out a certain number of patrons each month to keep it interesting. This power play wouldn't work if the food couldn't live up to the hype, but this sushi is so fresh it almost bites back.

Can you persuade others to obey you? Yes, you can. And if you use domination as keenly as the Sushi Dictators do, you'll even be tipped extra for it.

What Is "Power"?

One of the hardest tasks of leadership is understanding that you are not what you are, but what you're perceived to be by others.
—EDWARD L. FLOM

Power takes the alpha stance. It strengthens, earns respect, motivates, and guides action. Used intelligently and selectively, Power strengthens your reputation as a leader and earns respect. Power brands can serve as role models, even beacons within their category. With a strong point of view and a self-assured stride, these brands show us the way without pulling over to ask for directions.

POWER:
THE LANGUAGE OF CONFIDENCE
Power leads the way with authority and confidence. Power always has a plan, moves with purpose, and reaches its goals.

The Top Traits of Power

Assertive. Goal oriented. Decisive. Purposeful. Opinionated. These are some of the adjectives that describe your brand when you speak the language of confidence. As you develop messages, make sure that these traits fit your tone and attitude. To learn more, turn to the next page.

How Power Fascinates

Power is the difference between thinking and knowing. Power brands lead the pack, setting the tone of the business discussion.

Under the influence of extreme Power, individuals have little choice. Their behavior is controlled by someone (or something) else. People obey because they must, as a matter of survival. Classic example: the iron-fisted hand of a Communist regime. You'll work hard, and you'll like it!

FIVE ADJECTIVES TO DIFFERENTIATE YOUR POWER BRAND

ASSERTIVE

Power brands have a competitive spirit and pursue goals ambitiously to help consumers be on the winning team.

GOAL ORIENTED

They're focused on specific and ambitious outcomes—both for themselves and for their customers. Achievement matters.

DECISIVE

These brands take action rather than sit around and wait to see what happens next.

PURPOSEFUL

They're often looked to for answers and assistance, and they take this position seriously.

OPINIONATED

Power brands have strong beliefs and aren't afraid to express them with candor. No mincing of words here.

Yet lest you think Power is all hammer and sickle, take a look at the flip side. Power isn't necessarily overpowering. It can guide gently, even lovingly. It's a necessary ingredient in many forms of structure that use training and motivation to achieve higher results. A parent uses Power with an infant by shaping sleep patterns, feeding times, and language development. A parent might also use this Advantage with a high school student through a weekly allowance or the use of the family car. Either way, the goal is not to defeat the child, but to make her stronger. Similarly, strong brands often fulfill a parental role in guiding consumers' choices and behavior.

Every day, we allow organizations to control our personal environment. We agree to iTunes' terms of use, and take off our shoes for TSA officers at the airport. On Facebook, users operate within a regimented interface. iTunes, the TSA, and Facebook all use Power to control their environments, and we follow. Why? Because Power is pure confidence. Doubt is death, and hesitation loses.

How Brands Use Power in Their Marketing
To apply Power in your messages, you must establish a reputation as a confident, knowledgeable authority with the experience to guide your customers. What will you say to inspire this leadership? What do you confidently know is true, based on your unique knowledge and experience?

If you waver in your confidence or come across as wishy-washy, you'll fail to spellbind. To keep a steady flow of Power running through all of your communications, use at least three of the following four pillars in every form of communication:
- Lead the way.
- Take control.
- Pursue specific goals.
- Voice your Opinions of Authority.

If you're confident in yourself, we'll be more likely to have confidence in you. Play well with others, but submit to none.

Lead the Way

No matter where you rank on the pecking order, no matter what your age or gender, no matter which continent you call home, you're fascinated by Power. Our fixation on powerful leaders is embedded deep within our tribal psyche.

When powerful brands speak, the world listens. They set the rules for any event. In their presence, others follow. When others stare, they blink last.

Tesla Accelerates

Tesla car brand showrooms are "galleries" where consumers are allowed to look but not buy. All orders are taken online. Tesla retains control by requiring all visitors to its headquarters to sign an NDA, even if they are just visiting the company's corporate offices, and not its research and design facilities. When it comes to how cars are bought and sold, the company's CEO, Elon Musk, is taking the wheel.*

Any company, and any industry, can fascinate when it demonstrates clear actions and a strong, decisive voice of leadership. A kitchen company, for instance, can comment on the latest trends in kitchen design. A mortgage adviser can provide tips and trends in the most family-friendly neighborhoods. A financial planner can give clear direction and help make decisions on new tax laws.

Take Control

If you want to be powerful, you must be ready to make decisions for others. Exude total and complete assurance in all manner of execution. Don't submit or stumble, else you risk losing credibility.

---

* How's this for fascinating customer service: When I test-drove a Tesla, the dealer brought the car to the house. Afterward, he stayed for dinner. Then he helped my husband move the grill from the backyard to the porch. After that, we signed the contract.

Speak always without hesitation or ambivalence. Establish immediately that you are the last word, end of story.

Powerful companies, like powerful people, have a strong point of view. The same is true for your marketing. Powerful brands aren't afraid to lead. To describe this pillar of Power, let's see how people apply it in their brands to build a reputation for confident communication.

Star-Spangled Beyoncé

There's hell to pay when fans of a world-renowned R & B star discover that her blowout performance of the national anthem on the steps of the White House was no more than a cleverly disguised lip-synch routine. But they don't call her "Queen B" for nothing.

Beyoncé Knowles-Carter responded to the outrage of her fan base by performing the anthem again ten days later. This time, the star belted out the notes *live*, with a fierceness that left the audience convinced of her raw talent. And when she finished, she had just two little words for the millions of people watching: "Any questions?"*

Why We Play Follow the Leader

Why do we respond so strongly to leaders? Why do we follow them, admire them, imitate them, and even obey them? To understand, let's go back a few million years. You're about to learn a thing or two from celebrities with hairy backs and knuckles that drag on the ground.

The next time you're in the grocery store checkout line and find yourself inexplicably mesmerized by a cover story about a smiling athlete, a billionaire mogul, or a movie star, blame your DNA.

---

* Beyoncé's voice isn't her only fascinating attribute. A species of fly has recently been named after the singer, because of its distinctive golden booty. Any questions?

No matter where we rank on the social food chain, no matter the group with whom we align, our alpha members fascinate us. Our obsession with powerful people is far older than *People* magazine; in fact, we inherited it from our hairier ancestors.

Programmed deep into our social code is a need to "follow the leader," to find alpha idols and fixate on them. Dr. Michael Platt, a Duke University neurobiologist, proved this by offering thirsty rhesus monkeys a choice: a drink of their favorite beverage, or an opportunity to look at photos of dominant monkeys in their own pack, the ones with food, power, and sexual magnetism, which Platt dubbed the "celebrity" monkeys.

So strong was the fascination with these celebrities that the parched monkeys chose photo viewing over imbibing. Even the most celebrated monkeys were fascinated by images of fellow celebrity monkeys.

Similarly, our brain's innate fascination with "following the leader" sets us all up to be spellbound by sports hysteria, high school cliques, and other group activities that grip attention.

Pursue Specific Goals

By focusing on a specific outcome, Power companies stay focused until they reach the finish line. They sustain fascination over long periods of time by staying rooted in lasting qualities of substance, such as courage, intelligence, and work ethic.

Warren Buffett's singing voice might not be as strong as Beyoncé's, but his investing results are music to investors' ears. His company, Berkshire Hathaway, is ranked number four on the Fortune 500 (as of 2015). The company wholly or partially owns several world-class brands.

Buffett has consistently beaten the market by sticking to his own principles. He often ignores economic facts. He puts his money in businesses, not stocks. He shuns trendy themes. But when he's confident, so are investors.

What specific goals does your brand pursue? Revenue? Employee happiness levels? Shareholder profit? Media fame?

What goals do you want your audience to pursue? Do you want them to improve their lives? Switch to your product? Stay loyal (rather than being lured by a competitor)?

Be confident and clear in establishing goals, starting with Opinions of Authority.

Voice Your Opinions of Authority

Powerful companies have a strong point of view. The more clearly you can define your opinions, the more customers will see you as an authority. These are your "Opinions of Authority."

An Opinion of Authority is a strongly worded viewpoint that is not a statement of fact, but rather a firm belief that reflects your expertise. It must be rooted in your area of experience and reflect a core belief. It provides a clear point of view and is a very effective way to differentiate yourself from others in your market, so that your message will convince and convert.

Leading brands don't just get attention—they drive behavior. They incite action. If people don't change their actions as a result of your message, that message has failed.

Invest in establishing a reputation as a confident, knowledgeable expert with the experience to guide others. You must be prepared to lead. How will you speak the language of confidence? In many situations, if you want to gain influence, you must be perceived as a decision maker. You won't stand apart from your competition if you won't first take a stand.

Fascinating messages, like fascinating people, have the potential to consume us as almost nothing else can, sucking us into a vortex of intensity. Mihaly Csikszentmihalyi describes this as the addictive nature of flow, and "the state in which people are so involved in an activity that nothing else seems to matter; the experience itself is so enjoyable that people will do it even at great cost, for the sheer sake of doing it." Moments of fascination can become peak life experiences, calling us forth to engage more fully than at any other time, giving ourselves over to the vividness of complete and total engagement.

So compelling are such fascinations that in the extreme, only a thin line separates fascination from its evil twin: obsession. And with obsession fascination becomes dangerous.

Using Your Powers for Good, Not Evil

Like cults, fascinating brands speak to their followers in a clearly defined language. Rather than speaking to the maximum number of people, these brands identify their target, and then go deep.

Like cults, fascinating brands have the ability to bond people together, and to effectively tap into the human desire to be part of something bigger than themselves, to be loved and accepted by an alpha leader, to be part of a group, to feel wanted and admired.

Like cults, fascinating brands make their insiders *feel fascinating*. For instance, cults lavish new recruits with attention and praise, acculturating them. They make the insiders feel good about themselves because they are part of a particular group.*

Let's end on a positive note. What can you learn and apply from the dark lords of fascination?

If you have a core value or belief, don't be afraid to share it with your audience. Stand out, or don't bother.

Feeling more confident about communicating with strength? In our next chapter, I'll show you how to feel more excellent about communication excellence.

---

* Remarkably little is known about cult recruitment strategy, which is understandable considering the unpleasant consequences for those who violate these groups' ironclad bonds of secrecy. Details come only from the few individuals who successfully escape. Of those details, I found this one rather perplexing: cult recruiters actively seek out vulnerable individuals who appear to be outcasts. Telling signs include walking solo with a backpack, or carrying a musical instrument. (So if you're walking solo while carrying a musical instrument inside a backpack, you're a prime target.)

THE LANGUAGE OF CONFIDENCE

POWER

AT A GLANCE

Lead with authority.

DEVELOP MESSAGES THAT ARE:

Assertive • Goal Oriented • Decisive • Purposeful • Opinionated

PILLARS OF POWER BRANDS:

> Lead the way.

> Take control.

> Pursue specific goals.

> Own your opinions of authority.

Does your brand fascinate with Power?
Get your Brand Profile at BrandFascination.com.

Prestige

THE
PRESTIGE
ADVANTAGE

AMBITIOUS • RESULTS ORIENTED • RESPECTED
• ASPIRATIONAL • ELITE

Be Extraordinary

Welcome to a place that knows how to be extraordinary. Classical music follows your every step as you enter the tree-lined path. Around you, birdsong fills the air. Glancing down at your feet, inspiring quotes on the bricks put a skip in your step. Up ahead on the park bench, you can sit next to a life-size bronze statue of Mark Twain or William Shakespeare. You continue on to a Morton's-style steakhouse, where you dine on a five-course meal of international cuisine while learning from experts around the world. Once finished, your cart driver escorts you to your room, where you'll bask in the hot tub or pool, all protected by top-level security. Sleep soundly, knowing that if you wake up late, your breakfast will be served in your room. Extraordinary, no?

This is not a resort. It's a campus for college students.

Welcome to High Point University, the brainchild of business master Nido Quebein.

Most colleges today are struggling. Just as businesses are cutting costs in order to survive, many schools are losing enrollment, decreasing services, and nickel-and-diming students for everything from copies to meals. Yet in less than ten years, High Point University has transformed itself from a little-known North Carolina school into a boutique institution. Any business would turn green with envy for these results: enrollment jumped 197%, the number of faculty members increased by 152%, eighty-two new buildings were built, with a total investment of $1.2 billion. *US News and World Report* gave High Point University three number one rankings.

How did this unremarkable college soar over an economically depressed time and location? It applied Prestige to fascinate applicants, parents, teachers, and donors. Here, average is out. Extraordinary is in. Each corner of the campus is intended to inspire a positive and enlightened mind-set. Everything is intended to remind you, each step of the way, in each and every corner, that your life too can be extraordinary. Students are being prepared for the world as it is going to be, not for the world as it is.

For instance, that restaurant I described earlier? It wasn't created to pamper students, but to push their understanding of business-meeting etiquette. This dining room is a learning lab. There, the servers teach students dining protocol, and the menu illuminates a different international cuisine each month.

All visitors are welcomed with personalized signs printed with their name and city, and a student guide to escort them. Golf carts are available 24/7 for any student who wants a secure ride on campus. After all, the school believes, how can students reach their highest and best if they have to worry about security?

Success coaches guide each student through a four-year plan. After graduation, students can continue on in the college's funded business incubator, pursuing new business goals with capital and mentorship provided by the university.

Rather than merely differentiating itself as a school, High Point applies Prestige. It teaches students how to differentiate themselves.

What Is "Prestige"?

Athletes have medals. Bake-off champions display blue ribbons. Twitter stars have Klout scores. Mary Kay's top employees drive pink Cadillacs. Children collect autographs from Mickey and Minnie at Disney World. Girl Scouts wear badges on uniforms. Proud fathers of newborns have hospital bands. Alcoholics Anonymous members mark sobriety with medallions. Scholars frame Phi Beta Kappa keys.

Prestige is the mark of excellence, in every form. Fancy logos and designer brands might come to mind when thinking about excellence, but that's merely the obvious side of this respected Advantage. It's the line that forms when a local hero signs autographs. When Sephora gives exclusive early access to its top customers. When collectors show off a signed Jackie Robinson baseball from their childhood.

Prestigious people evoke admiration, competition, and envy. In corporate circles, fascination might be triggered by a framed Princeton diploma or an invitation to speak at a TED conference.

In high school, the same status might result from winning a Call of Duty tournament. Both represent achievement, and carry implied "value" to the group.

PRESTIGE:
THE LANGUAGE OF EXCELLENCE
Whether established or up to the minute, humble or high end, Prestige communicates exclusivity, achievement, and value.

The Top Five Traits of Prestige

While there are many ways a brand can apply Prestige, all earn admiration from their audience. Prestige is about rank, and elevating one's position to the highest level. Do your messages communicate with Prestige? Turn to the five adjectives on the next page to find out.

How Prestige Fascinates

If we aspire to the idea of high quality, excellence, or exclusivity, Prestige allows us to physically connect with objects that bleed those values. We're fascinated by how clothing, cars, neighborhoods, banks, and universities can act as an extension of our values. And Prestige has an uncanny way of instantly elevating status. We may not get too many second looks in a generic T-shirt, but a designer logo sends a message loud and clear. Prestige tells the world what we value while simultaneously increasing our perceived value.

FIVE ADJECTIVES TO DIFFERENTIATE
YOUR PRESTIGE BRAND

AMBITIOUS

It's not enough to be good. Prestige brands focus on being better.

RESULTS ORIENTED

These brands have very clear and specific goals.

RESPECTED

Prestige brands relentlessly earn top results.

ASPIRATIONAL

These brands create desire by being out of reach for most people.

ELITE

Prestige brands make people want to spend more or work harder, in order to get on the inside.

Prestige is the coveted university with a minuscule acceptance rate, the real estate company with a competitive spirit and Realtors highlighted in the trade press, Häagen-Dazs with its premium ingredients. It's the interior design firm with the famous clientele, or the consultant with a long waiting list. The product development company IDEO designed an insulin injector that looks like a Montblanc pen rather than a medical tool. Instead of being purely practical, this medical device now attracts with Prestige.

How Brands Use Prestige in Their Marketing

Apply at least three of the four pillars of Prestige in each and every communication to elevate yourself above the crowd:

- Increase perceived value.
- Set a new standard.
- Develop emblems.
- Limit availability.

Does your brand speak the language of excellence? If so, align your communication with these defining traits. Check your main messaging against these descriptors to make sure you are consistently setting higher standards.

Increase Perceived Value

Just as beauty is in the eyes of the beholder, value is in the mind of the consumer. But how do you put it there?

Your car loses value when you drive it off the lot, the DVD player is obsolete with the introduction of the next technology, and this season's must-haves become next season's has-beens. But that never stops Prestige from gripping consumers and investors. If we value the newest, the latest, and the greatest, we most likely value its second cousin, exclusivity. On the right day, and with the right mix, you can use Prestige to increase perceived value and therefore increase prices. This isn't a new concept. The Dutch, as we'll learn, were already quite good at it in the 1600s.

When a Tulip Is Worth More Than the House It's in Front Of

Centuries ago, a Dutch botanist introduced the tulip to the Netherlands from Turkey. His introduction created a hysteria for the flower. The frenzy for tulips became so extravagant, so delusional, so widespread, that modern economists have pinpointed it as the world's first economic bubble.

Tulips became a symbol of status, a sort of botanical Gucci bag. The rarer the bulb, the more expensive. A single tulip bulb was sold in exchange for four fat oxen, twelve fat sheep, four tons of butter, a thousand pounds of cheese, a complete bed, a suit of clothes, a silver cup, and large measures of rye, wheat, beer, and wine.

Investors traded tulip bulbs in the stock exchanges, with prices depending not on beauty or perfume, but on scarcity and fashion. At the market's height, an investor offered twelve acres of prime land for one prestigious Viceroy bulb.

The rarest tulips had spectacularly vivid petal colors, and scarcity increased their price. The most desirable varieties required years of investment.

Prices soared to such extraordinary heights that an entire network of values was flipped on its head. So ferociously had Prestige bewitched the community of tulip buyers that they became obsessed. At one point, a single flower could be worth more than the house in front of which it was planted.

The flowers themselves had no utility, of course. They couldn't be eaten, they had no medicinal use. Investors couldn't ride one to market, or pass it down as an heirloom.

On the other side of the world, the Salem Witch Trials were about to begin. But first, the Netherlands were gripped by marketing witchcraft.

Increase Prices by Spellbinding Your Customer

Under the spell of fascination, people don't always act rationally. That's how fascination is different from marketing. It creates such an intense desire that price can cease to be an issue.

Do you want to increase your prices? Build a dose of tulip hysteria. Or, as we'll soon see, a dose of Grey Goose hysteria.

Set a New Standard

Setting a new standard doesn't just change people's perceptions of a company; it shifts its entire category. Once set apart, a prestigious brand will have no alternatives, merely inferior substitutes.

Grey Goose and Black Magic

When Grey Goose vodka was introduced, it threw down the ultraluxury vodka gauntlet. The price tag, literally double that of other vodkas on the shelf, was unthinkably high. Yet more incredibly, the price was established before the bottle was designed, before the distillery was named, and even before the vodka recipe itself was invented.

That might seem like putting the cart before the goose, but not only did Grey Goose define a new ultrapremium vodka category, it closed the largest-ever single brand sale when Bacardi bought the spirit for $2 billion after its first eight years. Instead of dogfighting with others to gain status, it simply forced the entire category to realign.

What Happens When the World's Most
Dazzling Diamonds Lose Their Sparkle?

No royalty, dynasty, or government empire can surpass the House of Winston in its legacy of celebrated jewels. The brand's glorious past includes many of the most famous diamonds, and diamond wearers, in history.

As one fine example, the grande dame of gemstones, the Hope Diamond, began its dramatic life with Louis XIV. After peering down from its golden perch atop the crown jewels of France, it then spent time in the jewel boxes of Marie Antoinette and Countess du Barry before becoming the possession of the New York jeweler Harry Winston. Winston donated the forty-five carats of dark blue perfection to the Smithsonian, where it now sits on cushioned display as specimen 2177868. Diamonds from the Winston vault have commemorated some of the most renowned romances ever, from European royalty to Hollywood royalty. It was at Harry Winston that Richard Burton bought Elizabeth Taylor's engagement ring, and where Aristotle Onassis bought Jackie O's marquise.

And not without reason. The House of Winston was known for selecting only the rarest gems, with just 0.01% of the world's reserves deemed worthy to sell under its name. Yet what makes the Winston brand even more precious are the stories behind the stones themselves.

Mr. Winston once purchased a 726-carat stone in London, setting off a heated debate about the safest way to get it back to the States. A league of bodyguards? Chartered ship? Colossal insurance policy? Harry Winston wouldn't say which method he'd picked. Two weeks later, the priceless jewel arrived at his Fifth Avenue store, sent via standard registered mail, for 64 cents postage.

Shipping methods weren't Harry Winston's only nerve-racking decision. He cut many of his diamonds himself, often with tens of millions of dollars resting on a single mallet tap. Later in his career, when negotiating the largest-ever individual parcel sale of diamonds in history, Mr. Winston made one final request: "How about a little something to sweeten the deal?" His counterpart wordlessly took a 181-carat rough from his pocket, and rolled it across the table. The resulting D-flawless emerald-cut diamond has since been known as "The Deal Sweetener."

Harry Winston was Prestige incarnate, living and breathing in every single piece. Wearing jewelry from the House of Winston grants an absolute sense of excellence that nothing else possibly could. Yet after the passing of Mr. Winston himself, the House of Winston slipped into the realm of commodity.

"The Inside of a Coffin"

While the Harry Winston Fifth Avenue flagship store boasted exclusivity and discretion to older shoppers, for others, it was fussy and outdated. The gray silk decor was described as "the inside of a coffin." With the new abundance of cubic zirconia, five-carat earrings became rather passé.

Could the House of Winston reclaim its Prestige Advantage? As part of the team charged with updating the brand, I focused on the emotional experience of wearing gemstones of excellence.

While diamonds might be billions of years old, as with every product, their cultural context changes over time. To survive amid new competitors and a changing economy, we summoned Prestige cues. First, we wooed the world's most legendary portrait photographer, Richard Avedon. Next, we featured movie stars such as Anjelica Huston and Mena Suvari.

Then it was time to write the headlines for the ads, which ran in magazines such as *Vogue* and *Town & Country*. As the writer for the headlines, I had to fascinate with words. It wasn't easy. How to express just how exceptional these diamonds actually are?

To understand this experience myself, I visited the flagship store. There in the vault, I tried on some of the world's most iconic pieces of jewelry. A forty-carat ring once owned by Jackie O. A $10 million necklace worn by an actress as she accepted her Academy Award. Pieces that are loaned only to A-level stars and brides in Dubai. Adorned with those weighty gems, I found out that there's a thrill in wearing the Earth's most precious offerings. At that point, the headlines almost wrote themselves:

People will stare. Make it worth their while.

Watch the women watching the men watching you.

RSVP your regrets to the ordinary.

In 1867, Karl Marx had commented in *Das Kapital* that "If we could succeed, at a small expenditure of labor, in converting carbon into diamonds, their value might fall below that of bricks." Quite fortunately, the House of Winston proved him wrong.

Within your company, in the office, you can fascinate with Prestige by setting a new standard.

What emblems elevate your brand? As Napoleon said, "Men will go to battle and die for a scrap of blue ribbon." What blue ribbon could become your orange ticket?

Develop Emblems

Long before the establishment of Dior and Gucci, societies were fascinated by Prestige. In ancient times, coveted badges included coats of arms, specific colors, modes of wearing hair, wreaths, shoes, lineage, burial practices, certain seats, and insignia of office. In certain African tribes, scars prove one's bravery and valor. In Western societies, a fat, pale body once indicated wealth and success, because only outdoor manual laborers were tanned and thin; today, a tanned, thin body is a status symbol associated more with a spinning class than with spinning a combine harvester.

What's Your Emblem?

Just as they paid absurd prices for tulips 380 years ago, people today pay absurd prices for logos. Prestige emblems can cost a few billion dollars (a private island on the Palms of Dubai), or a few cents (a nifty new stamp), but they usually have little or no intrinsic value. Regardless of price tag or economy, these principles remain the same. Emblems themselves will change over time, but the human fascination with emblems will not.

Emblems fulfill a deep, instinctive need because they say something about us. The psychologist Abraham Maslow calls this "esteem": the need to feel important, respected, and recognized as an achiever. We satisfy this need by communicating our value to the world around us.

During the Japanese real estate boom, Ryoei Saito, an industri-
alist, paid world-record prices for a Van Gogh and a Renoir; then
he announced he planned to be buried with his paintings.

Simple or elaborate, all Prestige emblems share a degree of
unattainability. By developing symbols of value, your brand can
strengthen consumers' participation and commitment, and make
people eagerly work to acquire and show off emblems. Once companies develop emblems of value, they should protect those emblems at all costs.

Limit Availability

In 1837, at age sixteen, Louis Vuitton began his apprenticeship,
crafting trunks designed to withstand the rough carriage rides
of the time. His artisanal craftsmanship lives on. Today, rather
than discount its unsold bags, LV shreds them at the end of every
season, limiting their availability.

License to Drive

You might think of a license plate as a tedious piece of metal,
something to be tolerated. A "vanity plate" or "prestige plate" can
turn this up a notch, giving others something like YUHATIN or
HISNHERS to ponder while idling in traffic. (Think about those for
a moment.)*

How else could a lowly license plate be transformed into an
orange ticket by applying a heavy dose of Prestige? How about a
$14.3 million price tag? No, the plate isn't made of solid gold, and
it doesn't contain plutonium rocket fuel. It features the number 1.
In the oil-rich and car-obsessed culture of Dubai, license plates
are a matter of personal pride. Most plates have five digits. But the
lower the number, the higher the price tag.

---

* I'm embarrassed to admit that I once had a license plate that read CPYWRTR. Don't tell
anyone.

Price tags often rise along with scarcity. In return, scarcity leads to exclusivity. Luxury brands trade on a simple premise: a higher price tag isn't a barrier to purchase, but rather an incentive. Reports the *New York Times*, "In some cases, manufacturers adjust prices upward to make sure that their goods hang in good company, displayed alongside prestigious luxury brands."

Limiting availability isn't just confined to Persian Gulf emirates and chic boutiques. In many cities, Prestige can be described in five digits: the zip code.

You might not think of a number as a brand. Yet anything can become a brand, when it builds a strong connotation. For instance, you probably know 90210. But you might not know 31561 (Sea Island, Georgia), or 11771 (Oyster Bay, New York). These zip codes have reached the status of brand names to those in the know because they're among the most expensive. Those five digits communicate volumes of Prestige. Realtors report that increasingly, new residents "shop" for these numeric brands more fervently than for the house itself. In Long Island, the post office has received a flood of requests for neighborhoods to be annexed into more demographically desirable zip codes.

By making something rare, you can elevate its perceived value. For instance, doctors who steadily have a six-month wait for an appointment are perceived as more exclusive than those who can fit you in before 3:00 p.m. today. Schools that accept only 10% of their applicants can charge higher tuitions than those recruiting people off the streets. I've been part of several product launches that artificially limited the availability of a product. However, limiting availability works only when people get something worthwhile in exchange. Every detail must justify the heightened cost.

While a snazzy zip code may certainly impress many people on the return address of a letter, in many instances, Prestige is more about actions than purchases. Like respect, some of the most desirable status symbols must be earned.

THE LANGUAGE OF EXCELLENCE

PRESTIGE

AT A GLANCE

Set the standard.

DEVELOP MESSAGES THAT ARE:

Ambitious • Results Oriented • Respected • Aspirational • Elite

PILLARS OF PRESTIGE BRANDS:

> Increase perceived value.

> Set a new standard.

> Develop emblems.

> Limit availability.

Does your brand fascinate with Prestige?
Get your Brand Profile at BrandFascination.com.

Earlier we saw how Innovation can change the game with creativity, Passion can create an immediate emotional connection, and Power can lead with authority. But what if you want to build a quiet, long-term relationship?

In that case, look to Trust. This Advantage isn't about heart-thumping excitement or head-snapping attraction. Instead, Trust shows us how to gradually build stable and meaningful relationships over time.

Trust

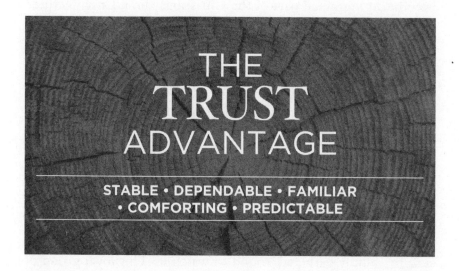

It Wasn't Always a Wonderful Life

Hum a few bars of "O Come, All Ye Faithful," sip your eggnog, and gather round the fireplace to roast chestnuts, kids. It's time to tell the story of how Trust brought us the traditional holiday classic *It's a Wonderful Life*.

Upon its release in 1946, *It's a Wonderful Life* wasn't nearly the success it is today. Actually, it flopped. Soundly. Earnings didn't come close to the cost of production, the studio was disappointed, and the director, Frank Capra, was criticized and humiliated. The holiday movie seemed destined to fade into obscurity. But then, serendipitously, Trust came into play.

In 1974, the film's copyright protection ended. It became public domain. Now television stations could air *It's a Wonderful Life* for free. And air it they did. Every year, the movie played throughout the Christmas season. Families gathered to watch. Children grew up with Jimmy Stewart and the angels. Americans saw the same images year after year. Jimmy Stewart and the angels became emblazoned on our collective concept of holidays, hope, and American optimism. From a marketing perspective, the movie has become an ingrained part of the Christmas "brand architecture" along with gift-wrapped toys, caroling, and the colors red and green. It's a tradition.

Yet like many traditions, one might argue, this one succeeds not because it's the highest-quality option, but because it's the most familiar. Familiarity and repetition have turned the movie into a fascinating holiday tradition. We love *It's a Wonderful Life* because, unlike the audiences in 1946, we're familiar with it.

Television stations took advantage of the freebie and inadvertently created a family tradition. Over time, viewers grew to expect to see the move each year around Christmas. They'd comb through the television guide to see when it was airing and make sure the family gathered 'round to watch it. This loyal group of viewers trusted the stations to air it. They knew that Jimmy Stewart would still be the star, that, in the end, another angel would get its wings, and that they would be suffused with the same wonderfully warm feeling they had the year before. Being familiar with the characters and the story is what they liked most about it. Now, seventy years later, it's one of the most popular movies of all time.

What could you do to create a feeling of comfort and familiarity with customers? When you speak the language of stability, and use Trust as an Advantage, you create familiarity with loyal, returning customers.

What Is "Trust"?

Trust is Twinings, the British tea maker, which has continued to use the same logo since 1706. It's the real estate agent who sends clients flowers or chocolates for their birthdays. It's Raymond James being the only major investment-services firm to be named to *Forbes* magazine's list of America's most trusted companies for its absolute consistency. It's Walmart matching prices from competitors without requiring customers to present the competing ad. It's Nordstrom, where consistent customer experience is so essential to the brand that the staff will even wrap a present you've purchased elsewhere.

> # TRUST:
> ## THE LANGUAGE OF STABILITY
> Trust delivers consistently and reliably. Ever dependable, it maintains expectations, and thrives on being loyal and worthy of your business.

The Top Five Traits of Trust

The following adjectives best describe how to speak the language of stability:

FIVE ADJECTIVES TO DIFFERENTIATE **YOUR TRUST BRAND**

STABLE

Even in a chaotic and fickle marketplace, Trust brands keep a steady demeanor.

DEPENDABLE

No matter what, they follow through on exactly what was promised.

FAMILIAR

They are usually known quantities, respected for their steadfast behavior and reliance on reproducible, proven ideas.

COMFORTING

Their communication feels like putting on your favorite pair of jeans.

PREDICTABLE

Trust brands develop patterns and strategies.

How Trust Fascinates

In a world in which the climate changes, the market fluctuates, and politicians betray constituents, Trust fascinates simply by doing what we, in a perfect world, would expect it to do. Trust is predictable. The more predictable a message, the more we rely on it—and the more we can rely on it. Trust brands demand very little of a learning curve, reassuring us by recognizing our expectations and reliably satisfying them. Trust is also consistent, with little conflicting information. While Innovation brands can be creatively inconsistent, Trust brands cannot.

How Brands Use Trust in Their Marketing

How to establish and enhance Trust? Trust messages will use different approaches depending on their stage and purpose, but drawing on these pillars can win the battle for attention. Trust relies on patterns, so using these four pillars consistently in all communication should come easy for Trust brands:

- Repeat and retell.
- Be authentic.
- Accelerate trust.
- Use familiar cues.

Trust messages are consistent, with very little conflicting information, because inconsistency breaks expectations. To build consistency, repeat your message, and retell your story.

Repeat and Retell

We're drawn to people and situations that feel familiar. They fit a pattern we already know. When we recognize them, not only do we rely on them, but we also develop preferences based on their repetition. Our brains use these patterns to map everything we see, hear, and experience, in order to establish an expectation for the future. The more you repeat and retell a message, the more familiar it becomes to your customers, and the more likely they are to believe, and even count on, it.

This isn't just marketing. It's a phenomenon of your brain, named the "exposure effect."

The Exposure Effect

In 1876, the German psychologist and physicist Gustav Fechner described how our brains respond more strongly to familiar cues; he called this the exposure effect. The more we're exposed to something or someone, the more we trust it. And the more we like it. Scientists have since used the exposure effect to describe why we might like a song more after hearing it a few times, why we feel more comfortable around friends than strangers, and why we're inclined to feel as though we personally know celebrities we see frequently in the media. Consistent and repeated exposure to celebrities such as Will Smith and Oprah Winfrey makes us more likely to trust and like them, because over time their images have literally created a neurochemical pattern within our brains.

These patterns can slowly accumulate over the course of years, as with *It's a Wonderful Life*. But does that mean that only adults experience trust? Do we experience the exposure effect early in life?

McNuggets, Milk, and the Golden Arches

Through repetition of messaging and consistency of experience, McDonald's builds trust in young diners. In a study designed to show the effects of marketing on young children, researchers at the Stanford University School of Medicine and Lucile Packard Children's Hospital presented children ages three to five with two different sets of chicken nuggets. They wrapped one set of nuggets in McDonald's packaging, and the other in plain, unmarked packaging. Which group of nuggets tasted better, they asked. The twist: the packaging was different, but the nuggets themselves were exactly the same.

Overwhelmingly, the young patrons rated the McDonald's-branded food as better than the unbranded food—even though the nuggets were identical. Thomas Robinson, the director of the Center for Healthy Weight at Lucile Packard Children's Hospital, reported, "Kids don't just ask for food from McDonald's, they

actually believe that the chicken nugget they think is from Mc-
Donald's tastes better than an identical, unbranded nugget." Kids
preferred the flavor of not only branded nuggets, but also the taste
of menu items not normally associated with McDonald's, such as
carrots, milk, and apple juice, when these foods were presented
in McDonald's-branded packaging. By age three, their taste buds
were already "tricked" into imagining superior taste.

To fascinate diners with Trust, Mickey D's doesn't just invest
in becoming the most familiar option. It also conditions people
to know what to expect from each encounter by maintaining
predictability.

Villains, Heroes, and Other Personal Brands

We measure how much we trust something by comparing our expectations against any deviations. The more similar something is
to our expectations, the more we count on it in the future. Human
reputations confirm this. We trust good guys to be good. (Notice
how few fairy tales illustrate Prince Charming embezzling from
the royal coffers.)

Note: This consistency doesn't *necessarily* mean "good." Trust
builds a strong expectation of future behavior based on past behavior. Now, that behavior could be bad. That college buddy who
always runs half an hour late, but you still meet him out for drinks
anyway? You've figured out his patterns, and can accurately judge
his behavior. His tardiness might annoy you, but it doesn't surprise
you. We also "trust" Darth Vader, Cruella de Vil, and Caligula to
be bad. We revel in the evil of Heath Ledger's Joker, and in the
innocence of Tom Hanks's Forrest Gump. If a character deviates
sharply from his or her established persona, we're confused, even
disappointed.

In marketing, predictable messages might become boring over
time, yet erratic action unravels the pattern. Reputations influence decision making. People make Trust judgments based on

comparisons with past experiences. If your success relies on instant gratification or surprise, then feel free to experiment. However, if your success relies on Trust, then you must, without question, deliver what people expect.

The more specific your promise, the more vital the need to deliver. We're indignant if a FedEx package shows up late (when it absolutely, positively needed to arrive overnight), or if a Timex watch takes a licking but doesn't keep ticking. Brands that fail to live up to their raison d'être earn negative fascination: bad word of mouth. The brands that we consistently trust are those that fulfill our expectations.*

Be Authentic

To be authentic is to be the genuine article, the gospel truth, the real McCoy. And no wonder we're fascinated by the real McCoy, with so many fake McCoys around. We want what's real, and honest, and genuine. We want transparency. Authenticity must be earned over time, making it one of the most difficult ways to fascinate. Authenticity must arise from your brand's story. All elements of your behavior, attitude, culture, beliefs, and benefits must tie back into this story. True authenticity is never contrived or manipulated—it lives within substance, not style. The more you attempt to force authenticity, the more surely it will elude you.

Flavor of the Month

Tempestuous by nature, fads can feel sexy and exciting. They whip up exaggerated, even zealous, discussion. However, trends are fickle mistresses. They're difficult to maneuver or maintain.

---

* People look to FedEx for urgency and punctuality. Yet when Fred Smith founded FedEx, the overnight shipping company didn't find overnight success. When the corporate bank account once dropped to $5,000 in the early years, Smith flew to Las Vegas and turned this meager pot into $27,000—enough to keep the company running for another week.

For iconic people and companies, fads erode credibility. Or worse, they damage Trust. If your brand speaks the language of stability, your messages are not mercurial. For a retailer, sustaining the same message may sound easy enough, but the reality is that tastes change, economies change, and companies change. Sometimes it's easy to give in to the temptation of cashing in on a fad.

Fashion Victim or Fashion Victor?

A quintessential classic, the Tiffany & Co. logo is engraved into 170 years of exclusivity. Yet in the late 1990s, Tiffany's lower-priced line of silver jewelry became a must-have sensation among teenage girls. In particular, one $110 charm bracelet became an essential fashion item. Other brands would rejoice at such brisk sales, yet Tiffany's executives knew that these trinkets could make the brand seem too accessible for older, wealthier patrons. As the company's stock prices rose, so did the concerns.

In a controversial move, Tiffany raised its prices on the silver pieces to put the brakes on this trend. This decision probably lost the company short-term profits from shoppers wanting an affordable look, but it preserved prestige from the company's long-term wealthy base.

It's a risk to remain unchanged. Ruts are sticky. But for companies that rely on long-standing Trust as a primary Advantage, every message must communicate stability.*

Accelerate Trust

Earning Trust demands an investment of time and effort, because predictability requires a guaranteed certainty. Trusted brands carefully pay attention to detail, reinforcing consistency between

---

* In twenty years, when those teenage girls acquire the spending power for lavish gold and diamonds, they won't associate the Tiffany & Co. logo with the one attached to that cute little sterling silver trinket they wore back in high school.

the expectations they set and the results they deliver. In return, the reward for earning trust is a big one: loyalty.

Loyalty acts as a rudder for decision making, because in certain circumstances, we want to know exactly what to expect. Surprises aren't fun when it comes to an auto manufacturer's warranty, the direct deposit of a paycheck, or the skill of our cardiac surgeon. In these types of relationships, we seek reliable options. Safety is paramount and excitement is bad, so we're drawn to stability. Year after year, we might return to the same accountant not for her keen fashion sense or witty banter, but because we won't have to worry whether our 1040 form will pass muster.

Reinventing Cues from the Past

Yesterday's tired facts can be reinvented anew. And just about anything from your past is fair game. Colt 45, the malt liquor favored by the urban poor, turned a flinch-worthy truth into a street-smart marketing tool. Instead of hiding from the fact that its oversized bottles are usually carried in small brown paper bags, the company created cool hand-drawn ads printed directly on small brown paper bags. The campaign used its heritage to do the seemingly impossible: reposition Colt 45 to hipster drinkers.

Companies occasionally rebuild trust by going back to their own history and resurrecting old marketing devices. Maxwell House returned to "Good to the last drop," StarKist tuna reintroduced Charlie the Tuna, and Burger King invited us to once again have it our way.

Companies lacking in perennial Trust cues often simply borrow someone else's. Senekot laxatives borrowed James Brown's "I Got You (I Feel Good)," and Viagra regaled us with "Viva Viagra." Sea-Bond denture adhesive brought back "Bye Bye Love."

If a song isn't quite exactly right in its original form, hey, why not take poetic license (as long as you pay to license the song)? For instance, Luvs diapers paraphrase the Beatles: "All You Need

Is Luvs." And Kraft Cheese Crumbles brought us their version of "Unbelievable," named "Crumbelievable."*

Are dead celebrities off-limits for conjuring Trust cues? Hmm. Maybe not. Using old footage, a 1997 Dirt Devil commercial featured Fred Astaire dancing with a vacuum cleaner, resulting in a public outcry. And although Orville Redenbacher died in 1995, through the wonders of computer graphics, a 2007 commercial featured him holding an iPod while touting his microwave popcorn.

Use Familiar Cues

Remember the exposure effect? We're drawn to people and situations that feel familiar. They fit a pattern we already know. This logic explains why "Crumbelievable" probably tested so well in focus groups. And it explains why we're more likely to extend trust to something that's similar to what we know.

By linking a new message to one that's already firmly trusted, we can shorten the time frame needed to develop trust. Real estate professionals often use the scent of baking bread or cookies when showing a home to buyers, because these nostalgic scents cue unconscious memories for many people. The scents bring familiar cues to an unfamiliar environment, making it seem more immediately homelike.

Beer Sommeliers Wanted

Anheuser-Busch takes predictability seriously. Their quality control might be renamed "predictability control." Members of an elite panel ensure the consistency of the beer's flavor from brewery to brewery, day to day. To guarantee uniformity, samples from each of the fifteen breweries are flown to the company's St. Louis

---

* Reportedly, a hemorrhoid cream was about to use Johnny Cash's "Ring of Fire" for a TV commercial, until Cash's family exerted their good taste.

headquarters, and are served to the tasters in identical glasses that have been cleaned precisely with filtered water. The panel samples every ingredient, including air, which they bubble through water and sip. Because of this, consumers can trust that every beer, from every brewery, will taste the same.

When you build your brand around the language of stability, customers stop being customers, and start becoming friends. Even family.

Become Familiar

The word "familiar" comes from the Latin *familia*, meaning "family." Family is more than just an emotional bond, and so is familiarity. Neurochemically, there's a lot going on with familiarity. Our minds look for patterns. When we recognize them, we not only rely on them, but we also develop preferences based on pattern repetition. Our brains use these patterns to map everything we see, hear, and experience in order to establish an expectation for the future.

Consider your own family's traditions. They usually are not focused on the "best" foods or the "biggest" gestures, but rather on a sense of continuity that draws on your home, your shared history, your favorite activities, and time spent around your kitchen table.

Our next chapter, Mystique, will make you curious. We'll explore unanswered questions, the secrets of poker, and the world's greatest unsolved mysteries. Cultures throughout history have always been captivated by the thrilling power of unanswered questions. Pandora had her box, Lot's wife's curiosity turned her into a pillar of salt, one bite of an apple got Adam and Eve booted out of paradise. And let's not forget the cat, whose curiosity proved her undoing.

And in the spirit of listening rather than speaking, I'll say no more.

THE LANGUAGE OF STABILITY

TRUST

AT A GLANCE

Build loyalty with consistency.

DEVELOP MESSAGES THAT ARE:

Stable • Dependable • Familiar • Comforting • Predictable

PILLARS OF TRUST BRANDS:

➤ Repeat and retell.

➤ Be authentic.

➤ Accelerate trust.

➤ Use familiar cues.

Does your brand fascinate with Trust?
Get your Brand Profile at BrandFascination.com.

Mystique

THE MYSTIQUE ADVANTAGE

OBSERVANT • CALCULATED • PRIVATE
• CURIOSITY PROVOKING • SUBSTANTIVE

The Nineteen Crimes

Panting, out of breath, you push your way through the night fog across cobblestone streets. You're fast, but not fast enough. The police cuff you in heavy shackles, and drag you away.

It's eighteenth-century England, and you have just been accused of larceny. You know your fate. You're being shipped away to a godforsaken island, facing near-certain death.

If lucky, your transport will take only five months, during which time you'll watch many of your shipmates perish from disease and thirst. If you survive the journey, you'll work up to eighteen hours a day or else risk being beaten into the ground. You're a prisoner, banished from your homeland. You might be guilty. You might not. At this point, it doesn't really matter.

Which crime did you commit? There are exactly nineteen crimes worthy of this inhumane treatment, including:

No. 1: Grand larceny, the theft above the value of one shilling
No. 5: Impersonating an Egyptian
No. 11: Stealing roots, trees, or plants, or destroying them
No. 13: Assaulting, cutting, or burning clothes
No. 16: Stealing a shroud out of a grave

If accused of stealing less than one shilling, you'll live on this island for seven years of labor. If you stole more than one shilling, you can look forward to dying in the penal colony after a life of hard labor.*

As you consider these options, sit back and take another sip of your wine. The wine is named 19 Crimes, in honor of this epic mythology. As you do, take special note of the cork. Printed on each cork, you'll learn exactly which one of the crimes you've committed. Did you steal a shroud from a grave? Cut or burn clothes? Was stealing plants your crime of choice? Or did you unwisely decide to imitate an Egyptian?

You and your dining companions are no doubt curious to know which crime you'll commit next. Open another bottle, and find out.

---

* Perhaps the convicts had the last laugh. The island was Australia, now one of the world's favorite tourist destinations.

What Is "Mystique?"

Fascination is black magic, mesmerizing your audience, capturing its attention as through hypnosis—in some cases, literally. In Part I, we learned that Freud described fascination as a "hypnotism." Mystique draws in your audience, making them curious to learn more, captivating their attention.

Of all seven Advantages, Mystique is the rarest. Unlike the thrilling creativity of Innovation, or the charismatic charm of Passion, it fascinates with intellectual curiosity. Instead of jumping up and down for attention, Mystique watches and waits, knowing that some things are better left unsaid.

Brands that use Mystique communicate selectively. They reveal information bit by bit. They listen first, take the time to think things through, then speak when ready. Only a select few are allowed inside. By sharing information in small doses, these brands control what the public knows (and doesn't know), in order to maintain control.

Curious to learn how to make people curious? Let's begin.

MYSTIQUE:
THE LANGUAGE OF LISTENING

Mystique reveals less than expected. It provokes questions. These brands know when to talk, and when to be quiet.

The Top Five Traits of Mystique

Does your brand watch and listen, rather than dominate the conversation? Do you maintain confidentiality? If Mystique is one of your top Advantages, you'll fascinate with these five traits:

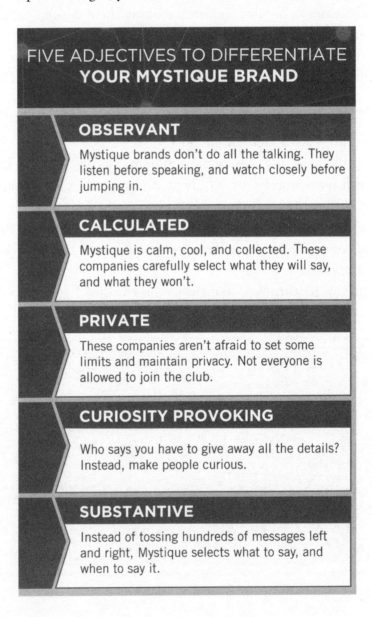

FIVE ADJECTIVES TO DIFFERENTIATE YOUR MYSTIQUE BRAND

OBSERVANT

Mystique brands don't do all the talking. They listen before speaking, and watch closely before jumping in.

CALCULATED

Mystique is calm, cool, and collected. These companies carefully select what they will say, and what they won't.

PRIVATE

These companies aren't afraid to set some limits and maintain privacy. Not everyone is allowed to join the club.

CURIOSITY PROVOKING

Who says you have to give away all the details? Instead, make people curious.

SUBSTANTIVE

Instead of tossing hundreds of messages left and right, Mystique selects what to say, and when to say it.

How Mystique Fascinates

Eye-catching enough to get noticed, yet complex enough to stay interesting. Open enough to start the conversation, yet elusive enough to leave you with questions. Mystique offers just enough, but not too much. It filters what it communicates, editing ideas and opinions, choosing what to reveal and what not to share.

We're fascinated by Mystique because of our natural desire to fill in missing information. If there's a question, we want an answer. "What happens next? How will the story end? Who gets the girl?" Maybe you'll get the answer. Or, maybe not.

How Brands Use Mystique in Their Marketing

Instead of jumping up and down and shouting for attention, Mystique is more subtle. Brands that use Mystique observe the following four pillars:

Protect information.
Spark curiosity.
Ask questions before giving answers.
Build mythology.

For our first pillar of Mystique, we'll examine how to protect information. And we'll do it with a high-stakes game of poker.

Protect Information

There's "poker," the game you play around a kitchen table with buddies. And then . . . there's poker. The kind without quotation marks. The real kind, at tournaments, in Vegas or Monaco. The win-it-or-lose-it kind. What's the difference between these two versions of poker?

At the highest level of play, poker is not a game of luck, or skill, or experience, or statistics, or even the cards. At the highest level of play, poker is an intimate understanding of human nature, and the secrets of Mystique.

Limiting information can be a valuable tactic for any professional. For some, it's a full-time pursuit. Jeff "Happy" Shulman is an expert in Mystique—and a world-class poker player. To achieve his impressive winnings, he's spent much of his life mastering Mystique, and observing rather than telling.

A Million-Dollar Drop of Sweat

Under conditions of stress, the human body responds in predictable ways: increased heart rate, pupil dilation, perspiration, fine motor tremors, tics. In high-pressure situations, such as negotiating an employment package or being cross-examined under oath, our bodies give us away, no matter how much we might try to play it cool. We broadcast our emotional state, just as Marilyn Monroe's voice broadcast passion.

We each exhibit a consistent pattern of stress signals. For those who know how to read such cues, we're essentially handing over a dictionary of our body language. To an expert eye, it can be easy to predict our thoughts, fears, and actions.

Tournament poker is no longer a game of cards, but a game of interpretation, masking impulse, and self-control. In an interview, Happy says that memorizing and recognizing your opponent's nuances can be more decisive than luck or skill. Imperceptible gestures can reveal a million dollars' worth of information. Players call these gestures "tells."

With a tell, a player unintentionally exposes his thoughts and intentions to the rest of the table. The ability to hide one's tells—and, conversely, to read the other players' tells—offers a massive advantage.

Happy spent his career learning how to read these tells. "If you know what the other player is going to do, it's easier to defend against it," he says. Like others competing at his level, Happy might prepare for a major tournament by spending hours reviewing tapes of his competitors' previous games in order to instantly translate their tells during live competition.

In other words, the more information you gain, and the less you reveal, the greater your control of the situation.

Poker players are fascinated by one another, obsessed even, in their quest for clues. Since they can't look at one another's cards, they have to hunt for any available information. At the same time, they're hiding information about themselves.

Away from the poker table, brands use Mystique the same way. They carefully watch (or rather, listen to) their customers. Unlike Passion brands, which can become chatty, Mystique brands will never be accused of overcommunicating. They selectively reveal strengths and rarely reveal weaknesses. As a result, their audiences search for information to answer their questions and predict their behavior, much like the way poker players compete to seek every morsel of information on their opponents.

The Invisibility Cloak

Mystique can act like a stealth tool, allowing you to selectively fly under the radar. It's like Harry Potter's invisibility cloak, allowing the wearer to move around without being noticed. You might use Mystique if you don't want the competition to be sorting through which patents you've filed, or what proprietary intellectual property you keep hidden in the vault. You might want to keep a low profile during a time of controversy, or while beta-testing a new system.

But more likely, you'll apply this form of witchcraft as a *visibility* cloak instead, wrapping your brand in fascination.

Finger-Lickin' Fascinating

Colonel Sanders, as you might recall from the company's advertising, uses "eleven secret herbs and spices" in KFC chicken. These spices are mixed separately, in two different factories, to minimize the number of people who know the whole recipe. Then the company combines all eleven ingredients at a third location.

Maybe KFC's recipe is more special than what you can buy at your local grocery store, maybe not. But Mystique seems to help people think so. From a brand perspective, it's hard to know which is more valuable: the recipe, or the secret.

Stories are often more fascinating messages than facts are. Stories allow others to participate, and to draw their own conclusions. Over time, a group's "tribal knowledge" turns into a mythology, creating an unspoken shorthand for bigger events and stories.

If you want to build mythology within your company, rather than circulate a PowerPoint presentation of data, cultivate legend and lore. As we know from poker, too much obvious information kills Mystique.

Spark Curiosity

David Copperfield is a modern-day Houdini, spellbinding audiences with feats such as making the Statue of Liberty disappear into thin air. In one of his most famous tricks, Copperfield floats acrobatically across a stage, suspended in midair, almost daring audience members to disbelieve. And yet the audience members do believe—unless they have read US Patent 5354238, which details how the trick is performed.

The magic trick ceases to fascinate once the audience knows how the white rabbit appears from the black hat.

Intriguing people and products make us curious to learn more. When a brand spellbinds us with Mystique, we might ask friends about it to hear their experiences, research it online, read product manuals, spend time learning about its history and process, and spend time in the store. If we're deeply fascinated by a brand, we go out of our way to learn insider tips, or travel to a conference where it's featured.

This level of intense speculation doesn't often happen by accident. More likely, it begins with a secret that sparks curiosity.

The Kitchen within a Kitchen

As you walk through the doors of the Beverly Hills restaurant Crustacean, it's clear that the establishment is less like a restaurant, and more like a sacred temple. Underneath your feet, gigantic orange koi fish swim beneath glass. To your left, you spot a face in the shadowy tables that may (or may not) be an A-list celebrity. All around you, the atmosphere is thick with Mystique.

Yet there is one secret that you'll never know.

Crustacean is famous for one signature dish: the garlic crab. I'd tell you the recipe if I could, but like every other devotee, I have no idea. This recipe is so religiously guarded that the restaurant's founding family built a special "secret kitchen" inside the restaurant's main kitchen.

Yes, a kitchen. Inside the kitchen.

In this sacred space, the founding family members make their famously secret garlic crab. No one but blood relatives of the family are allowed to enter. You can't beg or buy your way inside this kitchen (even if you marry into the family). Outside the kitchen, at Crustacean's coveted tables, the elite crowd is talking about the one thing they can't order on the menu: access.

It's not unusual for a restaurant to fascinate customers with creative cuisine, bubbly waitstaff, or trendy decor. Yet one little slice of mythology can build positive hype, not to mention revenue. The key to Mystique isn't always what you *do* offer customers, but rather, what you *don't*.

If you fascinate your audience with Mystique, they'll want more information. Reveal that information very carefully, if at all. Show a glimpse without giving away the money shot. When information isn't available, people become curious. Topics that spark our curiosity become discussed, debated, and dissected, often without ever being understood. We wait breathlessly during cliff-hangers and suspense thrillers. We wonder about conspiracy theories and unsolved mysteries: The Shroud of Turin. Area 51. From the Bermuda Triangle to crop circles, we're obsessed with certain phenomena specifically because we can't explain them.

The Attraction of Anticipation

Neuroscientists explored the science behind anticipation in a simple experiment. They examined brain scans of monkeys eyeing a luscious treat: a grape. Each monkey's brain was stimulated by the sight of the grape, and it became even more stimulated as the monkey held the grape, ready to eat it. However, its sense of reward didn't increase when the monkey ate the grape; it actually decreased. Maximum pleasure occurred at the moment of getting the desired object, rather than at the moment of consuming it.

The conclusion: as a motivator, anticipation is stronger than fulfillment.

If customers aren't returning to your website, or if millennials are bored by your same old story, it might be time to take a step back and build intrigue. Sometimes the chase really can be more exciting than the prize.

Don't Kiss and Tell

Too much information is, well, TMI. Like too much cleavage. Too much tongue. Eww. Make it stop.

Confidentiality is rare. We're living in a time of kiss-and-tell and tell-alls. A time when starlets race the tabloids to announce their own exposés. When companies confess to problems before the bloggers expose them. And then there's the Internet, which leaves little to the imagination.

Successfully mysterious people and groups limit access. They maintain control by making people feel special to be "on the inside." When people feel that they're part of a select few, they're more committed. And they make all those people on the outside want to get inside, to see what all the fuss is about.

Surprises, Suspense, and Spoiler Alerts
How much is a surprise worth?

Some brands can charge more for ordinary products simply because they build a surprise into the purchase experience. By heightening a delicious sense of anticipation and suspense, these brands don't spellbind by spelling out every detail, but rather, by eliminating certain details entirely.

Whatever and Anything
When we buy certain products, we're actually paying for something else entirely.

Imagine buying a can of soda, and having no idea what it will taste like. Only after that first swig will you find out what you're actually drinking. Open a can of Whatever, and you'll soon discover whether you're sipping grape tea, chrysanthemum tea, or one of the other four flavors. Pop open a can of Anything to find out if you'll be drinking cola, apple soda, or root beer.*

A Box of Mystique
What makes Loot Crate so fascinating isn't what's inside the box, but the moment of opening the box. "Unboxing" is the trend of unpacking new products on video.

Loot Crate might seem like a loony premise. Each month the company sends subscribers a box of gaming and geek gear, anything from T-shirts to comic books. The exact contents are a surprise. To heighten Mystique, Loot Crate teases consumers by releasing videos of people unboxing the month's package.

---

* Now when you ask guests what they'd like to drink, if they respond "whatever" or "anything," you can actually serve them Whatever or Anything.

The brand creates an experience that keeps people hooked. (Fair warning: if you don't want to know what's inside your next monthly shipment from Loot Crate, you'd better watch out for spoiler alerts!)

Where's Waldo? (And What Is He Doing??)

Banned material isn't always wrapped in plain brown paper wrappers. It also comes in covers with titles that read *The Catcher in the Rye*, *The American Heritage Dictionary*, or *Where's Waldo?* In 1882, the great American poem *Leaves of Grass* was banned for its obscene content. Sales increased so dramatically from the publicity that its author, the poet Walt Whitman, bought a house from the royalties.*

Ask Questions before Giving Answers

Instead of giving generic information, Mystique brands begin by asking questions. Here's how one company used questions to drive sales:

Victoria's Secret makes lingerie seem sexy and simple. In reality, that's not always the case. Which bra actually fits? Every woman is shaped differently (and few are shaped like a lingerie model). For many women, bra fitting is a major pain point in the process of buying a new bra, because getting measured can be complicated and even embarrassing. To avoid the process of finding a bra that fits, women often just keep wearing ones that don't fit at all. How could a company make the experience more private, and more simple?

---

* It's difficult to identify exactly how the Where's Waldo? series of children's books earned the distinction of being among the American Library Association's one hundred most challenged books between 1990 and 2000. Rumor has it that as young readers search to find Waldo amid the intricately drawn cartoon images, they can also find topless sunbathers and other naughty bits. Get out your magnifying glasses, kids.

True & Co. took the bra-fitting experience online by asking questions. Lots of questions. The company identified six thousand different body types and designed a questionnaire that pinpointed the ideal fit. The brand listened, and women responded, generating $22 million in sales. By asking questions, and offering privacy, this startup got people involved (and buying).

A good set of ears, a tape measure, and the cups no longer runneth over.

The Forty-Eight-Hour Wait

Years ago, when I first released the Fascination Advantage assessment for individuals, it took a while for my team and me to figure out how to automate profiles. Until we did, each profile was painstakingly hand-finished by our heroic designer. Each profile took hours of labor. As a result, customers had to wait two days from the time they took the assessment to the time they received their results.

Frankly, I was a bit worried that this delay would make people impatient, or even dissatisfied. Yet that wasn't the case. During that forty-eight hours, curiosity grew, and by the time people received their results, they couldn't wait to read them.

Too often, marketers rush in and smother consumers. Instead of a high-pressure pitch, what if you used a low-pressure (or anti-pressure) approach? Consider backing off a little. Pull customers in, rather than pushing them to buy. Build an anticipation gap.

Build Mythology

"Mythology" is the collection of stories, traditions, and beliefs belonging to a particular group or event. It can be strategically fostered, or it may just naturally build over time. What's the story behind your brand? Instead of spelling everything out in your marketing, what if you let people draw their own conclusions, and draw on your stories? Mythology is bewitching.

Private Passwords and Hidden Hideaways

A few pages ago, we explored the "kitchen within a kitchen" at the restaurant Crustacean. Trendy nightclubs have a velvet rope outside to limit access and build anticipation. Even better, you can build new marketing ideas around old mythology.

The Alchemy bar in Tallahassee operates like a Prohibition speakeasy. The entrance is hidden past a storefront of blacked-out windows. Even if you can find the location, you can't enter unless you know the secret password and whisper it to the correct doorman. When it's time to exit, you'll have to find the hidden doorway inside the bookcase. Are the drinks better than at other bars in town? Perhaps. Yet this bar doesn't compete on the usual terms. Instead, it spellbinds customers by turning an ordinary experience into a forbidden, thrilling game.

Think of your own brand. Can you offer certain people a secret password, or a private entrance? Once, I invited a small group of successful entrepreneurs to a private, insiders-only product launch. In order to learn about the product, prospective buyers had to sign an NDA. I didn't realize it at the time, but signing that NDA made the experience far more desirable for the invitees. What if your clients or customers had to sign an NDA before purchase?

Pop Rocks, Bull Testicles, and the Mysterious 33

In Part I, we discussed how Epcot's Mission Space ride uses an orange ticket to turn a plain ride into an unforgettable one. With the mythology of Mystique, you can build a memorable story line around otherwise boring products and services.

Rolling Rock beer has the number "33" on the bottle (supposedly for the year Prohibition was repealed). Dr Pepper's original bottle featured the numbers "10-2-4" (supposedly for the three main pick-me-up times of day). Other brands build mythology through a fictitious history, such as Bartles & Jaymes, which built a campaign around the idea that wine coolers were dreamed up by two old guys on a porch.

Legend has it that Pop Rocks are lethal if mixed with Coke. Green M&Ms are an aphrodisiac. And Red Bull lists "taurine" as an ingredient, which is reportedly made with either bull urine or bull testicles, depending on which urban myth you believe.

What story can you tell about your brand's background, culture, or products? What hidden pieces of background could become your orange ticket? Whether you're an old or new brand, you can draw on mythology, as long as you present it in a new way.

THE LANGUAGE OF LISTENING

MYSTIQUE

AT A GLANCE

Don't reveal everything at once.

DEVELOP MESSAGES THAT ARE:

Observant • Calculated • Private
• Curiosity Provoking • Substantive

PILLARS OF MYSTIQUE BRANDS:

> Protect information.

> Spark curiosity.

> Ask questions before giving answers.

> Build mythology.

Does your brand fascinate with Mystique?
Get your Brand Profile at BrandFascination.com.

On to Alert, the language of details. Sharpen your pencils, get your spreadsheets ready, and we'll dive into details that drive human behavior. We'll learn why deadlines cause customers to act quickly, and why details help make your products more convincing and captivating. We'll also learn why your brain freaks out when your computer freezes (and you haven't backed up the hard drive recently).

Alert

THE
ALERT
ADVANTAGE

ORGANIZED • DETAILED • EFFICIENT
• PRECISE • METHODICAL

What Gets Measured Gets Managed

What do you measure (and manage)? For instance, exactly how many steps do you walk each day? More than a thousand? More than ten thousand? As Peter Drucker famously said, "What gets measured gets managed." When details come to the forefront, behavior changes. Data can make people more likely to take action.

Until recently, I didn't have the faintest idea of my number of daily steps. Or my heart rate. Or my sleep cycles. That information didn't seem relevant, and certainly not fascinating. Then I got a Fitbit activity monitor—a souped-up pedometer on the wrist. This nifty device illustrates the principle that people work harder to improve performance if they can measure their progress. It collects precise stats about your daily activity, transforming minutiae into a storyline. By weaving the details together, the Fitbit causes dull facts to become an addictive scoreboard. I can see how many steps my family and friends have taken. Once a day, my wrist buzzes and lights up, telling me that I've walked my ten-thousand-step goal. Party on the wrist!

Even detail-averse folks can get sucked into this addictive gamification. As a result, Fitbit's market cap is approaching that of the NBA.*

What Is "Alert"?

Instead of being warm and fuzzy, Alert is clean and well lit. Less like a child's doodle, and more like a surgeon's checklist. Alert eliminates mess. It organizes. It categorizes. It implements. Alert lives inside spreadsheets and annual reports.

Black or white? There is no gray. Yes or no? There is no maybe.

You might have heard the expression "Don't miss the forest for the trees." Alert makes sure we don't miss the trees. And the twigs. And the grains of soil. And each and every spot on each and every leaf. Alert adds detail to the details.

With its mastery of precision, Alert drives urgency and clarity.

---

* My kids wanted a new video game. I gave them Fitbits, and made them a deal: if they walked one hundred thousand steps in five days, they'd get the video game. ("Pleeease, Mom, let us go on another walk!")

Adding Detail to the Details

Alert is the form of communication that helps you manage communication in a rigorously structured way. It dots the i's and crosses the t's.

ALERT:
THE LANGUAGE OF DETAILS

Alert follows the rules. It persuades us by defining deadlines and details. These brands get us to take action by increasing urgency.

Five Adjectives to Differentiate Your Alert Brand

If you're an Alert brand, you don't just include details—you revel in them. It gives meaning to otherwise meaningless information. If your brand speaks the language of details, your communication is methodical and exact. I'll give you five adjectives to describe the language of details. To learn more, turn to the next page.

How Alert Fascinates

Alert logic usually goes something like this: There is a limited quantity (scarcity). Unless you act now (urgency), you'll lose your opportunity (consequence).

The more clearly a message explains why action is needed, and the greater the evidence, the more urgently people focus on the message. By defining the threat of inaction, the Alert message prompts action.

FIVE ADJECTIVES TO DIFFERENTIATE
YOUR ALERT BRAND

ORGANIZED

Alert is methodical in all aspects of business planning and follows a clearly systematized plan of action.

DETAILED

These companies ensure that every detail is correct before releasing it. Nothing slips between the cracks.

EFFICIENT

Alert communicates with clarity and responds to problems with careful reasoning. This is not a touchy-feely emotional appeal.

PRECISE

Check and recheck. Test and retest. Double-check and triple-check. Fix mistakes. Then check it again.

METHODICAL

Alert brands watch over each individual moving part rather than getting lost in the bigger picture.

For example, tax forms are not widely considered fascinating. However, if you haven't completed them, they become positively riveting on April 14. How does the IRS convince you to willingly hand over a percentage of your income? It clearly defines the consequences of not meeting the deadline. All you have to do is sign on the dotted line . . . but do it now.

Fire drills might be boring; however, if someone shouts "Fire!" in a crowded theater, we'll use whatever means possible to flee the threat. Consequences determine the level of action.

"I've Fallen and I Can't Get Up!"

Many products prevent negative consequences. Their marketing usually demonstrates just how badly things can go without the product. Think of advertising for car seats, self-defense classes, liability insurance, and, of course, LifeCall. In the face of dire alternatives, consumers perk up and consider the consequences of inaction.

Who needs to be practically perfect in every way, other than Mary Poppins? The electrical contractor firm with a two-thousand-page health-and-safety manual. The pension provider warning that you're not saving enough in your IRA plan. The antivirus company Norton warning against scams, fraud, and other security threats on its blog. The legal firm that wins by drilling through minutiae.

Messy vs. Meticulous

Alert is not random, abstract, or emotional. Passion, on the other hand, is an experience of exploration and discovery. If Passion was a breakfast, it would be gooey chocolate chip pancakes with extra syrup. If Alert was a breakfast, it would be 250 calories of whole wheat toast (unbuttered) with exactly half a banana and 8 ounces of skim milk.

This fascination is always crystal clear. Waterford Crystal takes its crystal clarity seriously. Factory workers shatter imperfect serving bowls and wineglasses on the hard factory floor, inviting visitors to smash 99%-correct pieces into a thousand shards. By throwing misfits to the floor, the brand keeps imperfect pieces from drifting to the off-price mall.

Now let's "listen" to what Alert might sound like at any given company.

How Brands Use Alert in Their Marketing

Like each of the other six Advantages, Alert engages us with clearly defined patterns. Consistently deliver at least three of these four pillars of Alert, and you will be speaking the language of details:

Sweat the small stuff.
Create urgency.
Define consequences and deadlines.
Use rational facts.

Sweat the Small Stuff

Details are a very big deal if you're speaking the language of detail. Problems arise when people fail to pay attention to little details. Appointments are missed. Payments show up late. Typos glare from important documents. Or worse, patients get the wrong medication, or flights aren't synchronized. If your company deals with complex systems, sweat the small stuff before things spin out of control. Examine defects. Execute minutiae.

Consistently following the details reinforces your brand identity, indicating an uncompromising commitment to specific standards.

Even creative and powerful brands track the smallest details. Steve Jobs once called a senior executive on a Sunday because he noticed that the yellow gradient of the second "o" of the Google logo didn't show exactly right on the iPhone display. Google itself is no less finicky. When choosing a shade of blue for a toolbar, Google tested forty-one shades to see what tested best.*

---

* Google also reportedly rents goats to "mow" the grass at its corporate campus. This method might be less precise than a mower, but it's greener (and way cuter).

Create Urgency

Join me for a walk down memory lane (and as we walk, let's envision our knuckles scraping along the ground, since this stroll takes place a few million years ago). Suddenly, you and I spot a saber-toothed tiger staring at us, its fangs dripping with anticipation. "Hmm, this could go badly," you grunt to me. And right you are. We have approximately 0.03 seconds to decide whether to stand our ground or hightail it outta there.

Generations ago, humans experienced danger at every turn. A five-second burst of energy allowed us to act quickly. We experience this same involuntary response today, even when there's no immediate mortal danger. A stressful thought alone is enough to set bells ringing and survival juices pumping, prompting us to act.

We work hard to eliminate dangers in our environment. We sterilize, we vaccinate, we declaw, we bubble-wrap. We do this because under the spell of Alert, we feel a strong sense of urgency to act.

People don't always enjoy the effects of Alert. Who wants to get a late-payment notice in the mail, or face a parking fine? However, when positively applied, Alert is important for achieving constructive goals. By communicating clearly with your audience, you can more specifically shape its behavior. It's a simple equation: Alert shows us a direction. We act.

3 . . . 2 . . . 1 . . . Buy!

Maybe you've had this happen: It's late at night, you can't sleep, and you find yourself watching an infomercial, or maybe QVC. A spokesperson holds a snazzy new Blend-o-Matic blender for your kitchen, or a Hang-o-Matic hanger for your closet. She announces that she has just one hundred Hang-o-Matics remaining at this price, so whatever you do, call now (!!!).

Now let me remind you, it's late, and you're awake rather than asleep, perhaps eating a bowl of Cocoa Krispies cereal in bed.

Whatever. The point is, you don't need a Hang-o-Matic hanger—you found out what one is only a few minutes ago—but because they're apparently all about to be gone, forever, never to be available ever again, you, like millions of other people, might find yourself pausing to say, "Well, hold on now, maybe . . ." Infomercials demonstrate how Alert gives rational incentive for irrational decisions.

Even if you've never succumbed to a late-night infomercial urge, you've probably noticed the urgency in those ads for one-day department store sales ("Sale ends at midnight!"), for Ginsu knives ("Call now and we'll throw in the free wind chimes!") or for monster truck rallies ("Sunday! Sunday! Sunday!"). These ads use a frenzy of exclamation points to whip up a purchasing panic.

Scarcity invokes the fear that if we don't buy now, someone else will snag that last reservation, that last appointment, that last spot at a webinar. The window of opportunity is closing. The sale finishes tomorrow. Deadlines force people to make a decision in order to avoid missing out, or losing potential options.

Ever booked a flight because there was only one seat left? The travel site Booking.com uses Alert to prompt immediate action. First the company points out that there are only two rooms left in the hotel you're considering. Then you notice that the latest booking was one hour ago. Finally, a notice flashes up that fifteen people are currently looking at the same hotel.

Another example: Gilt.com is a flash-sale site, transforming a leisurely afternoon at the mall into a thrilling and urgent need to buy now. Slashed prices and plummeting availability indicate how many products are still in stock, heightening the urgency. With a surge of adrenaline, people shop until they drop (all their money, that is).

When your audience is stuck in apathy, invoke urgency or scarcity and nudge them to make a decision. eBay mastered this technique, whipping bidders into a frenzy during the final count-down phase of a hot auction.

What if the person who's stuck in apathy is . . . you? If you need to direct a specific action, deadlines create focus. If you're a pro-crastinator, Alert can be your best friend.

At What Point Does a Procrastinator Stop Procrastinating?

Do your customers procrastinate before a purchase decision, or a contract renewal? When a deadline is comfortably far away, pro-crastinators don't feel enough urgency to merit attention. As the deadline looms, the consequences of missing the deadline become more imminent. Studies show that's the point at which Alert reaches a critical mass, and the task becomes fascinating enough to motivate immediate action to avoid the consequences.

Increasing perceived danger increases fascination. However, there's a law of diminishing returns at play. If Alert gets dialed up to the point of panic, the benefits diminish. The body sweats and trembles in the presence of Alert, and at a certain point, the brain shuts down and we lose the ability to problem solve. Neurosci-ence shows that after the fear system of the brain kicks into over-drive, decision making stops. We stop thinking creatively, and we start reacting purely out of fear. Whether real or perceived, Alert brings a sense of readiness, or even danger.

In the face of too much pressure, with consequences that are too great, people can't perform. They simply shut down, thrust into a frozen deer-in-headlights confusion. For instance, a politi-cal message is no longer fascinating if citizens are paralyzed.

The greater the resistance to a task (e.g., paying taxes), the greater the consequences must be (e.g., prison shower stalls) in order to compel us to do it. For a customer waffling about a deci-sion, an Alert message can tip him over to your side. Define con-sequences, and ratchet them up for failure to act—but stop before the customer becomes paralyzed.

Define Consequences and Deadlines

At the airport, you might not enjoy following the rules of the TSA. But you do, in order to avoid negative consequences. The TSA publishes its most "distinctive" finds to its Instagram account. The craziest items confiscated by the agency have included knives hidden inside enchiladas, razor blades stuffed into greeting cards, and three pounds of hard drugs wrapped in soft, raw beef.

Want to persuade a client to take a specific action? To urge your prospect to sign on the dotted line? Or to direct your kids to clean up their room? Alert is here to help.

Consequences usually follow a similar formula: "If you don't do this, then that will happen." For instance, "If you don't pay your taxes, then you will go to prison." Another example: Kids aren't always so fond of cauliflower or brussels sprouts. Many parents (including me) persuade kids to eat veggies with this classic Alert warning: "If you don't finish your vegetables, you can't have dessert."

You experience this every day. That feeling when your computer freezes (and you haven't backed up the hard drive recently)? That's what makes you take action to avoid consequences. If you don't stop hitting the snooze alarm, you'll be late for work. If you don't train for that marathon, you'll fizzle halfway through. If you paint your house chartreuse, your neighborhood association will get cranky. And so on. Alert prompts us to act, and to act a certain way.

Many public health and safety campaigns warn us of the negative consequences if we don't follow their advice. Life insurance companies also use scare tactics to sell insurance—what would happen to your loved ones if you pass away? Would they have to sell the house because they lost their main breadwinner?

Alert isn't about threats. It's often about the negative effects of not taking action.

Will You Drive to the Prom, or Be Driven?

Physiologically, people are programmed to focus and act. When given the consequences, people know how to act to get a positive outcome. Here's an example from my early advertising career:

In the photo, it looks as though someone has turned the car inside out. Disemboweled passenger seats spill onto the ground, a smashed windshield hangs from the dashboard, the headlights grimace. The car's frame, frozen in time, seems to writhe on the ground around the lamppost.

There's a reason for the expression, "I couldn't look away . . . it was like a car accident." Organizations such as Mothers against Drunk Driving (MADD) frequently use explicit photos like this one in their advertising, shocking us into the reality of hitting a lamppost at eighty miles per hour. Many drivers feel so repelled by these graphic consequences that they either call a cab or stick to Diet Coke. Many drivers, that is—but not all. Teenage drivers aren't as concerned by the graphic threat of drunk driving, thanks to their adolescent sense of immortality.

This presents a peculiar problem for drunk-driving prevention. How can teens be convinced not to drive drunk if death doesn't top their list of concerns? What could possibly be more frightening than being inside a car turned wrong side out?

Luke Sullivan, a legendary advertising writer, solved the problem. Luke knew that teens don't fear death in the same way as adults. Through extensive research and focusing on the details of the average teen's life, he figured out what does create a sense of urgency among these drivers: losing their license. Armed with that fact, he threatened teens with the ultimate dire consequence.

In Luke's ad, we see a picture of a teenage guy on the way to prom, with his corsage-wearing date at his side. The headline reads: "If the thought of losing your life doesn't keep you from drinking and driving, imagine losing your license." In the photo, the boy is being chauffeured to prom—by Mommy.

Little details like that were far more compelling to teens who viewed the ad instead of ads depicting gruesome accidents.

Hit Hot Buttons

By identifying an audience's hot buttons, a brand can target which message will most effectively change behavior. Often the most terrifying risks are not the most likely.

As mentioned, to convince teens not to drive drunk, Luke Sullivan didn't use graphic implications of car accidents, but social implications of losing one's driver's license. Generating a sense of urgency often has less to do with utilizing rational threats, and more with understanding human behavior.

The same applies to everyday dangers. Many people have trouble staying fascinated by their diet and workout routine. Long-term health benefits, such as greater longevity and lower risk for heart disease, often fail to motivate people to the gym as quickly as the prospect of an unpleasant unveiling at bathing suit season. In fact, when it comes to staying fit, the fear of looking unattractive is more motivating than the hope of a slim physique.

Similarly, the hamburger you eat for dinner will be far more likely to kill you with heart disease than mad cow disease. Chainsaws injure 36,000 Americans each year, while clothing injures 112,000 (oops, careful with that zipper).

Use Rational Facts

Early in my career, I learned many wondrous things. I found out about a new way to send messages from one computer to another across the World Wide Web, called "email." The other big a-ha was hearing about a new campaign being developed for milk. This campaign focused on the rational need to keep milk in the house, combined with an irrational fear of going without. The tagline was dead simple: "Got Milk?" These two words identify a brilliant human truth: we're more fearful of running out of milk while eating chocolate chip cookies than we are fearful of having weak bones later in life. The threat of crippling osteoporosis might eventually encourage us to drink more milk, but the threat of running out of milk while eating chocolate chip cookies sends us dashing to the convenience store.

Prevent Problems before They're Problems

You don't want to run out of milk, and your kitty doesn't either. Amazon has an automatic pet food dispenser made with built-in sensors to measure the amount of pet food remaining in its container. Before Kitty's kibble runs dry, the new supplies arrive. Running low on toilet paper? Press one of Amazon's Dash Buttons, and get double-ply at your doorstep.

What problems should your brand anticipate and prevent? The answers can be surprisingly effective and inexpensive. For instance, in advance of a noisy job, one roofing company put notes on each neighbor's door, along with a set of earplugs, apologizing in advance for the disturbance.

How about your brand? Even if you prevent the same details as your competitors, package them in a new way. What information are you already tracking about your customers or market? Even people who don't tend to be numbers oriented will still become fascinated when you transform raw data into a plan.*

Alert shows us how details can be spellbinding. After all, practical doesn't have to be boring.

---

* Many companies encourage employees to think "out of the box." Yet when everyone is trying to be "out of the box," that box might just be empty. Instead of thinking of a far-out idea, you might be more fascinating by staying right smack dab inside the box.

THE LANGUAGE OF DETAILS

ALERT

AT A GLANCE

Protect with care.

DEVELOP MESSAGES THAT ARE:

Organized • Detailed • Efficient • Precise • Methodical

PILLARS OF ALERT BRANDS:

> Sweat the small stuff.

> Create urgency.

> Define consequences and deadlines.

> Use rational facts.

Does your brand fascinate with Alert?
Get your Brand Profile at BrandFascination.com.

Alert loves rules. As a result, it likes to follow rules in marketing. These messages usually adhere to this formula: *"There is a limited quantity of* [fill in the form of scarcity]. *Unless you act now by* [how to take action], *you'll lose your opportunity* [specific consequence]." For instance, if you're an airline: "We only have x seats left at this price [scarcity]. Unless you act now by buying a seat [action], you will lose your chance to get the sale price [consequence]."

Turning the Schoolmarm into the Sorcerer

On our journey thus far, we've visited the creativity of Innovation, and the emotion of Passion. We learned how Power builds confidence, Prestige sets a new standard, and Trust provides stability. We listened to Mystique, and followed the rules of Alert.

Now it's time to take your next step into the world of fascination. Time to stop marketing like a prim schoolmarm, and instead start performing a little black magic.

UNDERSTANDING THE SEVEN ADVANTAGES

IF YOUR BRAND ADVANTAGE IS	HOW YOUR BRAND OPERATES	YOUR BRAND IS	YOUR COMMUNICATION IS
INNOVATION	You change the game	Forward-thinking, surprising, bold	Invent creative solutions that tweak tradition
PASSION	You immediately create connections	Expressive, sensory, warm	Apply optimism and energy to build relationships
POWER	You're in command of the environment	Assertive, purposeful, decisive	Become the Opinion of Authority
PRESTIGE	You earn respect for your results	Respected, aspirational, elite	Use admiration to raise the value of your brand
TRUST	You build loyalty with stability	Stable, dependable, comforting	Repeat and reinforce patterns
MYSTIQUE	You make people want to listen closely	Calculated, observant, substantive	Edit what you reveal, to prompt curiosity
ALERT	You watch over the details	Detailed, precise, methodical	Carefully prevent problems

I'll show you how to be less like a traditional marketing school-marm and be more tangible about your own message, as it lives in the real world.

Along the way, we'll pause to consider an $8,200 cocktail, a forty-foot dragon skull, and, oh, those delightfully bright orange polyester Hooters shorts.

PART III

Tactics: A Practical System to Customize Your Message

TurboBranding with Tactics

The $100,000 Second

It's incredibly loud. People screaming in each other's faces. Fierce loyalties in conflict. Emotions becoming hotter, to the boiling point.

Where are we? Not a riot. Not a boxing match. We're at a Super Bowl party.

Welcome to the ultimate stage for advertisers.

For 364 days a year, television commercials are little more than an opportunity to grab a ham sandwich or a bathroom break. Yet during the Super Bowl, for thirty glorious seconds, one brand can have the opportunity to capture a nation's eyeballs and wallets. For a brief moment, no matter where they live or what they believe, viewers share an experience.

For that sliver of attention, the advertiser pays about $100,000 per second. And that may just be a bargain. One study reported that a single Super Bowl ad generates more sales than 250 regular commercials.

Super Bowl commercials have the ability to make cash registers ring, but they also have the ability to start trends and change opinions. An ad agency might spend an entire year coming up with hundreds of potential ideas for a Super Bowl ad before narrowing it down to one. Yet not all Super Bowl commercials are created equal. Certain ones will captivate hundreds of millions of people. Others will float by unnoticed, a wasted investment for the advertiser (and visual spam for the impatient viewer). What's the difference?

Most people watch the Super Bowl for the football. I'm the opposite. I study the commercials, then discuss and debate the most fascinating points on shows such as the *Today* show.

The Most Fascinating Option Wins

In a distracted and competitive environment, the most fascinating option wins. This applies at a boisterous Super Bowl party. It applies to billboards and banner ads. And it applies to you and your brand, every single time you communicate.

To understand how certain messages succeed and others fail, let's take a look at tactics.

Tactics, the Two in the One-Two Punch

Your brand's Advantage gives it its distinct flavor, but what about when your message needs more nuance? What about when you are competing for new business that requires a further point of differentiation? Without a clear road map, you might go in circles, get frustrated, or even give up. That's where tactics come in.

A tactic is an Advantage applied in a tactical way to achieve a specific outcome, reach a targeted audience, or solve a particular problem. Tactics combine with your brand's Advantage in distinct, predictable ways.

Seven Ways to Win the Game

The biggest mistake Super Bowl advertisers make is to water down their message, and run a commercial that's nothing but mush. In Super Bowl commercials, as in the football game itself, you can't afford to play it safe.

By clearly applying a tactic, a Super Bowl commercial will be more likely to stand out and be remembered. A review of the seven ways a message can fascinate, applied to Super Bowl commercials:

Innovation: When a brand needs to immediately break through, it can be worth it to take a risk. Whether it's humor or shock value, Super Bowl viewers talk about the unexpected. Some advertisers (ahem, GoDaddy.com) even make an effort to get their commercial banned before it even airs, because as we saw earlier, controversy can be inherently fascinating.

Passion: Puppies, polar bears, and babies get us gushing with sentiment and emotional connection. We're inspired by these messages.

Power: Perhaps the greatest commercial of all time aired in the 1984 Super Bowl. Apple hurled a sledgehammer smack into the face of its competitors. If you haven't seen the commercial, go find it.

Prestige: Spectacular special effects and celebrity appearances can elevate a brand in the eyes of viewers.

Trust: Simple, familiar ideas can earn recognition quickly. For instance, you already know what a Budweiser Clydesdale looks like, so when you see it on the TV screen, you get the point even if you can't actually hear the commercial over the din of people shouting in the bar.

Mystique: With the growth of social media, advertisers can use teasers and cliff-hangers to provoke curiosity, pulling viewers from the family living room to the Internet to continue their involvement long after the game is over.

Alert: Rather than use fancy clutter and dazzling special effects, the most memorable commercials sometimes reinforce just one specific detail. For example, Master Lock ran a commercial just once, many years ago. Consumers can still recall the image of a bullet being fired through the steel lock, yet the lock stayed put.

SEVEN TACTICS FOR
FASCINATING MESSAGES

	DO THIS	AND YOU WILL
INNOVATION *Tactic*	Invent solutions to tweak tradition	Change the game
PASSION *Tactic*	Connect with emotion	Build warm relationships
POWER *Tactic*	Define your position	Be an authority
PRESTIGE *Tactic*	Set higher standards	Earn respect
TRUST *Tactic*	Never waver	Build loyalty
MYSTIQUE *Tactic*	Reveal little information	Get people thinking
ALERT *Tactic*	Focus on the details	Prompt fast action

When to Use Tactics

Tactics help you tailor your brand's voice for situations that call for a more specific or higher-level message. They allow you to build better connections more quickly and to bring your message to life in relevant, meaningful ways.

Use tactics when:

- There's a short-term sales opportunity. You want to stay true to your brand and also recognize the individual needs of your prospect.
- You want to provoke a very specific action and infuse your marketing message with a fresh perspective.
- You are expanding into a new business category and/or using a new type of communication.

By applying tactics, brands can very carefully hone a message that stands out even in the most competitive environment.

Tactics give a marketing message a specific strategic application. They allow you to customize what you're saying, while maintaining a consistent voice in *how* you say it. Take special note of the three adjectives listed in each combination of Advantage and tactic in the illustrations found in the coming chapters. These three words are the strategy driving each specific message.

Using Tactics and Advantages Together

A tactic should accent your brand's Advantage. Together, these two modes of communication build a more compelling overall message.

If your brand's Advantage is Trust, you're building a reputation on consistency. Yet Trust can eventually begin to feel ho-hum and predictable. What if you laced a little Alert into the mix? You'd increase urgency and action around your message, and add just enough adrenaline to keep things interesting.

If you add a bit of Passion, you'll encourage people to step in more closely and participate.

If you use Prestige, you'll elevate your status and rank. Yet be careful not to become so aloof and unattainable that your target audience feels uncomfortable with your message.

Mystique will make people want to ask questions, learn more, and share what they know. That curiosity keeps your message from feeling cliché or status-conscious.

Is Power your thing? This is a favorite with corporations, because it establishes leadership. Yet messages with Power run the risk of feeling corporate and self-inflated, or worse, steely and detached. To avoid intimidating your audience, add just a drop or two of Passion for warmth and approachability in your message.

If your message is feeling stale or ponderous, consider a whit of Innovation, which encourages your audience to consider new alternative ways of thinking and behaving. This zesty little attitude helps people experience your message anew, rather than taking it for granted as the same old, same old.

I'm about to show you some simple formulas you can use to craft the message you want and need, and that your target audience will find most fascinating—whether you're promoting a star-studded Oscar-night gala or a sale on pencils and paper clips.

ADVANTAGE + TACTIC = YOUR SPECIFIC MESSAGE

Next Up: Tactics

HOW TO CUSTOMIZE YOUR MESSAGE

When you took the Brand Fascination Profile, you learned your brand's Advantage—what makes your brand fascinating. That's step one of building your marketing messages.

Next, you'll see how to customize your messages for different customers and selling situations. That's step two.

Before we dig in, let's take a quick look ahead. In this section, you'll learn how tactics give you an easy way to adjust your marketing without losing your overall voice.

An overview of tactics, and how they shape your day-to-day communication:

Overview of the Innovation Tactic

When to Use Innovation as a Tactic

- Your brand's message is becoming stale or irrelevant.
- Competitors are bringing new products to market faster than you.
- You need a new approach to solve a problem.
- You need to evolve in a rapidly changing environment (such as emerging technology).

Quick Tips for Applying Innovation as a Tactic

- Highlight what you're doing that's new and revolutionary.
- Use humor, even irreverence, in your communication material.
- Surprise your audience with unusual analogies, bizarre stories, or new perspectives on business.
- Create unusual marketing material. Stand out from the competition with cutting-edge design and noteworthy language.

Overview of the Passion Tactic

When to Use Passion as a Tactic

- You want consumers to feel more connected to your brand.
- You want employees to feel more engaged with their jobs and with each other.
- You want to deliver a more colorful experience.
- You're feeling out of touch with customers.

Quick Tips for Applying Passion as a Tactic

- Be enthusiastic and adopt emotion-rich language.
- Appeal to the senses with vivid words.
- Tell stories, because stories connect and engage with your audience.
- Use strong imagery to get to the heart and soul.

Overview of the Power Tactic

When to Use Power as a Tactic

- Your customers believe (mistakenly or not) that you are not a leader.
- You want to take charge of a certain situation.
- You want clients to pay closer attention to your professional advice.
- Your customers don't know what the company stands for.

Quick Tips for Applying Power as a Tactic
- Be knowledgeable; share insights and ideas your customer may not have considered.
- Stay focused; avoid rambling on and wasting time; always keep the purpose of your customer contact points in mind.
- Be confident; have a firm message, with a clearly defined game plan.

Overview of the Prestige Tactic

When to Use Prestige as a Tactic
- You want to position yourself as being above competitors.
- You want to promote an upscale product or event.
- Your prices are dropping.
- A competitor is eclipsing you in a luxury market or competitive space.

Quick Tips for Applying Prestige as a Tactic
- Develop top-notch marketing material.
- Pinpoint ways in which you will improve your customers' outcome.
- Prominently display all awards, ratings, and other third-party recognition so that the brand is seen to the viewer as already highly regarded by others.
- Highlight superior product features.

Overview of the Trust Tactic

When to Use Trust as a Tactic
- Your customer is nervous about change, and seeks stability.
- You want to highlight your heritage and legacy.

Quick Tips to Apply Trust as a Tactic
- Be consistent: use the same colors, fonts, and tone of voice across communication materials.
- Compare your product to something your customer is already familiar with.
- Avoid trendy buzzwords.

Overview of the Mystique Tactic

When to Use Mystique as a Tactic
- You want to be perceived as calm rather than emotional.
- Your message needs to be carefully phrased.
- Competitors are trying to copy your proprietary process (your "secret sauce").

Quick Tips to Apply Mystique as a Tactic
- Distill all marketing messages down to their essence.
- Do not spell out every detail, in order to keep your "secret sauce" a secret.
- Avoid oversharing and overexposure.
- Maintain an unemotional tone, even in times of chaos or conflict.

Overview of the Alert Tactic

When to Use Alert as a Tactic
- You're low on cash and need to drive immediate revenue.
- Your customers don't understand how to use your products and services properly (you need to find a way to get them to read the manual!).
- You need to slash unnecessary expenses.
- Customers don't take action on "closing the deal."

Quick Tips to Apply Alert as a Tactic
- Focus on the data.
- Show consumers how you test and retest your process.
- Give a step-by-step plan of how you'll follow through on delivery.
- Offer in-depth details, and even minutiae.
- Avoid using emotional language or imagery, and instead focus on the rational.

Tactics Solve Specific Problems

Each of the seven Advantages can be combined with a tactic to position your message more specifically. As you're learning about how tactics apply to Advantages, take special note of the four pillars for each Advantage used as a tactic. Create a message with the tactic that is consistent with your specific goals for the communication. These words describe *how you are different*.

Let's start with Innovation. How could an Innovation brand apply the six tactics of Passion, Power, Prestige, Trust, Mystique, and Alert?

Innovation Brands

HOW THEY CAN USE TACTICS

If you are an Innovation brand, tactics will help you determine exactly how you should change the game with creativity. Tactics help you work "inside the box" (even if you are an out-of-the-box thinker). Selectively applying tactics allows you to hone your message, pointing you in exactly the right direction, yet it also allows you the flexibility to customize your message for different instances and audiences.

For example, if you add the Power tactic, you'll bring a sense of confidence and authority to your message. Add the Passion tactic, and you will invoke a more enthusiastic response. Add Trust to stabilize your message over time.

If your brand's Advantage is Innovation, you defy expectation and surprise audiences. You change the game. Let's go through each way that Innovation can use a tactic, so you will get a clear idea of how to apply each one.

THE INNOVATION ADVANTAGE
CUSTOMIZE YOUR MESSAGE BY ADDING ONE OF THE FOLLOWING TACTICS

INNOVATION + PASSION
Excite and engage with messages that are:
BOLD ▪ ARTISTIC ▪ UNORTHODOX

INNOVATION + POWER
Invent strong ideas with messages that are:
PIONEERING ▪ IRREVERENT ▪ ENTREPRENEURIAL

INNOVATION + PRESTIGE
Develop a higher standard with messages that are:
CUTTING-EDGE ▪ ELITE ▪ PROGRESSIVE

INNOVATION + TRUST
Tweak tradition with messages that are:
DELIBERATE ▪ THOUGHTFUL ▪ FLEXIBLE

INNOVATION + MYSTIQUE
Inject wit and dry humor with messages that are:
CLEVER ▪ ADEPT ▪ CONTEMPORARY

INNOVATION + ALERT
Bring structured creativity with messages that are:
PROLIFIC ▪ THOROUGH ▪ DILIGENT

Innovation Is	Innovation Is Not
• Brainstorming sessions	• Communicating predictably within rigid boundaries
• Big ideas that surprise and take risks	• Linear, rational thinking ("A leads to B, which leads to C")
• Creating revolutionary products, forcing competitors to realign	• Blindly following traditional approaches

Innovation Brand Pillars

Remember to continue to use as least three of the four pillars of Innovation:

- Invent surprising solutions.
- Turn something old into something new.
- Do the opposite.
- Infuse a dose of vice.

How Innovation Brands Could Use the Passion Tactic

Be Bold, Artistic, and Unorthodox

- Create a program that invites customers to become "advocates" for new products.
- Post an office vision board where employees can share what the company means to them.
- Celebrate the moments in your clients' family lives, such as a child's birthday or graduation.

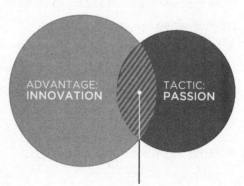

Create messages that are:
Bold
Artistic
Unorthodox

Innovation brands evolve quickly, and this rapid change can make it difficult for consumers to feel attached. Virgin Atlantic is an Innovation brand, but it infused a sweet dose of Passion into its messaging for Valentine's Day.

Love Stories at Thirty Thousand Feet

The billionaire Sir Richard Branson is Innovation through and through, but that doesn't mean he can't show some love. Virgin Atlantic, after all, was formed because of a woman. "I had a beautiful lady waiting for me, and a canceled flight wasn't going to stop me from getting to her," Branson wrote on his website. "So I wrote 'Virgin Airlines' on a blackboard, hired a plane, and filled it with other passengers who had been bumped." To keep the spirit of Passion alive, Virgin Atlantic encourages customers to tweet their love stories while aboard its planes.

How can you bring a kiss of romance to your brand? Even a small touch of Passion can spark infatuation with your brand.

How Innovation Brands Could Use the Power Tactic:

Be Pioneering, Irreverent, and Entrepreneurial

- Go against the grain with an unconventional stance.
- Challenge your audience to experiment.
- Hold a contest for rookie entrepreneurs, and back the top new idea, like *Shark Tank*.

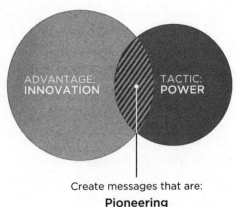

ADVANTAGE: INNOVATION

TACTIC: POWER

Create messages that are:

Pioneering
Irreverent
Entrepreneurial

We've covered some big brands so far. What if you're selling yourself? What if you are the product? This is the challenge facing many "solopreneurs," or solo entrepreneurs, today.

Entrepreneurs often speak the language of creativity. Yet often competitors have a bigger budget, higher awareness, or greater reach. By adding confidence to your creativity, you can build a strong presence. Don't shy from bold opinions. Don't mince words. Remember: have the biggest *budget*, or be the most *fascinating*.

If you're an entrepreneur in Silicon Valley, you may have easy access to fascinating ideas from friends and investors (not to mention funding). But how about if you sell tacos from a food truck in Michigan? You might offer free tacos for life, for a price . . . a visible tattoo of your logo on a customer's body.

Taco truck Vehicle City Taco offered a free taco per day for life for anyone who gets a tattoo of a taco with their logo somewhere on the body that can be seen in public. Pass the hot sauce, Kristopher Kimber, and congratulations on being the first winner.

How Innovation Brands Could Use the Prestige Tactic:
Be Cutting-Edge, Elite, and Progressive

- Use testimonials describing your company as an early adopter of a key trend.
- Write articles about how your company is pushing the curve to set new standards.
- Post customers' videos demonstrating how they improve results using your product.

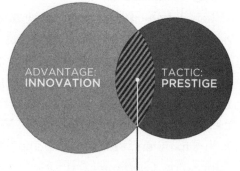

Create messages that are:
Cutting-Edge
Elite
Progressive

Ever heard of a T-shirt company offering a "breakfast special?" One T-shirt company did just that. They released a limited-edition tee that you could purchase only before noon. Innovation with a side of Prestige—coming right up!

How Innovation Brands Could Use the Trust Tactic:
Be Deliberate, Thoughtful, and Flexible

- Find an accepted norm in your category, and give it a twist.
- Introduce product updates gradually to avoid customer whiplash.
- Celebrate your oldest products.

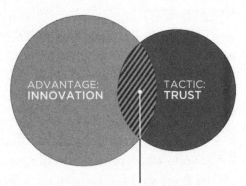

Create messages that are:
Deliberate
Thoughtful
Flexible

The Burn-Free Guarantee

When I helped the innovative brand 800razors.com build its product launch, we took things one step further by instilling some Trust. Market research told us that men felt irritated by the high prices of quality razors. Their skin felt irritated (literally) by the red bumps and rashes caused by cheap razors. They were either financially burned, or razor burned. Working closely with the company's founders, Phil Masiello and Steven Kane, we developed the "Burn-Free Guarantee." If for any reason you feel burned by their razors, you get a 100% refund.

What kind of creative guarantee could your brand offer? A money-back guarantee isn't a revolutionary strategy, yet there are all kinds of fascinating applications here. In the example above, we guaranteed that something would *not* happen (emotional and facial burn). With Innovation + Trust, you'll apply old formulas in new ways.

How Innovation Brands Could Use the Mystique Tactic:

Be Clever, Adept, and Contemporary

- Give a peek of new products to your core fans, before you reveal them to the public.
- Have team members act as "secret shoppers" to get feedback on new products.
- Reward smart questions from your customers by posting the answers directly online.

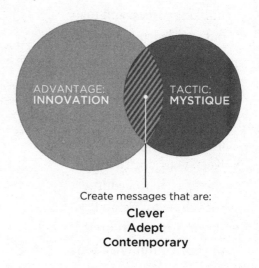

Create messages that are:
Clever
Adept
Contemporary

Gnarly Surf Bar and Grill

One of my favorite restaurants in New Smyrna Beach, Florida, is Gnarly Surf Bar and Grill. Gnarly's is located on the river side of New Smyrna, directly underneath the North Causeway Drawbridge. While many people would consider this location to be a death knell for a popular beach bar, Gnarly's uses the drawbridge to its advantage with the "Bridge Up Beer Deal." During the five to seven minutes that the bridge is up, beer is only twenty-five cents.

Boats in New Smyrna aren't on a schedule, and the bridge goes up only when a boat cannot safely clear it, so there's no telling if and when the turn-of-the-century beer prices will apply. When the bridge goes "ding, ding, ding," customers excitedly rush to the bar to get their beer. Gnarly's keeps its patrons guessing, and it's become a part of the bar's mythology.

How Innovation Brands Could Use the Alert Tactic:

Be Prolific, Thorough, and Diligent

- Take inspiration from unlikely places, and map out step by step how you will implement it.
- Solicit new marketing ideas from a wide range of sources, then execute one extremely well.
- Keep your creativity in check with procedures that allow for flexibility.
- Become more grounded in your communications, target specific audiences, and expand your creative influence.

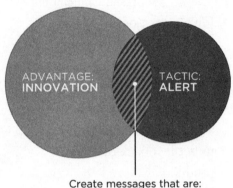

Create messages that are:
Prolific
Thorough
Diligent

Printing an Arm

Daniel was just fourteen years old when a bomb severed both his arms. Without arms, he could no longer support his family, or even feed himself.

When my brilliantly creative friend Mick Ebeling saw a photo of Daniel, instead of just thinking about doing something, he actually did it—and applied his creativity to prompt fast action. Mick and his team hauled 3-D printers, laptops, and spools of plastic high into the mountains of the war-torn country, to design a printable arm for Daniel. (Yes, print an arm.) Soon Daniel was feeding himself, for the first time in two years. And locals who had never seen a computer soon learned how to print prosthetic arms. The whole venture, sponsored by Intel, garnered the brand massive global attention. Sometimes the most fascinating advertising isn't what your brand says to the world, but what it actually does in the world.

Up Next, the Passion Advantage

We're exiting the realm of Innovation and heading into the land of Passion. Ah, Passion . . . the language of relationship.

Passion has a broad emotional spectrum. This black magic comes in a rainbow of bright colors. Passion messages range from a giddy bubble of excitement for a theme park, to a heartfelt plea for donations to a charity. What all Passion messages have in common is that they instantly strike a chord with the target audience, inviting them a step closer.*

---

* I don't like to play favorites among the seven Advantages. Yet Passion is my own primary Advantage, meaning that it's my own most persuasive form of communication. When I walk into a room and I quickly connect with the people around me, I feel energized and in the flow. Similarly, when I apply the language of relationship in marketing, the writing process is easy and fast. You'll probably find the same is true for you. It will be easier for you to create marketing messages that use your primary Advantage.

Passion Brands

HOW THEY CAN USE TACTICS

Brands with the Passion Advantage are expressive, colorful, warm, and engaging. These brands fascinate us through the experience of emotion, energizing people, encouraging them. Instead of selling simply on the basis of rational benefits, Passion focuses on building an attachment.

Passion Is	Passion Is Not
• Warm and engaging conversation	• Stiff or cold
• Colorful and expressive	• Passive or uninvolved
• Focused on emotion	• Numbers, tables, and text-based information

What happens when intensely expressive Passion needs to appeal to a more reserved or laid-back audience? It applies its arsenal of tactics.

THE PASSION ADVANTAGE
CUSTOMIZE YOUR MESSAGE BY ADDING ONE OF THE FOLLOWING TACTICS

PASSION + INNOVATION

Playfully engage with messages that are:
OUT OF THE BOX ▪ SOCIAL ▪ ENERGIZING

PASSION + POWER

Attract advocates with messages that are:
DYNAMIC ▪ INCLUSIVE ▪ ENGAGING

PASSION + PRESTIGE

Elevate first impressions with messages that are:
EXPRESSIVE ▪ STYLISH ▪ EMOTIONALLY INTELLIGENT

PASSION + TRUST

Build lasting bonds with messages that are:
NURTURING ▪ LOYAL ▪ SINCERE

PASSION + MYSTIQUE

Magnetically attract interest with messages that are:
DISCERNING ▪ PERCEPTIVE ▪ CONSIDERATE

PASSION + ALERT

Accelerate a group's focus with messages that are:
ATTENTIVE ▪ DEDICATED ▪ EFFICIENT

Passion Advantage Pillars

Tactics give flexibility to your message. However, don't lose your core brand. Remember to consistently rely on the pillars from Part II in all your communication:

- Woo with wow.
- Use the five senses.
- Put lust before logic.
- Create a strong and immediate emotional response.

How Passion Brands Could Use the Innovation Tactic:

Be Out of the Box, Social, and Energizing

- Tap into what your audience is already passionate about.
- Help people build enthralling new relationships.
- Invite customers to brainstorm new ideas with you via crowdsourcing.

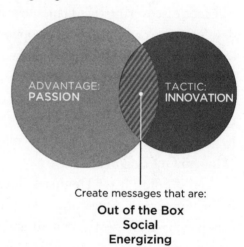

Create messages that are:
**Out of the Box
Social
Energizing**

Passion brands don't play it close to the vest. They use vivid emotional statements to inspire emotions in others. Apply the Innovation tactic, and you'll deliver delightfully surprising experiences. You may even increase the population of Denmark.

Surprising with Innovation

When you visit the website of a Danish travel agency named Spies, you might mistake the company for a standard vacation hub. After all, they have the requisite smorgasbord of photos tempting you with faraway tropical paradises and all too blissful families. That is, until one unusual headline catches your eye: "Do it for Denmark, Do it for Mom."

What exactly are you being asked to "do"? I'll give you a hint. It often results in a baby. (Or babies, if you're lucky.) Under the guise of a humanitarian effort—helping save Denmark's dwindling population—this travel company offers packages and promotions to help you get pregnant. Yep. Romantic city guide included.

Since discovering that Danes have 46% more sex while on holiday, Spies took advantage of the opportunity to kill two birds with one stone. Save the Danish population, and sell more vacations. Happen to be ovulating next week? Enter the date of your last menstrual cycle and the site will spit out an "Ovulation Discount" code. Not sure how this whole getting-pregnant thing works? Not to worry. They provide easy-to-follow instructions, aptly titled "How to Get Pregnant."

And if doing it for Denmark doesn't "do it" for you, then do it for your mom. Spies offers bundles that unfulfilled mothers can purchase to gently encourage a reproductive rendezvous. Pricing will vary . . . based on "how much you want to be a grandmother."

Not all countries want to increase their population. In Bangkok one restauraunt promotes family planning: Cabbages & Condoms proudly proclaims, "Our food is guaranteed not to cause pregnancy."

How Passion Brands Could Use the Power Tactic:

Be Dynamic, Inclusive, and Engaging

- Identify fans who could contribute to your brand's blog as industry experts.
- Put a great deal of energy into your social media program, to engage a wide audience.
- Don't become so overly emotional that you fail to inspire action.

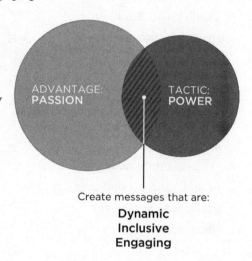

Create messages that are:
Dynamic
Inclusive
Engaging

Passionately Powerful

Let's say you're a personal trainer, and you want to sell an online program for physical fitness. With Passion + Power, you'll be loving but strong. When inviting prospects to sign up, you might take a firm stance: "If you're committed to play big and make serious improvements in your body, I'm interested in working with you. If you're still on the fence about making a serious change, I'm happy to direct you to other training programs."

How Passion Brands Could Use the Prestige Tactic:

Be Expressive, Stylish, and Emotionally Intelligent

- Add testimonials from favorite clients, including interesting facts about them.
- Toot your horn with a celebration of team accomplishments.
- Watch every nuance of style and attitude, to make sure you never disappoint.

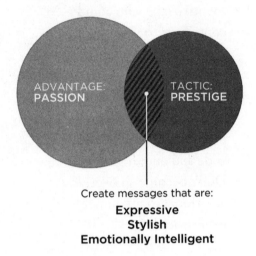

Create messages that are:
Expressive
Stylish
Emotionally Intelligent

Refreshing with Prestige

Not so long ago, the height of epicurean indulgence was a box filled with Godiva chocolates. The gold box became a glimmering icon, available only in metropolitan areas. Then, in an effort to expand, Godiva made a fateful decision to distribute in mass retailers such as Barnes & Noble. The chocolates began to include preservatives, and you could buy the gold box in suburban strip malls. I worked closely with Godiva to develop a new, exclusive blended chocolate drink to repair the brand's image, and put Lady Godiva back in her rightful place.

How Passion Brands Could Use the Trust Tactic:

Be Nurturing, Loyal, and Sincere

- Create timeless attraction by tapping into themes of love, parenting, and childhood.
- Build relationships slowly and gradually, with a focus on the long term.
- Go to extra lengths to thank devoted customers.

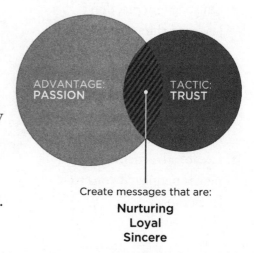

ADVANTAGE: PASSION

TACTIC: TRUST

Create messages that are:
Nurturing
Loyal
Sincere

Repairing a Broken Relationship

Trust can help you rebuild a broken relationship by spelling out a long-term commitment.

If you're a natural juice brand, and your brand promises to avoid pasteurization, then it's crucial that the apples used in your juice be picked from the trees, rather than from the ground. When gathering apples for Odwalla juice in 1996, a worker in the grove apparently took an apple off the ground. This led to an E. coli outbreak. Rather than explaining or hiding, Odwalla removed all its fruit juices from the shelves, and within just five weeks of the recall, it developed a safer "flash pasteurization" method.

No matter what your brand's primary Advantage, you can apply Trust to reestablish your commitments and rebuild your core principles.

How Passion Brands Could Use the Mystique Tactic:

Be Discerning, Perceptive, and Considerate

- On social media, don't just read the words; listen to what customers are actually saying.
- Engage customers in a game (a scavenger hunt?) to announce a launch.
- Create advertising that makes people curious to learn more.

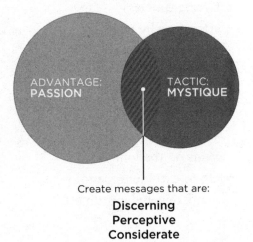

Create messages that are:
Discerning
Perceptive
Considerate

Follow the Bricks

In the nineteenth century, the showman P. T. Barnum demonstrated fascination at its finest. And not just with lions, tigers, and bears. He also knew how to spellbind potential customers. When an unemployed man came to his museum and asked for a job, Barnum gave him a seemingly meaningless one that managed to pay off. He instructed the man to take five bricks and set them outside the museum in different spots. Every hour, he was to enter the museum and pretend to pay for a ticket, then leave and move the bricks to different locations. The peculiar behavior caught the eyes of onlookers, who gathered in large numbers, debating the meaning of his actions, and paid to enter the museum. Before Barnum could count his receipts, the police asked him to stop the charade, because the crowds were too large to handle. Even small details can add curiosity and captivation.

How Passion Brands Could Use the Alert Tactic:

Be Attentive, Dedicated, and Efficient

- Create a quality-
  assurance process and
  ask your customers for
  feedback.
- Turn basic details into
  an engaging experience.
- Reward customers for
  finding errors on your
  website.

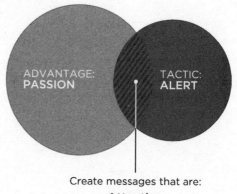

Create messages that are:
**Attentive
Dedicated
Efficient**

Of Mice and Manholes

If your customer experience revolves around emotion, it's also important to get the details right. And those details can be spellbinding. Walt Disney was a master of magical details. His legacy oversees everything at his theme parks, from the distinctiveness of their sections to the tiny Mickey Mouse on every manhole cover.

Power Brands

HOW THEY CAN USE TACTICS

Power leads the way, showing us which way to go, directing our actions and opinions. Yet there is no one "right" way to lead. Leadership can take many forms, from quiet certainty to boisterous cheerleading. Yet what all forms of Power have in common is a clear direction and a comfort with command.

Power Is	Power Is Not
• Confidently leading the pack	• Meekly asking permission, hesitating, second-guessing, or communicating with insecurity
• Voicing opinions in no uncertain terms	• Passive, indifferent, or neutral communication
• Decisive and ready to take action	• Being a follower, behind others in your category

Brands that use Power, like brands that use any other Advantage, need to communicate effectively with everyone from those with primary Mystique to those with primary Passion. To expand your audience, use your new arsenal of tactics.

THE POWER ADVANTAGE
CUSTOMIZE YOUR MESSAGE BY ADDING ONE OF THE FOLLOWING TACTICS

POWER + INNOVATION

Spark entrepreneurial spirit with messages that are:
INVENTIVE ▪ UNTRADITIONAL ▪ SELF-PROPELLED

POWER + PASSION

Inspire participation with messages that are:
MOTIVATING ▪ SPIRITED ▪ COMPELLING

POWER + PRESTIGE

Compete to win with messages that are:
AMBITIOUS ▪ FOCUSED ▪ CONFIDENT

POWER + TRUST

Build loyalty over time with messages that are:
PROMINENT ▪ GENUINE ▪ SURE-FOOTED

POWER + MYSTIQUE

Win strategically with messages that are:
METHODICAL ▪ INTENSE ▪ SELF-RELIANT

POWER + ALERT

Jumpstart urgency with messages that are:
PROACTIVE ▪ CAUTIONARY ▪ STRONG WILLED

Power Advantage Pillars

Whether you're a global brand or a local startup, you can speak the language of confidence. You don't have to wait to be asked for your opinion. Power is the means to the end.

Having an arsenal of tactics puts you in a position to get the attention of those you might not otherwise attract. Use them when called for, but remember to rely on at least three of the four pillars of Power in order to maximize your competitive Advantage:

- Lead the way.
- Take control.
- Pursue specific goals.
- Voice your Opinions of Authority.

How Power Brands Could Use the Innovation Tactic:

Be Inventive, Untraditional, and Self-Propelled

- Reinvent the accepted norm, and then lead the way.
- At client meetings, don't be afraid to offer a wide range of options.
- Reward your team with prizes for great new ideas.

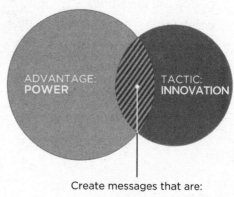

Create messages that are:
**Inventive
Untraditional
Self-Propelled**

Few small business owners have an in-house marketing department, or even a marketing person. But apply Innovation, and you'll stand out from the established options.

When to Emphasize Change

If you want your prospects to switch from a competitor, prompt them to be dissatisfied with their current situation. You want them to view you as a different road to success. For instance, if you're a financial adviser, apply Innovation by reinforcing the need for change. You might say: "The market is rapidly changing. Opportunities are shifting. You can't build a strong financial future with outdated strategies. I can help you intelligently adapt your financial strategy, and your mind-set, with a fresh look at your future."

How Power Brands Could Use the Passion Tactic:

Be Motivating, Spirited, and Compelling

- Take extra effort to inspire and encourage new customers.
- Institute an open-door policy for the whole company.
- Start staff meetings with an overview of recent team achievements.

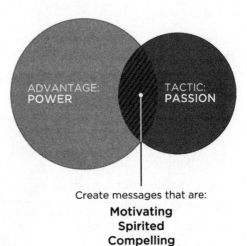

Create messages that are:
Motivating
Spirited
Compelling

Uberlicious

To celebrate its birthday, the car service Uber offered free "on-demand" cupcakes. Even if you'd never used Uber before, on this one day you could download its app and order a cupcake to be delivered, for free. The brand had thousands of new customers the next morning.

How Power Brands Could Use the Prestige Tactic:

Be Ambitious, Focused, and Confident

- Develop specific professional-development goals for your employees.
- Play big! Instead of aiming for fifty new clients this year, shoot for a hundred.
- Show your audience how to set ambitious goals, and give the tools to track them.

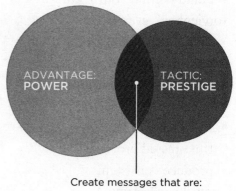

Create messages that are:
Ambitious
Focused
Confident

Lane Bryant's Cacique lingerie line, aimed specifically at plus-sized women (who make up well over half of the population of U.S. women), uses print and TV ads that show beautiful models of various shapes and hues with one simple statement, "I'm no angel"—taking a poke at and the lead against Victoria's Secret, which does not cater to plus-size women.

How Power Brands Could Use the Trust Tactic:

Be Prominent, Genuine, and Sure-Footed

- Stand behind your team
  members, even when
  they make mistakes.
- Honor longtime
  customers with benefits
  and extra privileges.
- Demonstrate how your
  time-tested processes
  produce consistent
  results over time.

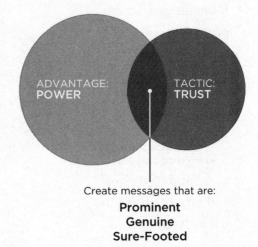

Create messages that are:
Prominent
Genuine
Sure-Footed

The FBI is a Power brand. It is normally associated with impervious strength. To show the organization's trustworthy, family-loving side, the FBI's official website has an entire section devoted just to kids. According to the FBI, "the Kids' Page is designed for children and their parents to learn more about the FBI."

Even if you have an intensely Power-oriented brand, the language of stability can help make your audience feel more safe and secure with you.

How Power Brands Could Use the Mystique Tactic:

Be Methodical, Intense, and Self-Reliant

- Treat marketing like chess. Stay two steps ahead by watching the competition.
- Ask insightful questions to provoke discussion within your industry.
- Strategically plan each step to avoid public errors.

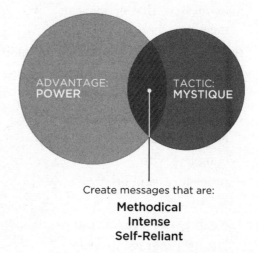

Create messages that are:
Methodical
Intense
Self-Reliant

Here's an example of how one Power brand used Mystique to take billboard marketing to the next level.

A Dragon Skull Washed Up on the Beach . . .

In Part I, we learned that traditional marketing is the school-marm of communication. Most marketers rely on expensive media buys to get their message across, but you could instead perform marketing witchcraft by planting a forty-foot dragon skull on a beach.

To announce the release of the third season of HBO's *Game of Thrones*, a mammoth dragon skull was planted on the shore of England's Charmouth Beach, already well known for its dinosaur fossils. No explanations were given. Crowds formed, media coverage ensued, and publicity skyrocketed. Turns out, this faux dragon skull came from a new UK streaming service called Blinkbox. In the end, the brand increased revenue by 632%, torching the usual model of marketing.

Want to ignite new interest in your brand? Have people stopped following your brand because you flood the airwaves? Develop a juicy mystery that people can solve with clues.

How Power Brands Could Use the Alert Tactic:

Be Proactive, Cautionary, and Strong Willed

- Ensure every employee has a copy of a detailed employee handbook, complete with procedures and other references.
- Keep a close eye on your clients' progress, making sure projects don't fall behind.
- Take a proactive approach to company progress by creating contingency plans.

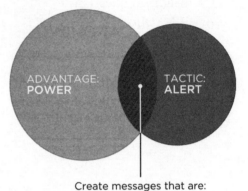

Create messages that are:
Proactive
Cautionary
Strong Willed

No Brown M&Ms

Let's see how the legendary rock band Van Halen used Alert to test the waters. Like all big acts, Van Halen requested items for their backstage comfort, such as beer, wine, food, and M&Ms— but no brown ones. Why would Van Halen care whether they were munching on yellow, red, or brown candies? Van Halen's seemingly uppity performance criteria was a test of sorts. If the band found brown M&Ms backstage, they assumed that paying attention to details was not the promoter's strength and that important aspects of the show, such as lighting, staging, and security, might suffer as a result.

If Power can use tactics to rule the world, Prestige can soar above it. By setting new standards, any type of communication can earn respect and elevate perceived value.

Prestige Brands

HOW THEY CAN USE TACTICS

If your brand's Fascination Advantage is Prestige, you carefully inspect new products before releasing them, provide ongoing customer service training, and add testimonials from your biggest clients to your website's home page. Prestige brands shine; in fact, they glow in the dark. People can't help but be drawn to Prestige for status symbols. If your company speaks the language of excellence, keep up the good work—then take it up a notch.

Prestige Is	Prestige Is Not
• Accustomed to raising the bar	• Hesitating to form an opinion
• Focused on specific outcomes	• Hiding from publicity or exposure
• Dedicated to excellence	• Content to accept situations as they are

As a Prestige brand, what do you do when you need to reach the less detailed Innovation personalities or the practical Trust customers? When stepping outside your normal circle, pull from your new arsenal of tactics to create the perfect message.

THE PRESTIGE ADVANTAGE
CUSTOMIZE YOUR MESSAGE BY ADDING
ONE OF THE FOLLOWING TACTICS

PRESTIGE + INNOVATION
Provoke a new perspective with messages that are:
ORIGINAL ▪ ENTERPRISING ▪ FORWARD-THINKING

PRESTIGE + PASSION
Attract a savvy audience with messages that are:
INSIGHTFUL ▪ DISTINGUISHED ▪ IN THE KNOW

PRESTIGE + POWER
Drive superior results with messages that are:
RESPECTED ▪ COMPETITIVE ▪ RESULTS ORIENTED

PRESTIGE + TRUST
Build timeless admiration with messages that are:
CLASSIC ▪ ESTABLISHED ▪ BEST IN CLASS

PRESTIGE + MYSTIQUE
Define a better structure with messages that are:
SKILLFUL ▪ RESTRAINED ▪ POLISHED

PRESTIGE + ALERT
Identify the correct path with messages that are:
INTELLECTUAL ▪ DISCIPLINED ▪ SYSTEMATIC

Prestige Advantage Pillars

Your new arsenal of tactics is an excellent resource for taking your communication to the next level. Remember, however, that to maximize your competitive differences as a brand, and to avoid the three threats of distraction, competition, and commoditization, you must continue to rely on your Prestige pillars:

- Increase perceived value.
- Set a new standard.
- Develop emblems.
- Limit availability.

How Prestige Brands Could Use the Innovation Tactic:

Be Original, Enterprising, and Forward-Thinking

- Establish brand iconography that is one of a kind.
- Make weekly status meetings fun and uplifting with bold thinking and dramatic style.
- Inspire clients to look ahead. Show them how to keep their business relevant.

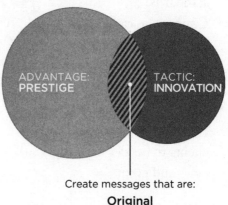

Create messages that are:
Original
Enterprising
Forward-Thinking

The Technology of Fashion

One of my clients, Cole Haan, had a legacy of Prestige. Everyone knew that its products were well crafted, but Cole Haan lacked the level of lust normally reserved for trendier Prestige brands such as Gucci and Jimmy Choo. To fight back, Cole Haan tapped new technology from its parent company, Nike, and engineered a breakthrough design of cushioned four-inch high-heeled shoes. With this invention, high heels weren't just for Town Car–cruising socialites and masochists. Women who do crazy things like walk could now wear shoes with Prestige. One appearance on Oprah later, and the early designs were sold out across the country.

How Prestige Brands Could Use the Passion Tactic:
Be Insightful, Distinguished, and In the Know

- Connect with your customers through enthusiasm over higher standards.
- Choose the right style, approach, and words to solve your audience's pain points.
- Show in-the-know expertise by tipping off clients to insider industry news and events.

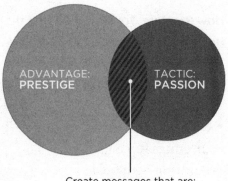

Create messages that are:
Insightful
Distinguished
In the Know

The Smell of Success

When Rolls-Royce started manufacturing vehicles using leather-clad plastic instead of wood, customers knew something wasn't right. The car just didn't smell the same. While owners couldn't see the plastic, they also couldn't smell the wood. Once the company determined the problem, they created a scent to match the 1965 Rolls-Royce Silver Cloud. Ah, the smell of success.

What if your brand had a signature scent to reinforce your experience? Singapore Airlines has created a strong visual brand identity and a corporate perfume for flight attendants—which is also used on the hot towels served to tired travelers.

How Prestige Brands Could Use the Power Tactic:

Be Respected, Competitive, and Results Oriented

- Demand higher results from everyone on your team, and reward them for their achievements.
- Set the bar by measuring customer satisfaction.
- Overdeliver in specific ways for key clients and prospects.

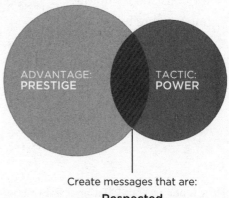

Create messages that are:
Respected
Competitive
Results Oriented

The Ultimate Driving . . . Plane?

BMW started making cars because it wasn't allowed to make planes after World War I. That led to "the ultimate driving machine." If a Prestige brand can grow respect, how could your brand grow its presence by applying the Power tactic?

How Prestige Brands Could Use the Trust Tactic:

Be Classic, Established, and Best in Class

- Avoid fads and buzzwords to keep your brand timeless.
- No matter what, maintain a reputation for consistently doing outstanding work.
- Make sure you overdeliver by following patterns that have historically performed well.

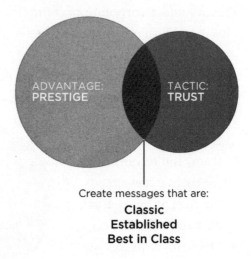

Create messages that are:
Classic
Established
Best in Class

How Much Is Your Customer Experience Worth?

The Ritz-Carlton hotel chain is an outlier in customer service. While it's not a formally acknowledged policy, any Ritz-Carlton employee is reportedly permitted to spend up to two thousand dollars to ensure that a guest's problem is handled immediately. (That's Prestige partnered tightly with Trust, to ensure credibility.) How far can you take your brand Advantage, and turn it into an extreme?

How Prestige Brands Could Use the Mystique Tactic:

Be Skillful, Restrained, and Polished

- Underpromise and overdeliver.
- Take time to master specific proficiencies rather than jumping from one to the next.
- Offer fewer products, focusing on top-notch, error-free delivery.

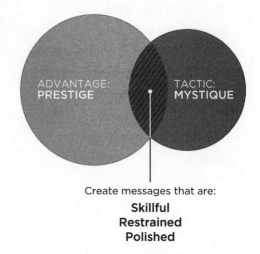

Create messages that are:
Skillful
Restrained
Polished

Imported Tile (and Imported Craftsmen)

When Epcot built its Morocco Pavilion, King Hassan II flew expert Moroccan craftsmen to Orlando. They installed tile, carved archways, and created the mystery of Moroccan culture. This level of perfectionism goes beyond the bazaar. This is my personal favorite pavilion at Epcot, thanks to the combination of Prestige and Mystique.

How Prestige Brands Could Use the Alert Tactic:

Be Intellectual, Disciplined, and Systematic

- Show a proven track record with details of awards and recognitions.
- Implement a systematic process in every area.
- Prepare carefully for failure; leave nothing to chance.

Create messages that are:
Intellectual
Disciplined
Systematic

When Economies Change, So Does Prestige

During an economic recession, luxury connotations can have a negative brand effect. The classic black Armani power suit can be pushed aside in the closet for the understated shirt and slacks.

During the Great Recession, high-end resorts backpedaled from their opulent descriptions. When belts tightened, they faced uncomfortable scrutiny. Loews Hotels even temporarily removed the word "resort" from its name. When budgets tighten during a cutback or recession, Alert enters the picture and Prestige cues can shift dramatically. Diversify beyond superficial name recognition to avoid taking a hit when people no longer want overt displays.

Next, on to the bedrocks of the business world: Trust brands. These companies leverage their consistency to captivate.

Trust Brands

HOW THEY CAN USE TACTICS

Trust is reliable and comforting. We know exactly what to expect. Yet, Trust can become a little dull and predictable for your audience. But by infusing Trust with tactics, such as Innovation or Power, you'll speak the language of stability in a variety of fascinating ways.

Trust Is	Trust Is Not
• Comforting in times of change	• Using fluffy or flowery language
• Being dependable	• Changing packaging, slogans, or locations
• Relying on reproducible, proven ideas	• Following the latest fads or trends

The other six Advantages can fascinate us in a short time. An approaching deadline instantly motivates us with Alert. A provocative headline on a magazine cover can fixate with Mystique. Trust, however, is fascination of a different sort. It's established consistently.

When you need to step outside your comfort zone to reach new and bigger audiences, rely on the various tactics outlined in this chapter to create spellbindingly trustworthy messages.

THE TRUST ADVANTAGE
CUSTOMIZE YOUR MESSAGE BY ADDING
ONE OF THE FOLLOWING TACTICS

TRUST + INNOVATION

Tweak traditions with messages that are:
CURIOUS ▪ ADAPTABLE ▪ OPEN-MINDED

TRUST + PASSION

Nurture consistency with messages that are:
APPROACHABLE ▪ DEPENDABLE ▪ TRUSTWORTHY

TRUST + POWER

Promise lasting quality with messages that are:
DIGNIFIED ▪ STABLE ▪ HARDWORKING

TRUST + PRESTIGE

Uphold enduring values with messages that are:
LEVELHEADED ▪ SUBTLE ▪ CAPABLE

TRUST + MYSTIQUE

Guarantee security with messages that are:
PROTECTIVE ▪ PURPOSEFUL ▪ ANALYTICAL

TRUST + ALERT

Reinforce each process with messages that are:
PRINCIPLED ▪ PREPARED ▪ CONSCIENTIOUS

Trust Advantage Pillars

Your new arsenal of tactics is a dependable way to expand your reach. Bear in mind, however, that your brand cannot violate the pillars of Trust. Use them as much and as often as possible to reinforce your brand promise.

- Repeat and retell.
- Be authentic.
- Accelerate trust.
- Use familiar cues.

How Trust Brands Could Use the Innovation Tactic:

Be Curious, Adaptable, and Open-Minded

- Make sure your brand is not falling behind or falling into a rut; schedule "rut checks."
- Keep the same logo over time, but update your tagline (or vice versa).
- Build flexibility into your promotional calendar, so you can customize tactics for holidays and current events.

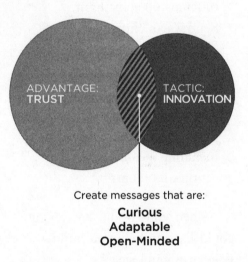

ADVANTAGE: TRUST

TACTIC: INNOVATION

Create messages that are:
Curious
Adaptable
Open-Minded

Here's an example: Accounting firms are classic Trust businesses. Because they're all using the same Advantage, and the same words and images, they often look the same and sound the same. If your brand doesn't stand out, it's at risk of becoming a commodity. How could an accounting firm stand out?

Bean Counters and Black Eyed Peas

Ever seen an accountant lip-sync a Black Eyed Peas song? Or bust a move in a flash mob? The CPA firm WithumSmith+Brown stands out in the Trust-saturated accounting category with videos starring their accountants lip-synching to "I Gotta Feeling."

In a commoditized category, employee personality can help you glow with a spark of Innovation.

How Trust Brands Could Use the Passion Tactic:

Be Approachable, Dependable, and Trustworthy

- Strengthen the relationship with each client; appoint a personal relationship consultant.
- Send warm chocolate chip cookies to clients on the anniversary of your working together.
- Create a welcome package for new clients, including a camera to capture moments.

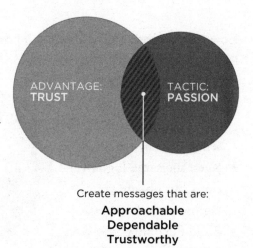

ADVANTAGE: TRUST

TACTIC: PASSION

Create messages that are:
Approachable
Dependable
Trustworthy

When your brand has operated the same way for years, how could Passion help you build a more emotional relationship with your own employees?

Closed on Christmas

Until 1988, most Denny's locations did not have locks installed on their doors, because the stores never closed. They were open 24/7/365. Then the company decided to give its employees Christmas Day off. The closing apparently cost about $5 million in sales, but many of its sixty thousand employees were so grateful that they sent cards and letters to their employers.

How Trust Brands Could Use the Power Tactic:

Be Dignified, Stable, and Hardworking

- Offer a consistent, money-back guarantee on all products.
- Explain the research behind your product development.
- Consistently publish white papers to establish your authority.

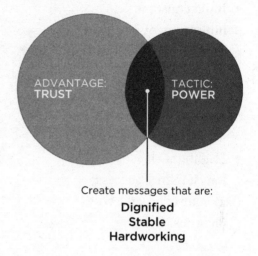

Create messages that are:
Dignified
Stable
Hardworking

Sometimes a symbol of Power is all you need to communicate.

Apply Some Muscle

You might not immediately recognize the name "Vulcan Spice Company." Yet in 1867 this brand created a distinctive logo of a muscular arm holding a hammer, in honor of the Roman god of fire and metalworking. Anyone know what it is yet? Here's a hint: the company makes baking soda. It's one of the most recognizable and trusted logos around the world: Arm & Hammer.

If you're communicating with Trust and a Power tactic, then demonstrate Power over an extended amount of time.

How Trust Brands Could Use the Prestige Tactic:

Be Levelheaded, Subtle, and Capable

- Build constant improvement into your core values.
- If you find a "bug" in your system, announce a clear timeline of when it'll be fixed.
- Highlight the longstanding success of your tried-and-true favorites.

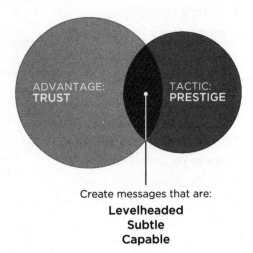

Create messages that are:
Levelheaded
Subtle
Capable

Flying Scot

She's a handcrafted vessel, designed in 1957. Her unsinkable shape glides effortlessly through the water. By leveraging Trust, Flying Scot has survived decades of sailing's so-called improvements, and its boats can still be found bobbing gently in most northeastern marinas.

Trust favors consistency and reliability. Flying Scots won't surprise you with a clever new rigging system or a flashy new hull. Here's the promise: each boat lasts a lifetime. Be sure to pick a color you like, because you'll have it practically forever.

Decide how your brand will be best in class, stick to it over time, and you'll earn everlasting respect.

How Trust Brands Could Use the Mystique Tactic:

Be Protective, Purposeful, and Analytical

- Rather than flashy parties or meetings, have low-key interactions with team members.
- Allow anonymous feedback with comment cards for customers and employees.
- Base your actions on solid research and long-term plans.

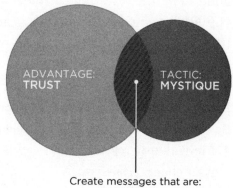

Create messages that are:
Protective
Purposeful
Analytical

Are you asking questions before rattling off answers that might not be helpful to your customer? Here's a smart way to give exactly the feedback your audience needs (nothing more, nothing less).

Questions Matter More Than Answers

When customers ask for tech support, the answer should depend on the expertise of the person asking. Beginners need simple language, while professionals want more sophisticated descriptions. DreamHost, a tech company, asks its customers to identify their own tech expertise before they receive an answer. Here are the choices:

1. Please explain everything to me very carefully.
2. I do know some stuff, but please don't assume too much.
3. Overall I know my stuff, but I'm a little shaky in this area.
4. I have a good understanding of this stuff.
5. Not to be rude, but I probably know more about this than you!

Me, I'd rate myself only 2 or 3 on this scale. So a 5-level response would feel overwhelming, and I'd be less likely to feel
good about the resulting customer service. How about you? Can
you ask questions before giving answers? DreamHost's Mystique tactic has translated into 1.2 million domain names hosted
worldwide.

How Trust Brands Could Use the Alert Tactic:
Be Principled, Prepared, and Conscientious

- Meticulously research
  your clients *before* you
  meet them.
- Use clear language to
  explain your values on
  your website or in your
  offices.
- Maintain a consistent
  schedule with your staff,
  rather than imposing
  unexpected deadlines.

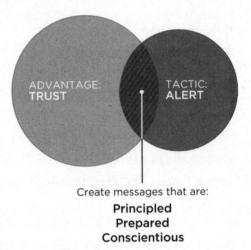

Create messages that are:
Principled
Prepared
Conscientious

Well-established banks, such as Wells Fargo, have a competitive edge when it comes to leveraging Trust. Over a hundred years
old, with a well-known logo, this monolithic bank almost has the
Trust market cornered. Almost.

No Asterisks Allowed
To accelerate Trust with new customers, Ally bank has a policy
to avoid any use of asterisks. This policy means that everything is
clearly spelled out, with no hidden fine print doublespeak inside its
financial documents.

If you're offering a complex product or service, remember that we're living in a world with a nine-second attention span. Your prospects can easily become confused or overwhelmed by disorganized nuances. Pick which details matter. Spell it out in plain English (or whichever language you prefer!). By streamlining with Alert, you'll be doing yourself, and your customer, a favor.

Mystique Brands

HOW THEY CAN USE TACTICS

If your primary mode of communication is Mystique, you already excel at influencing how your customers listen. Intentionally or not, your marketing avoids spelling out every detail. It isn't pushy or overt.

Heightening fascination while also maintaining privacy isn't always an easy balance. Earning attention is usually associated with talking *louder*, or talking *more often*. Yet this is not necessarily the case, if you can cast a spell with Mystique. In this section, you'll find simple methods for adjusting your message to specific situations by applying tactics.

Mystique Is	Mystique Is Not
• Knowing what to leave out of the conversation	• Superficial chitchat and banter
• Watching intently	• Communicating emotionally
• Enticing others to listen	• Pushing a hard sale

Combine a tactic with Mystique, and your message will become less veiled, and more accessible.

THE MYSTIQUE ADVANTAGE
CUSTOMIZE YOUR MESSAGE BY ADDING ONE OF THE FOLLOWING TACTICS

MYSTIQUE + INNOVATION
Bring an original viewpoint with messages that are:
NIMBLE ▪ UNASSUMING ▪ INDEPENDENT

MYSTIQUE + PASSION
Invite viewpoints from all with messages that are:
TACTFUL ▪ SELF-SUFFICIENT ▪ MINDFUL

MYSTIQUE + POWER
Keep a smart distance with messages that are:
REALISTIC ▪ INTENTIONAL ▪ TO THE POINT

MYSTIQUE + PRESTIGE
Earn respect with perceptive messages that are:
ELEGANT ▪ ASTUTE ▪ DISCREET

MYSTIQUE + TRUST
Stay calm, cool and collected with messages that are:
OBSERVANT ▪ ASSURED ▪ UNRUFFLED

MYSTIQUE + ALERT
Deliver careful execution with messages that are:
ON-TARGET ▪ REASONED ▪ PRAGMATIC

Mystique Advantage Pillars

Expanding into new marketing territory does not mean leaving home for good. Your brand pillars never leave your side. Use them consistently, adding tactics as necessary. Your pillars are as follows:

- Protect information.
- Spark curiosity.
- Ask questions before giving answers.
- Build mythology.

When Mystique applies different tactics to its marketing pieces, this understated Advantage can feel warmer, more powerful, and even revealing. We'll soon find out how, when we apply the six options, from Innovation to Trust.

How Mystique Brands Could Use the Innovation Tactic:

Be Nimble, Unassuming, and Independent

- Brainstorm solo or in small groups to avoid too many voices and opinions.
- Create a curiosity-provoking campaign with clues that gradually lead to answers.
- Keep new developments top secret.

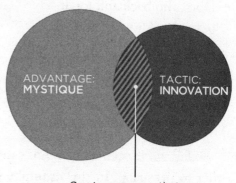

Create messages that are:
Nimble
Unassuming
Independent

Mystique is subtle and can risk being ignored. Stand out with intelligent tweaks to the norm. If your restaurant has an inconvenient location, you could offer 10% off for delivery service. If your retail location doesn't have ample parking, you could create your own version of a valet. Smart tweaks help you stand out without increasing your marketing budget. Humor works, too.

My family's favorite local ice cream shop has an unassuming storefront. Yet little creative touches bring Innovation to the experience. When peering through the glass screen to choose your ice cream flavor, a small sign puts a new twist on a familiar expression: "Please don't tap on the glass. It scares the ice cream."

How Mystique Brands Could Use the Passion Tactic:

Be Tactful, Self-Sufficient, and Mindful

- Be personable, yet not overwhelming.
- Put a real person on your customer support line, rather than an autoattendant.
- Don't flip back and forth between a "warm" and "cold" tonality.

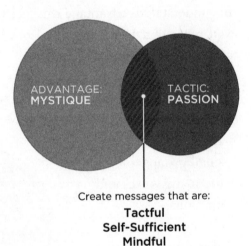

Create messages that are:
Tactful
Self-Sufficient
Mindful

So far, we've seen how brands can positively attract attention in order to persuade. In this example, we'll see how you can attract negative attention, yet do so potentially for your own reward.

Hollywooding

In "Mystique: The Language of Listening," we saw the inner workings of the poker table, and how professionals at the highest levels are experts at reading their opponents' tells. Yet there are newer (and more controversial) ways to tweak the game. "Hollywooding" is the practice of overdramatizing the decision process.

While every player at the poker table requires a certain amount of time to make a decision, the overly emotional player maliciously takes too much time, aggravating his opponents, intentionally trying to get them to reveal their strategy. It might not be a cool move, but it sometimes works.

If you're a Mystique brand, consider intentionally applying a little drama to throw your competitors off balance.

How Mystique Brands Could Use the Power Tactic:

Be Realistic, Intentional, and to the Point

- Give clear instructional guides and diagrams to tell your story.
- Keep messages brief, succinct, and to the point.
- Don't force customers to make a decision on the spot.

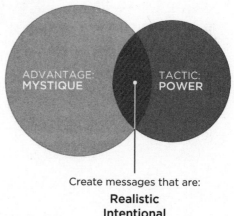

Create messages that are:
Realistic
Intentional
To the Point

Leadership can take many forms, from quiet certainty to boisterous coaching. Mystique brands might be understated, but they don't have to shy from directing with control and command. By adding Power tactics, you won't be mistaken for meekly asking permission, or hesitating. Power helps your communication avoid being seen as passive, indifferent, or neutral.

Earlier we talked about the trend of "unboxing" surprise gifts and deliveries. Birchbox delivers monthly goodies and beauty supplies each month; however, the customers don't pick the selections. Birchbox's editors do. They take control in selection.

(Interestingly, Birchbox's marketing says you can "buy with confidence"; however, you won't necessarily know exactly what you're buying with confidence until it arrives.)

How Mystique Brands Could Use the Prestige Tactic:

Be Elegant, Astute, and Discreet

- Analyze the structure behind your competitors' strategies (so you can outdo them).
- Quietly and steadily improve your behind-the-scenes process.
- Create messages that demonstrate superiority without showing off.

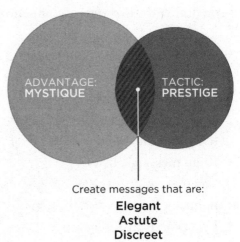

ADVANTAGE: MYSTIQUE

TACTIC: PRESTIGE

Create messages that are:
Elegant
Astute
Discreet

Walled Gardens

If you've used Facebook, a Kindle, or Apple iOS, you've been inside a "walled garden."

Almost anyone can use Facebook (and most of us do). Yet even with its freedom, there are boundaries and barriers. In a "walled garden," the provider controls the content, media, and applications that the user can access. If you do get access, such as an invitation to join a private group, that's an ego boost.

Just as dance clubs use the velvet rope, brands can use Mystique to maintain distance while selectively creating circles of insiders. The combination of Mystique + Prestige builds competition and desire to get into the walled garden.

How Mystique Brands Could Use the Trust Tactic:

Be Observant, Assured, and Unruffled

- Build long-lasting, sustainable messages, rather than trendy mentions on social media.
- Remind customers of how you've served them in the past.
- Remember that slow and steady wins the race when building relationships.

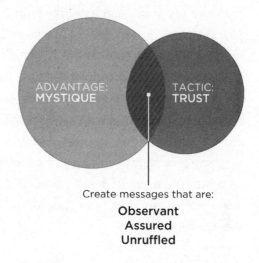

Create messages that are:
Observant
Assured
Unruffled

Merchandise 7X

The soda's secret ingredient, the cryptically dubbed "Merchandise 7X," has remained a secret since the beverage's invention in 1886. The company has kept its prized list of ingredients in a vault inside the Trust Company's bank since 1925.

This much is known. From there, it's difficult to tell fact from fiction, because Coca-Cola itself builds suspense and drama around its drink by feeding mythology to reporters and consumers.

One urban myth states that only two Coca-Cola executives know Coke's formula; however, they each know only half. The truth, apparently, is a bit different but no less mythologically lavish. Coca-Cola shrewdly builds mythology into its conversation and cultivates it in the media, boosting our perception of the drink's value and cachet. Executives who know the recipe cannot travel in the same airplane, because in case of a crash, the recipe would be lost forever.*

More mythological bang for your buck: When Cola-Cola employees were busted for trying to sell the company's secret formula to Pepsi for $1.5 million, Coke's CEO said that the breach "underscores the responsibility we each have to be vigilant in protecting our trade secrets. Information is the lifeblood of the company." But guess who turned the Coke employees in to the feds? Pepsi.

Secret formulas can turn an otherwise mundane recipe of any sort into a source of fascination. If Mystique is the lifeblood of sugar water, consider how your brand could avoid drinking from the mainstream.

---

* Spoiler Alert: In his book *For God, Country, and Coca-Cola*, Mark Pendergrast outs what many believe to be the classic Coke recipe. Coca-Cola's inventor, John S. Pemberton, kept it in a collection of formulas:

INGREDIENTS
1 oz. caffeine citrate
3 oz. citric acid
1 fl. oz. vanilla extract
1 qt. lime juice
2.5 oz. flavoring (*no further clarification here—could this be the mysterious Merchandise 7X?*)
30 lbs. sugar
4 fl. oz. powder extract of cocaine (*decocainized flavor essence of the coca leaf*)
2.5 gal. water caramel sufficient

FLAVORING
80 oil orange
40 oil cinnamon
120 oil lemon
20 oil coriander
40 oil nutmeg
40 oil neroli
Mix caffeine acid and lime juice in 1 qt. boiling water; add vanilla and flavoring when cool. Let stand for 24 hours.

How Mystique Brands Could Use the Alert Tactic:

Be On Target, Reasoned, and Pragmatic

- Answer complex questions directly, such as in bullet-point form.
- Outline clear purchase options, and explain the benefits of each.
- Carefully segment your target audience in order to be as specific as possible.

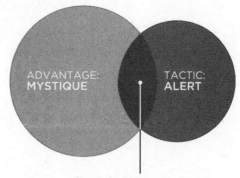

Create messages that are:
**On Target
Reasoned
Pragmatic**

Seeing a Brand "in the Flesh" (or Not)

For decades, Crayola has allowed kids to express themselves fully. Instead of dictating the game, it allows consumers to draw their own stage. Yet in one instance, it earned unwelcome attention. Years ago, Crayola had a color named "flesh." Today, happily, the same color is named "peach."

Should your brand be listening to customers, and hearing the details they need for fascination (in a good way)?

Alert Brands

HOW THEY CAN USE TACTICS

When your brand's Fascination Advantage is Alert, your brand sells by providing detailed information and by communicating what will happen if customers *don't* buy your product or order your service. Factual rather than flamboyant. But practical doesn't have to be prudish. If Alert is your brand's Advantage, you can shake things up while still being true to your core values.

Alert Is	Alert Is Not
• Clearly stating the facts	• Focusing on gut instinct to make decisions
• Delivering practical solutions	• Vague or wishy-washy
• Communicating the consequences for inaction	• "Just for fun"

The language of details can be spellbinding when it comes to messages that require promptness and practicality. Yet this form of fascination can also become so cut and dried that there's no heart and soul left. Add color and richness to your communication by applying one of the following tactics, so that you'll still apply the benefits of Alert while keeping your audience in mind.

THE ALERT ADVANTAGE
CUSTOMIZE YOUR MESSAGE BY ADDING ONE OF THE FOLLOWING TACTICS

ALERT + INNOVATION
Direct an alternative path with messages that are:
STRATEGIC ▪ FINE-TUNED ▪ JUDICIOUS

ALERT + PASSION
Keep people on track with messages that are:
CONSTRUCTIVE ▪ ORGANIZED ▪ PRACTICAL

ALERT + POWER
Incite bold action with messages that are:
DECISIVE ▪ TIRELESS ▪ FORTHRIGHT

ALERT + PRESTIGE
Focus on important details with messages that are:
PRODUCTIVE ▪ SKILLED ▪ DETAILED

ALERT + TRUST
Prompt predictable action with messages that are:
STEADFAST ▪ COMPOSED ▪ STRUCTURED

ALERT + MYSTIQUE
Reinforce specific details with messages that are:
CLEAR-CUT ▪ ACCURATE ▪ METICULOUS

Alert Advantage Pillars

All brands, regardless of their primary Advantage, benefit from reviewing their marketing communication guidelines and monitoring marketing pieces to ensure they contain the four pillars unique to their brand. Tactics will come and go, but your four pillars are constants. As a reminder, here are the four pillars for Alert:

- Sweat the small stuff.
- Create urgency.
- Define consequences and deadlines.
- Use rational facts.

The rational information in an Alert message (such as a safety report) can create an emotional bond by helping people interpret your data, so that you'll be communicating more than just dry facts. If your brand relies on an overwhelmingly rational message, the following tactics offer new ways to dial up your powers of persuasion.

How Alert Brands Could Use the Innovation Tactic:

Be Strategic, Fine-Tuned, and Judicious

- Establish a clear process for idea development, so you can replicate it.
- Find new ways to demonstrate how you improve customers' results.
- Customize every ad message to its exact target audience (e.g., by zip code or age).

Create messages that are:
Strategic
Fine-Tuned
Judicious

The Details of Creativity

If you played with Lego bricks, you know how neatly they all interlock with each other. That's not a coincidence. In an astonishing demonstration of finely tuned detail, Lego makes sure that every single brick fits neatly together with every other Lego brick *ever built*. That includes four hundred billion pieces since 1949. With their ultrastrict specifications, only eighteen bricks per million fail Lego's quality test.

When your brand speaks the language of detail, it can allow your consumer to speak the language of creativity.

How Alert Brands Could Use the Passion Tactic:

Be Constructive, Organized, and Practical

- Add visuals and colorful design to explain your research.
- Empathize with your audience's pain points.
- Offer online support throughout your purchase process.

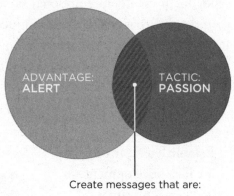

Create messages that are:
Constructive
Organized
Practical

Earlier in the book I compared vanilla and pistachio ice creams: vanilla is the lowest common denominator, and the obvious choice. Pistachio is highly desirable to a small but intense following. Let's get another scoop of fascination from Baskin-Robbins' thirty-one flavors.

The Inside Scoop

How many flavors does Baskin-Robbins offer? Yep, exactly thirty-one flavors. Or . . . maybe not. The brand has created unique flavors on special request, in honor of a famous fan, or just to connect more closely with a local palate. For example, the Shooting Star flavor is available only in South Korea, and the Red Bean and Green Tea flavors are available in Japan. ("Shooting Star" sounds so exotic, it makes pistachio sound vanilla by comparison.) You can apply this same principle. Bond with your customers by giving them personalized or locally specific versions of your product or service.

How Alert Brands Could Use the Power Tactic:

Be Decisive, Tireless, and Forthright

- Defend the company's intellectual property against copycats.
- Make decisions efficiently by focusing on the bottom line.
- Expand to new markets with a detailed export strategy.

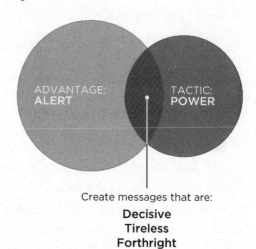

Create messages that are:
Decisive
Tireless
Forthright

Sears introduced the first replacement guarantee of its kind, for any tool bearing the Craftsman name. This new guarantee wasn't limited to one year or ten years, as other competitors offered; it was a lifetime replacement guarantee, reaching out to the edge, becoming a Power tactic.

What can your brand promise for a lifetime? The degree to which you are willing to step outside your category's norms is the degree to which you'll fascinate others.

How Alert Brands Could Use the Prestige Tactic:

Be Productive, Skilled, and Detailed

- Pay impeccable attention to detail with your products, like a watchmaker.
- Coach new team members to quickly close gaps in knowledge and skill.
- Put in the time to produce quality results. Let that midnight oil burn!

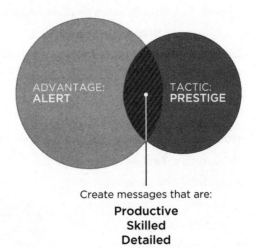

Create messages that are:
Productive
Skilled
Detailed

High Standards, Higher Heels

What happens when problem solving meets status? Egyptian butchers were among the first to wear high heels, so as to not have entrails or blood touch their feet. Your employees might not wear exotic footwear, but could you look to your past to find notable nuggets of skilled detail?

How Alert Brands Could Use the Trust Tactic:

Be Steadfast, Composed, and Structured

- Hire vendors and partners with long-term commitment.
- In difficult customer service situations, keep calm and respond logically.
- Map out a step-by-step, systematized, sustainable plan for clients.

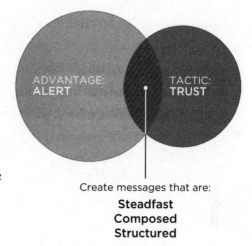

Create messages that are:
Steadfast
Composed
Structured

Even the most reputable Alert companies benefit from adding a little Trust now and then.

Decades of Details

Remember CliffsNotes from school, the "original study guide"? For CliffsNotes, getting the facts right and creating meaningful and concise guides are primary. But what good is all that content if consumers don't trust it? To elevate trust, CliffsNotes relies on its long history, and emphasizes that it is the "original—and most widely imitated—study guide." (And possibly the most plagiarized by students cramming to write a book report? No, not you—never!)

How Alert Brands Could Use the Mystique Tactic:

Be Clear-Cut, Accurate, and Meticulous

- Create ideal customer profiles to identify low-hanging fruit.
- Cross-reference results to see exactly what's working (or not).
- Don't reveal your company's strategy and next steps to outsiders.

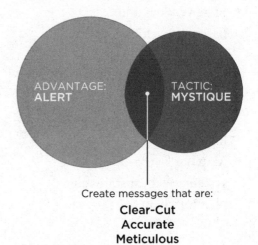

Create messages that are:
Clear-Cut
Accurate
Meticulous

Editing a book manuscript requires a tremendous use of Alert. After fact-checking and spell-checking fifty thousand words, an editor often finds everything swirled together. Here's a little trick that editors developed to help make sure that there's no missing content in the manuscript.

"TK"

In publishing, the symbol "TK" stands for "to come." As an author, I was confused by this. Why wouldn't the abbreviation be "TC"? Turns out, the letters TK are easier to spot when proofing a document, so the missing content won't remain a mystery. (Hopefully my copy editor will not remove this section, thinking that it is TK!)

Applying Multiple Tactics

The truth is, marketers can get into ruts. Our television commercials can get into ruts: we rely on winding roads to sell cars, cute animals to sell toilet paper, and ethnically nondescript families sitting around a dinner table to sell spaghetti sauce. We also get into ruts with tactics: we use Prestige to sell expensive items, Innovation to sell energy drinks, and Passion to sell perfume. It's all a bit trite, really.

Sometimes it's important to play against type, and apply unexpected tactics. In this what-if example, we'll apply a range of tactics to a small business in a highly commoditized category.

How Can a Small Business Stand Out in a Commoditized Category?

Let's say you're marketing a small neighborhood bookshop. Obviously, you'll be competing against a massive market leader: Amazon. How could you convince people to go out of their way to visit your store, pay higher prices, and forgo services such as automatic billing? By applying the tactics, of course.

What If You Used Trust as a Tactic?

Could you apply it relatively quickly, through a frequent-buyer program? Or apply it more intensively, by interacting with every customer on a first-name basis?

What If You Used Passion as a Tactic?

Your small bookshop could offer an intimate fireplace, or ergonomic reading chairs.

What If You Used Alert as a Tactic?

Alert uses consequences or a deadline to prompt fast action. You might carry a hard-to-find book, and stock just ten copies of it, giving customers a reason to shop immediately.

What If You Used Mystique as a Tactic?

Change your stock once a week, each week with a different theme, and always a surprise. One week, you might line the shelves with books about the ocean (from marine biology to *The Old Man and the Sea*), and the next you might delight consumers with a monkey-related theme (*Planet of the Apes*, *Tarzan*, and *Curious George*).

What If You Used Power as a Tactic?

Power controls the environment. A bookstore could develop its own unique system of evaluating books; for example, your store's own "100 Best Books" proprietary selection.

What If You Used Innovation as a Tactic?

Innovation entices people away from their routine behavior. Encourage customers to take one day a year to turn off the computer, stay home from work, and read their favorite new books— purchased from your shop, of course.

What If You Used Prestige as a Tactic?

Carry exclusive first editions and autographed copies. Or make your entire store accessible to a membership-only elite.

Cautionary Tale: Use Care When Switching

If you choose to alter your tactics, that's fine, but stick to your core Advantage unless you're ready for a massive overhaul. Even if you piggyback on trends, don't violate your core values.

Strolling the aisles of the grocery store, you might see a Wolfgang Puck can of soup or frozen pizza. Yet while the Wolfgang Puck brand is now in airports and strip malls, it had elite origins. Celebrity chef Puck opened his illustrious restaurant Spago in 1982, and since then, has often been credited with inventing "California cuisine." By releasing supermarket soups and airport pizzas, he shifted to a broader audience. Yet compared to other mainstream brands such as Campbell's Soup, he still retains his core Prestige Advantage, but now for a broader market.

Similarly, when the Lilly Pulitzer clothing brand offers pieces with accessible prices at Target, it brings luxury to the masses. Yet it's critical for a Prestige brand to avoid getting away without losing its core values.

On the other hand, a brand can occasionally apply a surprising tactic for an amusing twist. Ever been to Hooters? Take a closer look at the menu. The chain restaurant, whose tagline is "Delightfully tacky, yet unrefined," offers a meal package with twenty chicken wings and a bottle of Dom Perignon. (That's Prestige using the tactic of . . . um . . . orange dolphin shorts and tan pantyhose.)

At certain growth stages, messages that were once fascinating can become boring and meaningless. This might be because your audience has changed, or your category evolved, or technology leaped ahead; in any case, tactics are a means to an end and can change accordingly. As we saw, Harry Winston relied on Prestige for decades, but when new competitors emerged and the category shifted, the brand incorporated Power.

Club Med faced a similar need for change. The brand's former tagline neatly summed up a generational wild streak: "The antidote to civilization." For years, Club Med was the place to rid yourself of civilization's many irritating conventions (moderation, marital vows, etc.). Over time, Club Med fell out of sync. It refocused the brand on parents and families, adopting Prestige (attracting a laid-back international coterie) and Passion (cuisine, scenery, spa treatments). Club Med's transition is successfully complete.

Yet not all brands can switch so successfully. As we saw, when people buy a product, they're often actually paying for the *experience*. If you fail to deliver the expected experience, you could face a backlash.

When Kelly Clarkson became the first *American Idol* winner, her fans' expectations were clearly defined: she was the newly christened American pop princess, bubble gum and sparkles. But then Clarkson threw the world a curveball with her third album, *My December*. The new darker, grittier Clarkson broke her Trust core values. Songs such as "Haunted" and "Sober" were deemed "too negative" by her own label. Failing to fascinate fans, Clarkson canceled her tour due to underwhelming ticket sales, and sought new management.

Madonna, on the other hand, reinvents herself by the day; Innovation is her primary Advantage and a core value of hers. She has evolved from bad girl to street-smart eye candy to Jean Paul Gaultier couture fashion icon, and beyond.

It's good and necessary to evolve your message over time. However, changing yourself entirely and without warning might just end up creating the opposite reaction than the one you intended. Do it strategically, not randomly or as a knee-jerk reaction. Your brand belongs to your consumer.

PART IV

*How to Get Started Today
Your 5-Step Action Plan*

Cheap, Fast, or Good:
Pick Any Two

One of my favorite time-honored expressions from my days in advertising: "Cheap, fast, or good . . . pick any two." What does this mean? To explain, let's go with a food metaphor. Chipotle could be a rare example of cheap, fast, and good. It's less expensive than a sit-down restaurant, as well as speedy and delicious.

Similarly, Old Navy jeans are also cheap, fast, and good. They cost less than many other brands, they are easy to buy, and they are good quality. MINI Cooper and Timex watches are also cheap, fast, and good.

An agency can deliver two out of these three criteria, but not all three. Whether or not the clients realize it, the agency is shaping each project and relationship based on these three priorities.

Say you hire a marketing firm. What can a client expect from this rule of thumb?

Option 1: Results that are *cheap* and *fast*, but won't be as *good* as if there was a higher budget and more time.

Option 2: Results that are *fast* and *good*, but won't be *cheap*. You'll probably pay a premium for marketing fees and expensive but not necessary add-ons.

Option 3: Results that are *good* and *cheap*, but slow. The agency will take its time to do things right, and avoid cutting corners. However, it will take more time.

Sometimes brands and entrepreneurs need a deep-dive approach with intense market research, layers of departments, and a vast creative exploration process. That's where ad agencies shine.

However, there isn't always the time, or the budget, or the necessity for an elaborate marketing process. Sometimes what's needed is a smart, fast answer. Enter the Fascinate System. While not a substitute for a full-service agency, it condenses the time-honored marketing process into a streamlined and straightforward process for identifying your brand's message and key competitive advantage.

In my twenty years of working inside and around brands, I've discovered ways to identify the essence of a brand without a big learning curve. (This was a handy skill for a freelance writer, because it meant that I could fill tall orders on short deadlines.) With a bit of research and the right steps, your team can jump from start to finish. It's like a brand hack.

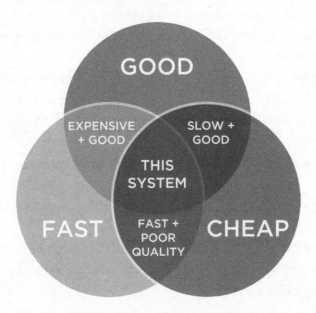

Now I want to share this system with you, so that you have a practical system that allows you to create marketing that's good, fast, and cheap (or as my mom would say, "it's not cheap—it's good value!").

A Quick Trip Down Memory Lane

In Part I of this book, we took an intimate look at both the art and science of fascination and revealed why fascination is the ultimate key to a powerful marketing message. We demonstrated how the quickly shrinking attention of prospects and customers actually *requires* that we fascinate in order to succeed. Disney World and ice cream helped make my point.

In Part II, we took an up-close and personal look at the seven Advantages—the seven different ways in which a product (or service, or person) can fascinate. We examined how each of the different modes of fascination possesses its own characteristics, speaks its own language, and yields its own mystifying results.

And in Part III, we learned about tactics—Advantages applied in a tactical way. We explored how tactics can be used to create marketing messages that achieve specific outcomes, reach targeted audiences, or solve a particular problem.

In other words, we covered a ton of ground. And now, it's time to put all this information to good use.

Introducing the Fascinate System, your fast track to a fascinating brand that is impossible to resist. I'll take you through the five steps for creating a memorable brand, and also share important insights about some of the steps (building a brand Anthem, choosing a tactic) so that you and your team can fully appreciate how the system works. And in the end, you will emerge with a fascinating brand message and a plan of attack that ultimately will allow you to win more business, retain more customers, and create a company culture that fascinates.

The Fascinate System for Brands

Your Fast Track to a Fascinating Brand

Creating a brand that is impossible to resist is as easy as following the five steps outlined below. (We will go into more detail on these steps in just a moment.)

1. Assemble your Fascinate Team.
2. Identify your brand's Fascination Advantage (by taking your free online assessment at BrandFascination.com).
3. Build a brand Anthem.
4. Apply tactics to hone your message.
5. Create a culture of fascination.

The Fascinate System for Brands

STEP 1: ASSEMBLE YOUR FASCINATE TEAM

You're ready to fascinate, but it's important to keep in mind that fascinating *brands* are born out of fascinating *people*. (If you're a one-person show, you likely already know who your Fascinate Team is.)

To assemble a Fascinate Team, look within your organization for those individuals who frequently rise to the surface as positive agents of change. Ideally, you should select an individual to represent each of the departments because while fascination is about developing a refined brand message, it's also about a unified company culture.

Individuals involved in marketing as well as the execution of the marketing message (sales, service) should be represented. And although you might not think of your receptionist as being a critical emblem of your brand, if he or she is a person who has frequent (and often the first) client contact and is also a long-term team member, your receptionist might, in fact, be a key member of the Fascinate Team. The bottom line is to have a group of individuals who work well together and have demonstrated a personal investment in the organization's success.

Prior to your Fascinate Team meeting, everyone in attendance should have familiarized themselves with the Fascinate philosophy and the seven Advantages by reading this book. (CliffsNotes not yet available.) Determine who will be the team leader—the person to work through the Fascinate System and take responsibility for completing tasks. Then set aside a morning or afternoon to begin your journey toward identifying and leveraging your brand's fascinating message.

Step One: Write down the names of your Fascinate Team members below. Assign a Team Leader to lead discussions and record the outcomes of each step (including this one!).

_____

Team Leader _____

Members _____

STEP 2:   IDENTIFY YOUR BRAND'S FASCINATION ADVANTAGE

Your brand's Advantage is the consistent voice of your communication. It shouldn't change day to day. It helps people understand what your brand stands for, and why they should build a relationship with your company, and buy your products. Focusing your marketing message around your brand Advantage is what allows you to distinguish yourself from the competition and not compete on price. Chanel can charge up to four times more for the same glasses as its competitors by leveraging Prestige. Morton's Salt can charge 187% more by promoting Trust. A packet of five gummies can be worth 1,000% more when Innovation turns it into Dinosaur Food candy.

And Now, Welcome to Your First Fascinate Team Meeting

Your initial task is taking the online assessment, the Brand Fascination Profile. This serves as an excellent team-building exercise and a jumping-off point for implementing the Fascinate System. The Team Leader is ultimately responsible for the responses, but I recommend you gather informal input from the entire group as you complete each question. (Make a note if there are questions that inspire excitement or disagreement.) After completing the assessment but before revealing your result, offer the group an opportunity to guess what language they think your brand will speak. Then (with or without drum roll) reveal your brand's Fascination Advantage to the group . . .

TIME TO DISCOVER YOUR BRAND'S FASCINATION ADVANTAGE!

Start here:
BRANDFASCINATION.COM

Every brand can become impossible to resist. How? Start by getting your **Brand Fascination Profile.** It's a fast, free guide for this book.

Share your customized results with your team and clients. Use it in marketing meetings, presentations, and social media. It's your quick guide to inspire better ideas.

GO FORTH AND FASCINATE!

#FASCINATE by @SALLYHOGSHEAD

HOWTOFASCINATE.COM   HOWTOFASCINATE
                            DISCOVERED BY SALLY HOGSHEAD

Step Two: Take the assessment and get your profile, and write your brand's Advantage below (go to <u>BrandFascination.com</u>).

_____

Our Brand's Advantage _____

| STEP 3: | BUILD YOUR BRAND ANTHEM |

(But first, a brief history of the importance of Anthems . . .)

At the highest level, Nike's brand has one focus: "Empower the athlete in all of us" (or more succinctly, "Athletic Empowerment"). This isn't a tagline, or a headline. It's a purpose. A rallying cry. It's Nike's greatest point of differentiation. This is the brand's Anthem.

In advertising, an "Anthem" describes a brand's highest value. It's the marketing version of a mission statement or a tagline, clearly explaining why people should buy this brand over others. An Anthem clearly identifies how the world sees a brand, at its best.

Your Brand Anthem

The Shortcut to Persuasion

Your Anthem is your filter, helping you decide what is "on brand" and what is "off." It's the essence of your company's communication strategy. By developing your Anthem, we're not just building a phrase; we're establishing your key competitive difference.

Once you build your Anthem, you'll have a strong, accurate and persuasive phrase to confidently describe how your company benefits your target audience.

When you can effectively articulate how you're most likely to add value, you'll attract ideal customers. This is because you'll be making it very easy for them to see why they should choose you over your competition.

In its simplest form, an Anthem is a combination of two words: *an adjective* that describes how your brand is different from competitors, and *a noun* that describes what your brand does best.

A Look at Other Brand Anthems

Let's see what an Anthem for Southwest Airlines would look like. An adjective that describes what makes it different would be "friendly." A noun that describes what it does best is "practicality." Here's how that works in the Anthem formula:

What makes it different: FRIENDLY
What it does best: PRACTICALITY
Southwest Airlines might have the Anthem "FRIENDLY
    PRACTICALITY."

With this Anthem, Southwest Airlines can make sure that every piece of marketing, from its in-flight announcements to its newspaper ads, aligns around this point of difference. Everything the brand delivers should tie back to "friendly practicality" in some way. When new employees join the company, they will have a quick filter to evaluate their corporate social media messages or customer service approach.

Brooks Brothers has a different position. An adjective that describes how it is different is "traditional." What it does best is a tightly curated set of "classics." Here's how that works in the Anthem formula:

What makes it different: TRADITIONAL
What it does best: CLASSICS
Brooks Brothers could have the Anthem "TRADITIONAL
    CLASSICS."

If a new designer at Brooks Brothers wanted to release a line of trendy shirts, that would get filtered out. On the other hand, when employees are being trained for the retail environment, the Brooks Brothers training manual could refer back to traditional, classic service.

Important note: You don't need to literally insert your brand Anthem into your marketing messages. Instead, allow your brand Anthem to guide you, and use it as a "gut check" to make sure that your marketing is aligned with your brand positioning.

Your Second Fascinate Team Meeting: Build Your Anthem

To complete Step 3, have your Fascinate Team select the adjective and noun combination that will form your brand Anthem. For inspiration turn to Appendix C for a list of adjectives based on your brand's Fascination Advantage, or revisit the five adjectives to differentiate your brand in Part II of this book. A list of nouns can be found in Appendix C.

Step Three: Select the words that will form your Anthem. Write them here:

Adjective _____

Noun _____

STEP 4: **APPLY TACTICS TO STRENGTHEN YOUR ADVANTAGE**

A tactic doesn't replace or override your overall point of view. It supports it. It targets it toward a particular opportunity, challenge, or specific goal. Individual marketing or sales messages can apply tactics to customize and make themselves more relevant. A brand will sell better, and be more valuable, when it tunes in to both the Advantage and the tactic that will be most fascinating to its target audience in a given situation.

Ask Yourself: Which Tactic to Apply?

You might be surprised to see how specific you can make your message, simply by applying a tactic.

Here's an example. Lexus is a Prestige brand, and it speaks the language of excellence. Its long-standing tagline was "The relentless pursuit of perfection."

Yet Lexus also adapts its message for different customers (for example, sports car drivers versus families with kids). And beyond building awareness, the brand also needs to get people to act quickly during a sales event, or during a new product launch. So while Lexus primarily speaks Prestige, the brand also adjusts its communication in order to get a specific outcome.

How can a brand that speaks Prestige also apply Passion, or Power, or Alert, in day-to-day communication?

If Lexus wants to heighten urgency around a weekend sale, it might run a newspaper ad applying the tactic of Alert to prompt immediate action. Or let's say that Lexus wants to tout sumptuous leather seats that envelop the passengers in rich softness. In this case, it might apply the tactic of Passion, to heighten sensory cues. And when launching a new 340 horsepower engine, it might emphasize the tactic of Power.

In all these examples, Lexus is still a luxury brand that defines itself by Prestige. However, its specific marketing messages incorporate other tactical cues.

Lexus uses Prestige as the thread that ties all of its communication together. It's how Lexus communicates most effectively, authentically, and often. Tactics, on the other hand, allow Lexus to achieve a specific purpose, such as bringing more customers into a dealership or launching a new feature.

Apply tactics to customize individual marketing pieces or sales messages, to make them more relevant.

Quick Tips for Applying Individual Tactics

Innovation Tactic

- Highlight what you're doing that's new and revolutionary.
- Use humor, even irreverence, in your communication material.
- Surprise your audience with unusual analogies, bizarre stories, or new perspectives on business.
- Create unusual marketing material. Stand out from the competition with cutting-edge design and noteworthy language.

Passion Tactic

- Be enthusiastic and adopt emotion-rich language.
- Appeal to the senses with vivid words.
- Tell stories, because stories connect and engage with your audience.
- Use strong imagery to get to the heart and soul.

Power Tactic

- Be knowledgeable; share insights and ideas your customer may not have considered.
- Stay focused; avoid rambling on and wasting time; always keep the purpose of your customer contact points in mind.
- Be confident; have a firm message, with a clearly defined game plan. Speak to the confidence you build in customers.

Prestige Tactic

- Develop top-notch marketing material, use expensive-looking paper, and pay attention to design details such as correct alignments of pictures and text.
- Ensure that your writing is impeccable; never dash off a quick email, because a spelling mistake will surely be noticed.

- Prominently display all awards, ratings, and other third-party recognition so that the brand is seen to the viewer as already highly regarded by others.
- Highlight superior product features.

Trust Tactic

- Be consistent: use the same colors, fonts, and tone of voice across communication materials.
- Use analogies, because they link something new to something your customer is already familiar with. Avoid buzzwords.
- Highlight the brand's traditions.

Mystique Tactic

- Distill all marketing messages down to their essence.
- Do not spell out every detail, in order to keep your "secret sauce" a secret.
- Avoid oversharing and overexposure. Incite curiosity.
- Maintain an unemotional tone, even in times of chaos or conflict.

Alert Tactic

- Focus on the data.
- Show consumers how you test and retest your process.
- Give a step-by-step plan of how you'll follow through on delivery.
- Outline in-depth information about one particular detail you track.
- Avoid using emotional language or imagery, and instead focus on the rational.

HOW TACTICS APPLY TO MARKETING PROBLEMS

IF YOUR PROBLEM IS	APPLY THIS	FIRST ACTION STEP
You need to compete against bigger, established category leaders	**INNOVATION** *Tactic*	Pinpoint an established norm then run in the other direction
Employees or customers feel only a lukewarm connection with you	**PASSION** *Tactic*	Communicate your messages with strong emotion and energy
You're not seen as the leader or authority	**POWER** *Tactic*	Establish decisive opinions and beliefs to become the voice of authority
You need to increase the perceived value of yourself or your products	**PRESTIGE** *Tactic*	Overdeliver in one area
Clients and teams aren't loyal to you	**TRUST** *Tactic*	Repeat and reinforce patterns, eliminate chaos and uncertainty
People aren't curious to discover your ideas and insights	**MYSTIQUE** *Tactic*	Carefully vet all communication, sharing only the minimum necessary
Your audience isn't taking fast or organized action	**ALERT** *Tactic*	Focus on negative consequences to accelerate urgency and drive action

Your Third Fascinate Team Meeting: Use a Tactic to Build a Message

You've made it to Step 4—only one more to go. To complete Step 4, have your Fascinate Team write down at least one big marketing challenge your brand is facing. (You can use the chart on page 266 for inspiration.) For example, your challenge might be promoting customer loyalty, establishing your brand as an industry leader, increasing the perceived value of your products and services, or closing out last year's inventory.

Now, select the tactic you will use to overcome this challenge.

Then build your message using your brand's Advantage and your chosen tactic. For this step, we are combining what you've done in Steps 1 through 3, to create a marketing message with a specific purpose. Remember to check this message against your Anthem to ensure that the message is still "on brand." Your messages should always sound like they are coming from *you*—not from your competitor.

Step Four: Write down your brand's Advantage and the five adjectives used to describe this Advantage. Then identify the biggest marketing challenge you currently face, and the tactic you will use to solve it. Once you've crafted a specific marketing message using your brand Advantage and your chosen tactic, add the message below.

Brand's Advantage and Adjectives _____

_____

Marketing Challenge _____

_____

Tactic _____

_____

Message _____

_____

STEP 5: CREATE A CULTURE OF FASCINATION

So far you've gathered a Fascinate Team, and with that team identified your Advantage, built an Anthem, and evaluated current (and potentially future) opportunities for applying tactics. So now what? How do you speak your fascination language and make it a part of everyday business?

Take a close look at your organization and determine what is the best way of disseminating information and getting the company to rally around a cause. Is it a company meeting, a group email, cool posters around the office? All three? The bottom line is that the Fascinate Team needs to establish an effective way to communicate with the rest of the organization what the brand's voice is, and how to best use it.

Of course you'll want to customize your message based on your existing company culture, but I recommend challenging employees to have your company's Advantage be the guiding light for all communication in the following ways:

1. All emails, proposals, and written communication should embody the brand's voice.
2. All social media should reinforce the company's Advantage. (Social media, being the easy-to-tweak medium that it is, should also be the jumping-off point for the application of any tactics.)
3. The company website's look and feel should be adapted to be consistent with the established marketing message and must *reinforce how you fascinate.*
4. As you design company materials, brochures, product packaging, office décor, and other points of customer contact, your company's Advantage must guide the process.

5. To ensure that your fascinating brand becomes not just a marketing ploy but a company-wide culture that you live and breathe, encourage all internal communication to speak your brand's language of fascination. Your Fascinate Team should lead the way.

As you bring your Fascinate Team meeting to a close, carefully review Step 5 and discuss ways to include and inspire the staff. I also recommend determining the frequency for future Fascinate Team meetings or online "check-ins" to ensure that the Fascinate System is continuing to grow with your organization. To be sure, the application of tactics will be something that continues to evolve and must respond to changing market pressures. It is key that as a team you are evaluating these opportunities and brainstorming about ways to keep your brand's fascinating message *fascinating*.

Step Five: Make a list of the ways in which you will incorporate your brand's Fascination Advantage, Anthem, and tactical marketing messages into your existing company culture. Also include ways to involve and inspire the rest of your team.

_____

_____

_____

_____

_____

_____

Go Forth and Fascinate!

That's it, you're on the way to a fascinating brand. A brand that has a specific position with tactics designed to solve a specific opportunity or challenge facing the brand.

Author's Note

The world is not changed by people who *sort of* care.

The same is true for brands. The world is not changed by brands that *sort of* care. Or that *sort of* have a message. Or that *sort of* engage and inspire.

You can do this. Your brand doesn't live inside of an agency. It doesn't live inside the products you build, the service you offer, or the office you inhabit. It lives inside you. And your customer. And your employees. Nobody can live and breathe it like you. And with this book, I hope you can bring your message to the world.

The world is changed by the companies and people with the courage to say something that matters. With this book, I hope everyone has the opportunity to do exactly that. To say something that matters.

Appendix A:
The Kelton Study of Fascination

Women will spend more to be fascinating than they spend on food. In fact, women will spend more to be fascinating than they spend on food and clothes combined. They will pay an average of $338 per month to become the most fascinating person in the room, or roughly 15% of their net income. This finding was on page 46 of the Kelton Study of Fascination, a survey conducted by the national public opinion company Kelton Research. Developed for this book, this extensive study surveyed 1,059 people in the United States.

To our knowledge, there's never been an in-depth national survey on this topic. The survey included a lengthy list of questions on the relationship between fascination and decision making: brand choices, careers, relationships, and personal self-image. Our goal was to define the role of fascination in people's lives, measure it in tangible terms, and learn more about its general themes.

- How much is fascination actually worth, in dollar amounts?
- Are people willing to pay more for fascinating products?

- In what ways do people differ in their levels of fascination (men versus women, CEOs versus college students, New Yorkers versus people in the Midwest)?
- What exactly determines if a message or product is fascinating?
- What measurable behaviors do people exhibit when fascinated?

Some answers surprised us, some didn't. On a deeper level, the numbers reveal people's vanities and insecurities, love lives and work lives, secret obsessions and public personae.

Later in this section, I'll share some of the top research findings from *How the World Sees You*.

Top-Line Findings
- People will pay a great deal of money if you can help them feel fascinating at work, on a date, or on social media. Give your customer new tools to feel fascinating, and you can charge more.
- People will spend up to 400% more for your product or service if you can build a fascinating experience. (This is the principle behind the "orange ticket" experience discussed in Part I.)
- People will go to surprising lengths to have a more fascinating life. They want to feel more engaged than they currently do, and if your brand can help them feel more involved in their life or community, they'll reward you for it.

How Can Fascination Shape Decision Making?
- If you want to measure whether you're fascinating someone: When fascinated by a product, 80% report behaving differently: doing research, talking to friends,

protecting the product, touching it, or even reporting a physical response when in contact with the item of their fascination. (If you're a marketer, track tangible behaviors to know whether your product is effectively fascinating consumers.)

- If you're interested in communicating to millennials: They are more interested in being *fascinating* than *fascinated*. (By giving them opportunities to captivate others, you open the door to higher sales or a higher price point for your brand.)

- If you're thinking about abandoning the personal touch: While the digital space offers endlessly unique experiences, 81% of us have our most fascinating conversations in person rather than online. In-person contact is still the most compelling form of communication, and it can drive deeper relationships.

- If you're thinking about hiring a celebrity spokesperson: We think of celebrities as fascinating; however, 78% of Americans are more fascinated with the lives of their families than with celebrities. (Yet as we'll see below, Americans are still bored by their own lives.)

- If you're wondering about customizing your message for different parts of the country: People respond to messages differently, based on their geography. Passion is more fascinating on the West Coast. Trust is the most fascinating Advantage in the Midwest. And in the Northeast, it's about Power. (Those lucky northeasterners also report having more fascinating lives than anyone else in the country.)

- If you want to align yourself with something that's already fascinating: An overwhelming 96% of parents find their own children fascinating.

- If you're still wondering if fascination matters for marketers: People will pay up to three times as much for a product or experience that they find "intensely captivating."

The Fascination Study at Work

Fascinating your bosses, employees, coworkers, and clients: Fascinated employees are more engaged with their work, and more loyal to their bosses and companies. Still, there's no such thing as one-size-fits-all fascination.

- Who is most fascinated by work? Those at the beginning of their careers, and those at the peak of their success. Those in their twenties are highly fascinated by their careers, as are CEOs and senior managers.
- Married employees are also likely to be "extremely fascinated at work." Maybe married employees have a greater appreciation for stability. Or maybe the singles scene makes work seem less interesting by comparison?
- A fascinating personal life is three times more important than a fascinating work life—another reason companies should support a healthy work-life balance. (Our company gives employees the day off on their birthday.)
- We're at our peak of fascination with work while in our forties. Members of this group say they become the most engrossed in their work, compared with the rest of the population. Of workers in their forties, 55% are fascinated at least once a day and sometimes more. (Replacing your more "expensive" employees with cheap young talent could end up costing more than enhancing the workplace experience for experienced players.)
- The higher you climb the corporate ladder, the more the Power Advantage becomes important. There's a

clear and steady increase in the desire to be perceived as powerful (starting at entry level to C level). People who make over $50,000 a year are twice as likely to be fascinated by Power as those who make under $50,000; if you're trying to fascinate a senior manager, reread the section about the Power Advantage.

- Lower-level employees are more fascinated by attractiveness than by power. (Among this group, appearance is more important than influence.)
- Only 9% say their bosses are "extremely fascinating." The majority of people don't find their bosses even mildly fascinating. Management training to help leaders engage and inspire their subordinates might help increase workplace morale.
- A few generational differences: Generations are fascinated differently by work, and by personal life. In order to best persuade and influence your employees' behavior, it's important not only to evaluate which Advantage to use with your groups, but also to customize messages for their age and professional level. Our priorities change throughout our careers. For instance, eighteen- to twenty-nine-year-olds think having a fascinating career is more important than having a fascinating personal life. Looking at the older set, we see a different story. C-level employees say they're more fascinated with their spouse than any other group is.
- Good news if you're hiring: People would rather be fascinating on a job interview than a first date.
- Good news if you're firing: Unemployed people think their lives are more fascinating than those who are employed.

The Role of Brands in Personal Decision Making

- If you're considering having a baby: Parents think their lives are far more fascinating than nonparents. Four in five parents become "completely engrossed" in an activity or conversation with their children at least a few times a week.
- If you're reaching out to someone: People find in-person conversations four times more fascinating than conversations online. In marketing, make sure your message doesn't just live in advertising or social media. Create opportunities for people to meet face-to-face, such as retail spaces or live events.
- If you're thinking about texting someone: It depends on his or her age. Baby boomers aren't very fascinated by their mobile devices, but for younger people their cell phones are "completely engrossing." The learning? While fascination is deeply rooted and timeless (remember the ancient Romans and the evil eye), be careful to adjust how you deliver your message, and in which media.
- If you're thinking about dishing the dirt on divorce: 82% say they're more fascinated by what keeps couples together than what breaks them apart. This could be because of the state of the country, with such a high divorce rate. And it may represent an opportunity for a brand or TV show that celebrates healthy relationships.
- If you're considering cosmetic surgery: People rated "reading books and newspapers" as making someone more fascinating than having cosmetic surgery. In addition, people would rather have a conversation with someone who's trustworthy than someone who is attractive.

- If you're considering stretching the truth: 64% of people are more interested in fact than fiction. (Embellishment also breaks the Trust Advantage. Find interesting ways to present the truth.)
- If you want to tempt people to break their rules: 60% say they'd be willing to bend morals and standards to live a more fascinating life. (For unmarried people, the figure goes up to 68%.) Midlevel managers, for instance, are less worried about telling the truth than other professionals. Now, this doesn't mean your brand should be dishonest (although people trust advertisers only slightly more than used car salesmen). It means that occasionally, people want to experience a novelty and surprise. You can do this by applying a different tactic to your Advantage, bringing refreshing novelty to your overall language.
- If you're thinking about breaking someone's trust: People rate trust in their personal relationships as most important.
- If you're nervous about taking a risk in your life: Spectacular success is more important than spectacular failure. Risks may be less risky than you think. A big success is a much bigger deal than a failure. When trying to impress the CEO, the news is even better: Among leaders, 93% find spectacular success to be more fascinating than failure.

Conclusions

A few final notes from the study:

- We're bored. We're overwhelmed with messages, but we're unsatisfied with the ones we do have. We're doing too much, but we're not fascinated by the things we are doing. All those messages and experiences aren't getting the job done. Only 40% of us found our lives fascinating in the past year.

- Most people don't feel fascinating. We feel shy about admitting that we want to be fascinating, but we do. On a personal level, we want to attract the respect and attention of others. We go to great effort and expense for products and experiences that can help us become more fascinating in the eyes of others.
- Fascination makes us feel more alive. In the presence of someone or something that fascinates us, we talk more, act more, and reconnect more. Get people to feel involved in activities, conversations, and communities.
- Consumers intensely value relationships. Relationships, especially with family, fascinate us and make us feel more engaged in general. We feel "intensely fascinated" more often while spending time with the people we love than while doing anything else.

Despite the billions of dollars spent by music companies, fashion designers, and movie directors to capture our attention, what we find most fascinating is time spent with our children and significant others.

Participants read the following opening statement at the top of the very first page of the survey:

For the purpose of this survey, we are describing fascination as an intense captivation. When something is fascinating, it captures your attention in an unusually intense way. It's more than "interesting." It distracts you from other things around you, and makes you want to pay complete attention. You might be fascinated by a favorite book, a project at work, or even a new love. Note that when something is fascinating, it is not inherently good or bad, only that it captures your full attention.

By the end of the research, it became apparent that the role fascination plays in our lives is more than that which is described above. The respondents told us that fascination is a fundamental part of our relationships and our quality of life. It affects how hard we work, whom we marry, and even how we feel about ourselves.

Appendix B:
Fast Facts about
the Advantages

Fast Facts about Innovation
- Innovation is an especially effective competitive edge for small businesses, entrepreneurs, and commoditized categories (such as mortgage and insurance).
- Innovation companies are the first to adopt new technologies.
- Innovation brands tend to generate multiple new ideas very quickly.
- Danger for Innovation: These companies often resist playing by the rules (even following deadlines).

Fast Facts about Passion
- Passion is most likely the most common language among the women in your consumer base.
- This form of communication is especially effective for products and services that aren't rational purchases (such as concert or theme park tickets), because it focuses on experience rather than rational benefits.

- Passion allows you to jump-start the "chemistry check" stage of a new business.
- Danger for Passion: Too much emotion can be seen as overly dramatic and unreliable. Add tactics such as Trust to avoid this.

Fast Facts about Power

- The use of the Power Advantage increases with rank within an organization. The higher the rank, the greater the use of Power.
- Important for women: The correlation between Power and rank is even more pronounced for women. Power is *three times* more frequent as a primary Advantage among women VPs than among women staff members.
- Danger for Power: You risk being perceived as a bully or an aggressor.

Fast Facts about Prestige

- Prestige is the most common Advantage for highly competitive organizations.
- To persuade with Prestige, you do not necessarily have to charge more or be a luxury brand, but you must unfailingly earn respect.
- Danger for Prestige: Too much superiority can alienate prospects by being perceived as arrogant, cold, or imperious—not to mention showy.

Fast Facts about Trust

- Of all seven Advantages, Trust is the hardest to earn, the most precious to hold, and the easiest to lose. Especially if your brand is not the oldest and most established.
- Trust looks to the *past*, whereas Innovation focuses on the *future*. Within teams, people whose primary

Advantage is Trust (the language of stability) often conflict with those whose primary Advantage is Innovation (the language of creativity), and often experience miscommunication with those individuals.
- Trust is most fascinating to midwesterners.
- Danger for Trust: Don't get stuck! If you do, you'll become irrelevant and outdated.

Fast Facts about Mystique
- Mystique is the least common language of marketing.
- Technology firms are six times more likely to use Mystique than marketing firms are.
- Male consumers are 30% more likely to respond to Mystique than women are.
- Danger for Mystique: If you're noncommunicative, your brand can risk being written off as uninterested, uncaring, or unsympathetic.

Fast Facts about Alert
- Alert relies on verbs for messages with action-oriented language.
- Dentists score highest in the Alert category.
- Danger for Alert: Alert brands can be perceived as the "control freaks" of their category. That's sometimes a bad thing, but perhaps a good thing when details matter!

Appendix C:
Adjectives

Specialty Adjectives for Each of the Seven Advantages

Specialty Adjectives for Innovation Brands

Surprising: Innovative brands feel at home brainstorming. If something isn't working, they reinvent their business model from the ground up, and they depart from traditional methods.

Visionary: Brands that rely on Innovation tend to be prolific idea generators. Teams behind these brands often find sudden flashes of insight, rather than carefully deliberate forever. They discover multiple paths to success to leverage their Advantage, even in a competitive market.

Entrepreneurial: These brands are always coming out with new ideas and projects. If sales start to drop, they'll try something new.

Forward Thinking: They always stay relevant. If their products and services fall behind the times, they'll do their best to give them a fresh outlook.

Bold: When the market seems to be shifting and everyone is nervous about what lies ahead, these brands drive forward and don't shy away from risk.

Specialty Adjectives for Passion Brands

Sensory: Confident and articulate, these brands communicate their ideas in a highly engaging style. When engaging with fans and customers, these companies will appeal to an audience's five senses.

Social: These brands are able to find common ground with stakeholders. They get the conversation going easily. This allows them to sense how the audience is receiving their message and adjust that message to resonate with the audience.

Expressive: Intuitive and engaging, they keep listeners interested. They share colorful examples. They tell vivid stories to explain their benefits.

Warm: Teams from these brands always have their ears to the ground. They know the issues that concern their customers and they quickly grasp how to resolve these issues.

Optimistic: These companies inspire those who follow them. They almost always find it easy to get others involved. Their excitement is contagious.

Specialty Adjectives for Power Brands

Assertive: These brands have a game-loving competitive spirit. You'll find them regularly exceeding their target goals. They like to win over competitors.

Goal Oriented: These companies appear to be intensely focused on achievements. Their drive to succeed fosters confidence in their clients and customers.

Decisive: Power brands know what they want, and they go after it without hesitation. If their audience isn't responding to their latest efforts, they can size up the situation and quickly determine a course of action.

Purposeful: As leaders in their category, these brands are often looked to for how to operate. They frequently set the standard for others to follow.

Opinionated: Companies that are high in Power generally have very strong beliefs. They are known for their candor with the public and they always follow their mission statement.

Specialty Adjectives for Prestige Brands

Ambitious: Brands with a heavy dose of Prestige set high goals and always push themselves to reach the next level of performance.

Results Oriented: They don't just want to get the job done. These companies want to excel. They never rest, because their methods and business plan can always be better.

Respected: Their impeccable presentation style earns them immediate respect from clients and fans. You'll never see these brands looking like a fish out of water.

Elite: Their audience depends on them. Their demeanor and distinguished reputation keep their customers coming back for more.

Aspirational: These brands are always focused on the company objective. They don't get distracted, because they always know exactly what they want to achieve.

Specialty Adjectives for Trust Brands

Stable: Even in a chaotic and fickle marketplace, they keep a steady demeanor. Clients depend on their sound judgment.

Dependable: These companies always appear to be on a stable and consistent path—even when the competition heats up.

Familiar: They are usually known quantities, respected for their steadfast behavior. Unlike brands that tap into Passion and Innovation, these companies choose reproducible, proven ideas rather than new, creative ones.

Comforting: In an always changing environment, Trust brands provide relief for those loyal to them. This helps their clients and customers feel free from worry or disappointment. They always know what to expect from a Trust brand.

Predictable: Trust brands develop patterns and strategies that they always follow. They typically believe that if a method or formula has worked in the past, there's no need to change it.

Specialty Adjectives for Mystique Brands

Curiosity Provoking: Brands that use Mystique are comfortable with charting their own course in the marketplace. They aren't easily swayed by the latest trend or fad. That's why they come up with new solutions while everyone else is stuck.

Calculated: These brands change course by weighing the pros and cons. They always have a game plan before trying something new.

Observant: They notice customer behavior and can tell when something is up. They spot obstacles that put their projects at risk before their competitors notice. These brands perceive subtle diversions from the standard process.

Substantive: These companies don't act impulsively. They are comfortable with their ability to make the right decisions. Thoughtful and steadfast, they rely on experience and analytical market research to make the right decision.

Private: They captivate audiences because they don't explain all the details. Everything they say to the public is carefully considered. They are always attentive and aware of their surroundings.

Specialty Adjectives for Alert Brands

Methodical: These companies typically appreciate predictability and are known to form patterns. This reduces the quantity of unknowns that they have to encounter.

Organized: They are methodical in their business plan. When deciding where to cut costs and where to move forward, they follow a systematized plan of action. It's always based on fact and not speculation.

Detailed: These companies make sure every detail of a product is correct before releasing it. They follow an ordered process to ensure the best quality. Nothing slips between the cracks.

Precise: They communicate their ideas with clarity, and respond to problems with careful reasoning.

Efficient: These brands see all the moving parts that form the bigger picture, and they keep them highly organized.

Rather than trying to constantly reinvent how your brand speaks and writes and works, you can use these words as a compass.

The goal here is to help you shape your entire communication strategy on your brand's key traits, so that you can feel relaxed and confident when you communicate.

Appendix D: Nouns

What Is Your Brand's Key Area of Performance?

Creativity

Experience

Expertise

Ideas

Insights

Problem Solving

Relationships

Reputation

Results

Standards

Thought Leadership

Vision

Profits

Goals

Management

Programs

Training

Entertainment

Trends

Techniques

Communication

Solutions

Procedures

Analysis

Principles

Leadership

Originality

Glossary

Advantage: A hardwired response in communication. There are seven Advantages: Innovation, Passion, Power, Prestige, Trust, Mystique, and Alert. In every piece of communication, whether you realize it or not, your brand uses at least one Advantage to elicit a response in the listener.

Alert: The language of details. Alert follows the rules. It persuades us by defining deadlines and details. These brands give us peace of mind, getting us to take action, in order to be safe.

Brand Advantage: The Advantage your brand most naturally uses when communicating. It's what makes your brand most persuasive and compelling. When you communicate using this Advantage, people are more likely to listen to and remember your message, because you are communicating in the way that is most natural for your brand.

Brand Anthem: The equivalent of a marketing mission statement. Though it is only comprised of two or three words, it instantly communicates how your brand is different from competitors. Your Anthem is shorthand for how your brand creates value for your customers.

Brand Fascination Profile: A fast, easy way to evaluate how your brand fascinates.

Commoditization: The threat of becoming so similar to your competition that you are no longer distinct. Once commoditized, you're in a vulnerable position, because you'll likely have to compete on price.

Competition: The threat of losing in a crowded environment in which others are competing for the same resources, recognition, or rewards.

Distraction: The threat of divided attention. Today, shortened attention spans make it increasingly difficult to capture and retain the attention of your listener.

Fascination: A state of intense focus. When you fascinate your listeners, they become completely engrossed so that they're not distracted. In this neurological state, they are more likely to listen to you, remember you, and take action.

Innovation: The language of creativity. Innovation changes the game with a new approach. It challenges assumptions, pushing people to think in new ways. Say good-bye to the status quo.

Mystique: The language of listening. Mystique reveals less than expected. It provokes questions (without giving all the answers). These brands know when to talk, and when to be quiet.

Passion: The language of relationship. Passion generates contagious excitement. Engaging, heartwarming, and inspirational, Passion elevates emotions and connects us to something bigger than ourselves.

Personal Brand: A traditional approach to packaging yourself, based on the impression you want to create. Your personal brand is based on the impression you want to project to others.

Power: The language of confidence. Power leads the way with authority. Sure and confident, it commands respect and has the track record to prove it. Power has a plan, moves with purpose, and reaches its goals. Competitors either follow, or get out of the way.

Prestige: The language of excellence. Prestige earns our attention, and respect. Whether established or up-to-the-minute, humble or high-end, Prestige communicates exclusivity, achievement, and value.

Tactic: An Advantage applied in a tactical way to achieve a specific outcome, reach a targeted audience, or solve a particular problem. Tactics combine with your brand's Advantage in distinct, predictable ways. Use tactics to create marketing or sales messages that elicit a desired response in your customer.

Trust: The language of stability. Trust delivers consistently, reliably, exactly the same way, over and over, in the safety of the tried and true. Ever dependable, it maintains expectations. Trust thrives on being loyal—and worthy of your business.

Acknowledgments

In my last book, I wrote these words:

> To become more successful, you don't have to *change* who you
> are. You have to become *more* of who you are, at your best.

For this revised edition of *Fascinate*, I might tweak it a bit:

To become more successful, this book didn't have to *change*
what it was. But it definitely had to change. After two years of re-
visions, the content became more of what it is, at its best.

If I could thank every single person who helped this book
become more of what it is, I would. You offered brilliant ideas and
input. You encouraged me when I wanted to gouge my eyes out
with a mechanical pencil. If I mentioned you all by name, it would
add another hundred pages.

Instead, I'll make this fit the nine-second attention span.

First, to my beloved Ed, and our kids.

To my dearest parents, Mutti and Big D. To Andy and Lynn,
Alex, Scott, and Max. To Nancy and Scott, and Aaron and the
twins, Millicent and Helen Clare. Love you so much.

Next, there are not enough baskets of chocolate chip cookies
to adequately thank my editor, Stephanie Hitchcock, as well as
Hollis Heimbouch and the team at HarperCollins.

Thank you to my team at How to Fascinate. I am ridiculously grateful to each of you.

To the team at SpeakersOffice, my speaking management company, for propelling this message into the world.

To Sabrina Lee, my dear editor and friend.

To my visionary clients and community. And to everyone who has participated in our research over the past ten years.

I do not thank my Microsoft Word document, which kept freezing and quitting in the final throes of the manuscript.

I definitely do thank you, my beloved reader.

Notes

Start Here

xix   national Chinese kickboxing championship: Rebecca Mead,
"Better, Faster, Stronger," *New Yorker*, September 5, 2011, http://
www.newyorker.com/magazine/2011/09/05/better-faster-stronger.

The Origin of Fascination Witchcraft

1   stones upon his chest: "The Man of Iron: Giles Corey,"
University of Missouri-Kansas City Law, accessed September
22, 2015, http://law2.umkc.edu/faculty/projects/ftrials/salem/
gilescoreypage.HTM; " 'Pressed' to Death—Giles Corey
and Fascination," GetaLegUp.Wordpress.com, October
28, 2010, https://getalegup.wordpress.com/2010/10/20/
pressed-to-death-giles-corey-and-fascination/.

1   others are powerless to resist: "Fascination," Dictionary.com,
accessed September 22, 2015, http://dictionary.reference.com/
browse/fascination.

5   which led to modern timekeeping: "Pendulum Clock," The
Galileo Project, accessed September 22, 2015, http://galileo.rice
.edu/sci/instruments/pendulum.html.

The Science of Fascination

14   fifty-six herbs, spices, and blooms: "Origins—The Very First
Jägermeister," Jagermeister.com, accessed September 22, 2015,
http://www.jagermeister.com/en-int/jaegerpedia/origins/.

15   churches around the world: "St. Hubert," NewAdvent.org,
      accessed September 22, 2015, http://www.newadvent.org/
      cathen/07507a.htm.

15   So it began: Sidney Frank, "How I Did It," *Inc.*, September 1,
      2005, http://www.inc.com/magazine/20050901/qa.html.

16   deer's blood: "The Jägermeister Legend," Jagermeister.com,
      accessed September 22, 2015, http://www.jagermeister.com/
      en-int/jaegerpedia/stags-blood/.

26   biologists Steven Gangestad and Randy Thornhill: Randy
      Thornhill and Steven W. Gangestad, "Human Facial Beauty."
      Abstract. *Human Nature* 4 (1993). doi:10.1007/BF02692201 http://
      philpapers.org/rec/THOHFB.

26   body symmetry measurements: PT Staff, "The Orgasm Wars,"
      Psychology Today (last modified May 12, 2014), https://www
      .psychologytoday.com/articles/199601/the-orgasm-wars.

26   literally smell different: A. Rikowski and K. Grammer, "Human
      Body Odour, Symmetry and Attractiveness," PubMed.gov,
      266 (1999). PMID: 10380676, http://www.ncbi.nlm.nih.gov/
      pubmed/10380676.

The Biology of Fascination

30   What he saw changed developmental psychology: Robert L.
      Fantz, "Pattern Vision in Newborn Infants," *Science*, April 19,
      1963, http://home.fau.edu/lewkowic/web/Fantz%20Infant%20
      Preference1963.pdf.

32   6% fearful and 2% angry: Toby Sterling, "Scientists Figure Out
      Why Mona Lisa Smiles," *USAToday*, December 15, 2005, http://
      usatoday30.usatoday.com/tech/science/discoveries/2005-12-15
      -mona-lisa-smile-solved_x.htm.

32   the way it makes *our voice* sound: John J. Ohala, "The Acoustic
      Origin of the Smile," Linguistics.Berkeley.edu, November 19,
      1980, http://linguistics.berkeley.edu/~ohala/papers/smile.pdf.

Fascinate the Goldfish

37 sales messages and posters: Zoe Fox, "The Evolution of Advertising: From Stone Carving to the Old Spice Guy," Mashable.com, December 26, 2011, http://mashable.com/2011/12/26/history-advertising/.

38 he reached the center: Howard Eichenbaum and Norbert J. Fortin, "Bridging the Gap between Brain and Behavior: Cognitive and Neural Mechanisms of Episodic Memory (Abstract)," US National Library of Medicine, National Institutes of Health, November 2005, http://www.ncbi.nlm.nih.gov/pmc/articles/PMC1389783/.

39 "My god, am I underwhelmed": David Pogue, "Appeal of iPad 2 Is a Matter of Emotions," *New York Times*, March 9, 2011, http://www.nytimes.com/2011/03/10/technology/personaltech/10pogue.html?_r=0.

41 "the same as a goldfish": "Turning into Digital Goldfish," BBC .co.uk, February 22, 2002, http://news.bbc.co.uk/2/hi/science/nature/1834682.stm.

41 eight seconds, or seven, or six: Consumer Insights, Microsoft Canada, "Attention Spans," ITWeb, Spring 2015, http://www.itweb.co.za/images/PDF/Microsoft_AttentionSpansResearch.pdf.

41 "swim away" like goldfish: Joshua Conran, "How to Grab Your Target's Attention in 8 Seconds (or Less)," *Inc.*, October 13, 2014, http://www.inc.com/joshua-conran/how-to-grab-your-target-s-attention-in-8-seconds-or-less.html.

The Schoolmarm and the Sorcerer

49 October 2, 2009, 9:47 am: "Florida Bar, Motel Made Famous by Serial Killer Aileen Wuornos Attracts Visitors from Across Country," *New York Daily News*, January 9, 2013, http://www.nydailynews.com/news/national/public-fascinated-serial-killer

-aileen-wuornos-article-1.1236968; James Nye, " 'Home of Ice
Cold Beer and Killer Women': Ghoulish Sightseers Flock to
Bar Where Notorious 'Monster' Serial Killer Prostitute Aileen
Wuornos Had Her Last Drink," *UK Daily Mail*, January 10,
2013, http://www.dailymail.co.uk/news/article-2259933/The
-Last-Resort-Ghoulish-sightseers-flock-bar-serial-killer-Aileen
-Wuornos-stayed--Home-ice-cold-beer-killer-women.html.

A Million Years of Personal Branding

53   a full-blown celebrity obsession: Michael R. Hyman and
      Jeremy J. Sierra, "Idolizing Sports Celebrities: A Gateway to
      Psychopathology?" New Mexico State University, 2007, http://
      business.nmsu.edu/~mhyman/M454_Articles/Idolizing_Sports_
      Celebrities.doc.

55   Mother Nature herself: Daniel Goleman, "For Man and Beast,
      Language of Love Shares Many Traits," *New York Times*,
      February 14, 1995, http://www.nytimes.com/1995/02/14/science/
      for-man-and-beast-language-of-love-shares-many-traits.html.

55   just how all women flirt: Joann Ellison Rodgers, *Sex:
      A Natural History*, 2003, http://www.amazon.com/
      Sex-Natural-Joann-Ellison-Rodgers/dp/0805072810.

56   cues about his reproductive fitness: Joann Ellison Rodgers,
      "Flirting Fascination," *Psychology Today*, January 1, 1999, https://
      www.psychologytoday.com/articles/199901/flirting-fascination.

57   *Love Sick: Love as a Mental Illness:* Frank Tallis, "Is Love a Mental
      Illness?" FrankTallis.com, http://www.franktallis.com/lovesick
      .htm.

58   risks that might otherwise seem unthinkable: Judy Dutton,
      "Love, Explained," Chemistry.com, accessed September 22, 2015,
      http://www.chemistry.com/datingadvice/LoveExplained.

58   "built to fall in love": Helen Fisher, "The Brain in Love," TED.com,
      2008, http://www.ted.com/talks/helen_fisher_studies_the_brain_
      in_love?language=en.

59   more than $100 million a year: "Al Capone Biography,"
      Biography.com, accessed September 22, 2015, http://www
      .biography.com/people/al-capone-9237536.

59   "a level never seen before": Ricardo Salinas, "Why Mexican
      Billionaire Ricardo Salinas Thinks Drugs Should Be Legalized,"
      Reuters, July 9, 2015, http://blogs.reuters.com/great-debate
      /2015/07/09/why-mexican-billionaire-ricardo-salinas-thinks
      -drugs-should-be-legalized/.

Innovation: The Language of Creativity

77   most popular and creative toys: Play-Doh: Daven Hiskey, "Play-
      Doh Was Originally Wallpaper Cleaner," TodayIFoundOut
      .com, November 12, 2011, http://www.todayifoundout.com/index
      .php/2011/11/play-doh-was-originally-wallpaper-cleaner/.

Passion: The Language of Relationship

84   "how you made them feel": Carmine Gallo, "The Maya
      Angelou Quote That Will Radically Improve Your Business,"
      Forbes.com, May 31, 2014, http://www.forbes.com/sites/
      carminegallo/2014/05/31/the-maya-angelou-quote-that-will
      -radically-improve-your-business/.

Power: The Language of Confidence

96   "in the form of a uni handroll": Katy McLaughlin, "Sushi
      Bullies," *Wall Street Journal*, October 24, 2008, http://www.wsj
      .com/articles/SB122480233710964683.

96   "what you're perceived to be by others": "Leadership Quotes,"
      Decision-Making Solutions, accessed September 22, 2015, http://
      www.decision-making-solutions.com/leadership_quotes.html.

101   "Any questions?": Associated Press, "Beyonce: I lip synced
      at Inauguration," Politico.com, January 13, 2013, http://www
      .politico.com/story/2013/01/beyonce-admits-she-lip-synced
      -at-inauguration-087017.

102   which Platt dubbed the "celebrity" monkeys: Jake Tapper,
       "Status-Conscious Monkeys Shed Light on Celeb Obsession,"
       ABC News, March 30, 2005, http://abcnews.go.com/WNT/
       WaterCooler/story?id=623557.

102   ranked number four in the Fortune 500: "Berkshire Hathaway,"
       Forbes, accessed September 22, 2015, http://fortune.com/
       fortune500/berkshire-hathaway-4/.

Prestige: The Language of Excellence

108   gave High Point University three number one rankings: "High
       Point University," *US News & World Report*, accessed September
       22, 2015, http://colleges.usnews.rankingsandreviews.com/best
       -colleges/high-point-university-2933; "Office of the President,"
       HighPoint.edu, accessed September 22, 2015, http://www
       .highpoint.edu/president/.

109   a different international cuisine each month: "1924 Prime,"
       HighPoint.edu, accessed September 22, 2015, https://1924prime
       .highpoint.edu.

113   the world's first economic bubble: Charles Mackay, *Extraordinary
       Popular Delusions and the Madness of Crowds* (Barnes & Noble,
       [1841] 2004), 73–80; "History of Tulips in Holland," Holland
       .com, accessed September 22, 2015, http://www.holland.com/us/
       tourism/article/history-of-tulips-in-holland.htm.

114   forced the entire category to realign: Tom Bruce-Gardyne,
       "Grey Goose: A Brand History." TheSpiritsBusiness.edu,
       January 8, 2015, http://www.thespiritsbusiness.com/2015/01/
       grey-goose-a-brand-history/.

114   on display as specimen 2177868.: "The Hope Diamond,"
       Smithsonian, January 2003, http://www.si.edu/encyclopedia_si/
       nmnh/hope.htm.

115   bought Jackie O's marquise: "Heritage," HarryWinston.com,
       accessed September 22, 2015, http://www.harrywinston.com/en/
       history.

115   for 64 cents postage: "Harry Winston," Macklowe Gallery,
       accessed September 22, 2015, http://www.macklowegallery
       .com/education.asp/art+nouveau/Artist+Biographies/antiques/
       Jewelry+Artists/education/Harry+Winston/id/116.

115   known as "The Deal Sweetener": Laurence S. Krashes,
       "Harry Winston: A Story Told in Diamonds," *Gems &
       Gemology*, Spring 1983, 21–29, http://www.gia.edu/cs/Satell
       ite?blobcol=gfile&blobheader=application%2Fpdf&blobhea
       dername1=Content-Disposition&blobheadername2=MDT
       -Type&blobheadername3=Content-Type&blobheadervalue1=
       attachment%3B+filename%3DHarry-Winston-A-Story-Told-in
       -Diamonds&blobheadervalue2=abinary%3B+charset%3DUTF
       -8&blobheadervalue3=application%2Funknown&blobkey=id&
       blobtable=GIA_DocumentFile&blobwhere=1355958490048&
       ssbinary=true.

118   to be buried with his paintings: Terry McCarthy, "The Last
       of the Big Spenders: Ryoei Saito Last Week: Under Arrest
       and in Deep Trouble, a Far Cry from His Coup at Christie's,"
       Independent, November 16, 1993, http://www.independent.co.uk/
       life-style/the-last-of-the-big-spender-ryoei-saito-last-week-under
       -arrest-and-in-deep-trouble-a-far-cry-from-his-coup-at-christies
       -1504552.html.

118   rough carriage rides of the time: "Why Trunks?" LouisVuitton
       .com, accessed September 22, 2015, http://us.louisvuitton.com/
       eng-us/la-maison/a-legendary-history#how-it-all-began.

118   limiting availability: Smitha Reagan, "Top 10 Things You Didn't
       Know about Louis Vuitton," LuxuryLaunches.com, March 21,
       2013, http://luxurylaunches.com/fashion/top-10-things-you-did
       -not-know-about-louis-vuitton.php.

118   the higher the price tag: Sammy Said, "Dubai Auction: Most
       Expensive License Plates in the World," TheRichest.com, April
       23, 2013, http://www.therichest.com/luxury/most-expensive/
       dubai-auction-most-expensive-license-plates-in-the-world/.

119   "alongside prestigious luxury brands": Ruth La Ferla, "When High Price Is the Allure," *New York Times*, August 9, 2007, http://www .nytimes.com/2007/08/09/fashion/09STICKER.html?oref=slogin.

Trust: The Language of Stability

122   Families gathered to watch: Jennifer M. Wood, "25 Things You Might Not Know about 'It's a Wonderful Life'," MentalFloss .com, http://mentalfloss.com/article/60792/25-things-you-might -not-know-about-its-wonderful-life.

123   the same logo since 1706: Tina Mailhot-Roberge, "Meet Twinings, the Oldest Logo Still in Use," VeoDesign .com. May 5, 2012, http://veodesign.com/2012/en/05/05/ meet-twinings-the-oldest-logo-still-in-use/.

123   for its absolute consistency: John J. Ray, "The Most Trustworthy Mid-Cap Companies," RaymondJames.com (Reprint from *Forbes*), March 27, 2008, http://www.raymondjames.com/pdfs/forbes_ most_trustworthy_companies.pdf.

123   to present the competing ad: "Our Ad Match Guarantee," WalMart.com, accessed September 22, 2015, http://corporate .walmart.com/ad-match-guarantee.

126   a present you've purchased elsewhere: Evan Hamilton, "Why Is Nordstrom Known for Their Good Customer Service?" Quora.com, May 4, 2011, https://www.quora.com/ Why-is-Nordstrom-known-for-their-good-customer-service.

126   the exposure effect: "Mere Exposure Effect," OxfordReference .com, accessed September 22, 2015, http://www.oxfordreference .com/view/10.1093/oi/authority.20110803100151249.

126   celebrities we see frequently: Kendra Cherry, "The Mere Exposure Effect," About.com, accessed September 22, 2015, http://psychology.about.com/od/socialpsychology/fl/The-Mere -Exposure-Effect.htm.

126   nuggets themselves were exactly the same: Krista Conger, "Old McDonald's Has a Hold on Kids' Taste Buds, Stanford/Packard

Study Finds," Stanford Medicine. August 6, 2007, http://med
.stanford.edu/news/all-news/2007/08/old-mcdonalds-has-a-hold
-on-kids-taste-buds-stanfordpackard-study-finds.html.

127   "an identical, unbranded nugget": Ibid.

129   so did the concerns: Jim Prevor, "Wal-Mart Needs to Take
        Lessons from Tiffany and HEB," PerishablePundit.com,
        January 12, 2007, http://www.perishablepundit.com/index
        .php?date=01/12/07&pundit=2.

130   reposition Colt 45 to hipster drinkers: Jeremy Mullman,
        "Challenge: Make Malt Liquor Look Good on Paper," Adage
        .com, January 28, 2008, http://adage.com/article/news/challenge
        -make-malt-liquor-good-paper/123367/.

130   "Good to the last drop:" Stuart Elliott, "Maxwell House, Aiming
        to Reclaim Coffee Crown, Starts Makeover," *New York Times*,
        April 13, 2014, http://www.nytimes.com/2014/04/14/business/
        media/maxwell-house-aiming-to-reclaim-coffee-crown-starts
        -makeover.html.

130   reintroduced Charlie the Tuna: Tanya Gazdik Irwin, "StarKist's
        'Charlie' Gets Makeover," MediaPost.com, January 12, 2014,
        http://www.mediapost.com/publications/article/217065/starkists
        -charlie-gets-makeover.html.

130   "All You Need Is Luvs": Chantal Todé, "In Luvs Campaign,
        'All You Need Is Love,'" *Direct Marketing News*, July 2,
        2007, http://www.dmnews.com/multichannel-marketing/
        in-luvs-campaign-all-you-need-is-love/article/96107/.

131   named "Crumbelievable": Catherine Taylor, "Kraft
        Uses 'Unbelievable' Unbelievably," AdWeek.com,
        December 2, 2005, http://www.adweek.com/adfreak/
        kraft-uses-unbelievable-unbelievably-19852.

131   dancing with a vacuum cleaner: Kara Kovalchik, "Dead
        Celebrities Brought Back to Sell Stuff," MentalFloss.com,
        January 20, 2009, http://mentalfloss.com/article/20659/
        dead-celebrities-brought-back-sell-stuff.

131   touting his microwave popcorn: Stephanie Thompson, "'Deadenbacher' Creeps Consumers but Drives Massive Traffic," AdAge.com, January 22, 2007, http://adage.com/article/news/deadenbacher-creeps-consumers-drives-massive-traffic/114434/.

131   flown to the company's St. Louis headquarters: "Budweiser Taste Testers," CNBC.com, July 2, 2008, http://video.cnbc.com/gallery/?video=787608627.

Mystique: The Language of Listening

136   wine is named 19 Crimes: "To the Banished," 19Crimes.com, accessed September 22, 2015, http://19crimes.com.

140   "it's easier to defend against it": Jeff "Happy" Shulman, email message to the author, August 2003.

142   ingredients at a third location: Alan MacNeill, "How Does KFC Manage to Keep Its 'Secret Recipe' a Secret?" Quora.com, January 30, 2013, https://www.quora.com/How-does-KFC-manage-to-keep-its-secret-recipe-a-secret.

142   how the trick is performed: John Gaughan, "Levitation Apparatus," Google.com, October 11, 1994, https://www.google.com/patents/US5354238.

143   the restaurant's main kitchen: Eddie Lin, "Behind the Scenes: The Mysterious Story of Crustacean's 'Secret Kitchen,'" *Los Angeles Magazine*, May 19, 2014, http://www.lamag.com/digestblog/behind-the-scenes-the-mysterious-story-of-crustaceans-secret-kitchen/.

146   watch out for spoiler alerts: "How It Works," LootCrate.com, accessed September 22, 2015, https://www.lootcrate.com/how_it_works.

146   banned for its obscene content: "Walt Whitman House," Wikipedia.org, accessed September 22, 2015, https://en.wikipedia.org/wiki/Walt_Whitman_House#cite_ref-12.

147   pinpointed the ideal fit: Jillian Goodman, "Cup Size Isn't Everything," FastCoDesign.com, September 9, 2014, http://

www.fastcodesign.com/3035228/innovation-by-design-2014/
cup-size-isnt-everything.

148   to the correct doorman: "Alchemy—A Speakeasy in . . .
Tallahassee," World of Deej.com, October 2012, http://www
.theworldofdeej.com/2012/10/alchemy-speakeasy-tallahassee.html.

148   year Prohibition was repealed: Rich. "What Does the '33' Mean
on the Rolling Rock Label?" Beer-FAQ.com, accessed September
22, 2015, http://www.beer-faq.com/rolling-rock-label-33/.

148   pick-me-up times of day: "History of Dr. Pepper,"
DrPepperMuseum.com, accessed September 22, 2015, http://
www.drpeppermuseum.com/about-us/history-of-dr-pepper.aspx.

149   lethal if mixed with Coke: "Death of Little Mikey," Snopes
.com, June 24, 2015, http://www.snopes.com/horrors/freakish/
poprocks.asp.

149   M&M's are an aphrodisiac: "Randy Candy," Snopes.com,
accessed September 22, 2015, http://www.snopes.com/risque/
aphrodisiacs/mandms.asp.

149   bull urine or bull testicles: Hemi Weingarten, "That Taurine
in Your Energy Drink: 10 Things to Know," Fooducate
.com, July 12, 2012, http://blog.fooducate.com/2012/07/12/
that-taurine-in-your-energy-drink-10-things-to-know/.

Alert: The Language of Details

152   approaching that of the NBA: "Fitbit," Yahoo! Finance, August
28, 2015, http://finance.yahoo.com/q?s=FIT; "The Business of
Basketball," *Forbes*, accessed September 22, 2015, http://www
.forbes.com/nba-valuations/list/.

156   to see what tested best: "Google Equates 'Design' with Endless
Testing. They're Wrong," FastCoDesign.com, accessed
September 22, 2015, http://www.fastcodesign.com/1662273/
google-equates-design-with-endless-testing-theyre-wrong.

158   need to buy now: Gilt.com, http://www.gilt.com, accessed
September 22, 2015.

159   decision making stops: Jean-François Coget, Christophe Haag, and Donald E. Gibson, "Anger and Fear in Decision-Making: The Case of Film Directors on Set," CalPoly.edu, accessed September 22, 2015, http://digitalcommons.calpoly.edu/cgi/viewcontent.cgi?article=1015&context=mgmt_fac.

160   most "distinctive" finds to its Instagram account: Sophie Forbes, "The 20 Craziest Posts from the TSA Instagram," Yahoo! Travel, April 27, 2015, https://www.yahoo.com/travel/the-20-craziest -posts-from-c1429903461024.html.

163   pet food remaining in its container: "Wellness Natural Pet Food Dash Button—Limited Release," Amazon.com, accessed September 22, 2015, http://www.amazon.com/Wellness-Natural-Food-Dash-Button/dp/B00WJ145MW.

Next Up: Tactics

169   about $100,000 per second: Dave Mosher, "Secrets of Success for Super Bowl Ads," LiveScience.com, January 31, 2008, http://www.livescience.com/9580-secrets-success-super-bowl-ads.html.

169   more sales than 250 regular commercials: Tim Arnold, "Super Bowl Ads Work (Almost Every Time)," AdWeek.com, February 4, 2011, http://www.adweek.com/news/advertising-branding/super-bowl-ads-work-almost-every-time-125654.

Innovation Brands: How They Can Use Tactics

184   "passengers who had been bumped": "Why Did Richard Branson Start an Airline?" Virgin.com, accessed September 22, 2015, http://www.virgin.com/travel/why-did-richard-branson-start-an-airline.

186   get a 100% refund: "Burn Free Guarantee," 800Razors.com, accessed September 22, 2015, https://www.800razors.com/burn-free-guarantee.

187   beer is only twenty-five cents: "Gnarly's 'Bridge Up' Beer Deal Everyday," GnarlySurfBar.com, July 2, 2012, http://gnarlysurfbar.net/gnarlys-bridge-up-beer-deal-everyday/.

189 how to print prosthetic arms: "Project Daniel," NotImpossible
.com, accessed September 22, 2015, http://notimpossible.com.

Passion Brands: How They Can Use Tactics

197 an apple off the ground: Sanford Nax and Dennis
Pollock, "Suits Against Odwalla Mount in E. coli
Case," Reprinted from the *Fresno Bee*, January 6,
1998, http://www.marlerclark.com/case_news/detail/
suits-against-odwalla-mount-in-e-coli-case.

197 a safer "flash pasteurization" method: Jessica Marati,
"Behind the Label: Odwalla Juices as Healthy as They
Claim?" Ecosalon.com, June 27, 2012, http://ecosalon.com/
behind-the-label-odwalla-juices/.

198 crowds were too large to handle: "The Brick Man," PTBarnum
.org, accessed September 22, 2015, http://www.ptbarnum.org/
humbugs.html.

Power Brands: How They Can Use Tactics

204 thousands of new customers: "We're Delivering Munch Cupcakes on
Demand," Uber.com, November 29, 2014, http://newsroom.uber.com/
jeddah/ar/2014/12/were-delivering-munch-cupcakes-on-demand/.

205 does not cater to plus-size women: "#ImNoAngel," LaneBryant
.com, accessed September 22, 2015, http://www.lanebryant.com/
content.jsp?pageName=redefine-sexy.

206 "learn more about the FBI": "Kids Page," FBI.gov, accessed
September 22, 2015, https://www.fbi.gov/fun-games/kids/kids.

207 well known for its dinosaur fossils: Ellie Walker-Arnott, "*Game
of Thrones* Comes to Dorset as Giant Dragon Skull Appears on
Beach," RadioTimes.com, July 15, 2013, http://www.radiotimes
.com/news/2013-07-15/game-of-thrones-comes-to-dorset-as
-giant-dragon-skull-appears-on-beach.

209 might suffer as a result: Jacob Ganz, "The Truth about Van
Halen and Those Brown M&Ms," NPR.org, February 14, 2012,

http://www.npr.org/sections/therecord/2012/02/14/146880432/
the-truth-about-van-halen-and-those-brown-m-ms.

Prestige Brands: How They Can Use Tactics

214   four-inch high-heeled shoes: "Fit High Heels: Cole
      Haan Nike Air," PopSugar.com, February 12, 2007,
      http://www.runningwithheels.com/index.php/2008/07/
      cole-haan-and-nike-air-fashion-fusion/.

214   sold out across the country: "Cole Haan and Nike Air—
      Fashion Fusion!" RunningWithHeels.com, July 28, 2008,
      http://www.runningwithheels.com/index.php/2008/07/
      cole-haan-and-nike-air-fashion-fusion/.

214   1965 Rolls-Royce Silver Cloud: "New Rollers Get Old Scent of
      Success," *Telegraph,* July 10, 2000, http://www.telegraph.co.uk/
      news/uknews/1347753/New-Rollers-get-old-scent-of-success.
      html.

215   towels served to tired travelers: Suzy Strutner, "Airlines
      Infuse Planes with Smells to Calm You Down (and Make
      You Love Them)," *Huffington Post,* March 25, 2015, http://
      www.huffingtonpost.com/entry/airlines-infuse-planes
      -with-smells-to-calm-you-down-and-make-you-love
      -them_551028d0e4b01b796c526510.

215   "the ultimate driving machine:" Jim Henry, "BMW Still The
      Ultimate Driving Machine, Not That It Ever Wasn't," *Forbes,*
      May 31, 2012, http://www.forbes.com/sites/jimhenry/2012/05/31/
      bmw-still-the-ultimate-driving-machine-not-that-it-ever-wasnt/.

216   problem is handled immediately: Robert Reiss, "How Ritz-
      Carlton Stays at the Top," *Forbes,* October 30, 2009, http://
      www.forbes.com/2009/10/30/simon-cooper-ritz-leadership
      -ceonetwork-hotels.html.

218   temporarily removed the word "resort": Kris Hudson, "Don't
      Use the R-Word: Hotels Find Trick to Business Bookings," *Wall*

Street Journal, January 26, 2010, http://www.wsj.com/articles/SB1
0001424052748703822404575019212570293060.

Trust Brands: How They Can Use Tactics

222 "I Gotta Feeling": "Withum, Smith + Brown," YouTube.com,
accessed September 22, 2015, https://www.youtube.com/user/
WithumVids.

222 cards and letters to their employers: "Diner Chain Has to Buy
Locks for First Holiday Closing," *New York Times*, December 20,
1988, http://www.nytimes.com/1988/12/20/us/diner-chain-has
-to-buy-locks-for-first-holiday-closing.html.

223 Arm & Hammer: Cindy Y. Hong, "Socialism, Baking Soda, and
Armie Hammer," *Slate*, November 8, 2011, http://www.slate
.com/blogs/browbeat/2011/11/08/armie_hammer_the_origin
_of_his_name.html.

224 in most northeastern marinas "History of the Flying Scot,"
FlyingScot.com, accessed September 22, 2015, http://flyingscot
.com/history.html.

225 identify their own tech expertise before they receive an answer:
"Dreamhost Review: Why We Recommend Dreamhost,"
CheapWebHostingReport.com, accessed September 22, 2015,
http://www.cheapwebhostingreport.com/content/dreamhost
-review-why-we-recommend-dreamhost; "DreamHost Survey
Reveals a Horde of Web Professionals," Dreamhost.com,
accessed September 22, 2015, https://www.dreamhost.com/press/
dreamhost-survey-reveals-a-horde-of-web-professionals/.

226 inside its financial documents: "Ally Bank Kicks the Asterisks in
New Campaign," Ally.com, May 19, 2009, https://media.ally.com/
index.php?s=20295&item=122684.

Mystique Brands: How They Can Use Tactics

234 buying with confidence until it arrives: "What Is Birchbox?"

Birchbox.com, accessed September 22, 2015, https://www
.birchbox.com/about/birchbox.

236   who turned the Coke employees in to the feds? Pepsi: "3 Arrested
       in Coca-Cola Trade Secret Scheme," CNN Money, July 5, 2006,
       http://money.cnn.com/2006/07/05/news/companies/coke_pepsi/.

237   the same color is named "peach": "5 Times Crayola Fired Their
       Crayons," MentalFloss.com. August 1, 2009, http://mentalfloss
       .com/article/22405/5-times-crayola-fired-their-crayons.

Alert Brands: How They Can Use Tactics

243   versions of your product or service: "Fun Facts," BaskinRobbins
       .com, accessed September 22, 2015, https://www.baskinrobbins
       .com/content/baskinrobbins/en/funfacts.html.

243   bearing the Craftsman name: "Warranty Information,"
       Craftsman.com, accessed September 22, 2015, http://www
       .craftsman.com/en_us/customer-care/warranty-information.html.

244   blood touch their feet: "Origins of High Heels," Weebly.com,
       accessed September 22, 2015, http://history-of-heels.weebly.com/
       origins-of-high-heels.html.

245   creating meaningful and concise guides are primary: "About
       CliffsNotes," CliffsNotes.com, accessed September 22, 2015,
       http://www.cliffsnotes.com/discover-about.

Applying Multiple Tactics

249   for a broader market: "Gourmet Foods," WolfgangPuck.com,
       accessed September 22, 2015, http://www.wolfgangpuck.com/
       shop/Gourmet-Foods.

249   wings and a bottle of Dom Perignon: "Best White-Trash
       Bargain Gourmet Dinner," SFWeekly.com, accessed
       September 22, 2015, http://www.sfweekly.com/sanfrancisco/
       best-white-trash-bargain-gourmet-dinner/BestOf?oid=2202515.

250   transition is successfully complete: "All Inclusive Family
       vacations," ClubMed.com, accessed September 22, 2015, http://

www.clubmed.us/cm/all-inclusive-family-vacations_p-115-l-US
-pa-SELECTIONS_ENFANTS_115US-ac-ps.html.

250 Clarkson broke her Trust core values: Nekesa Mumbi Moody,
      "Drama Accompanies New Clarkson Album," *Washington Post*,
      June 27, 2007, http://www.washingtonpost.com/wp-dyn/content/
      article/2007/06/27/AR2007062701543.html.

The Fascinate System for Brands

263 "relentless pursuit of perfection": "About Lexus," Lexus
      .com, accessed September 22, 2015, http://www.lexus.com/
      search?q=pursuit+of+perfection.

Index

About the Author

Sally Hogshead became the most award-winning copywriter in the United States by age twenty-four. Her campaigns for brands such as MINI Cooper, Nike, and Coca-Cola have fascinated millions of consumers.

To develop the science of fascination, Hogshead measured 700,000 people over the course of a decade. Using this research, she built a practical marketing system that now lives inside organizations such as IBM, Twitter, and the YMCA, as well as thousands of small businesses.

Hogshead has been named one of the top ten brand gurus in the world, and has been inducted into the CPAE National Speaker Hall of Fame. Her previous book *How the World Sees You* was a number one *Wall Street Journal* bestseller.

She lives in Orlando, Florida, with her husband and kids (and a dog named Bacon).

THE BRAND FASCINATION SYSTEM

ADVANTAGE + TACTIC = **YOUR MESSAGE**

BOLD,
ARTISTIC,
UNORTHODOX

PIONEERING,
IRREVERENT,
ENTREPRENEURIAL

ELITE,
CUTTING-EDGE,
PROGRESSIVE

FLEXIBLE,
DELIBERATE,
THOUGHTFUL

ADEPT,
CLEVER,
CONTEMPORARY

PROLIFIC,
THOROUGH,
DILIGENT

SOCIAL,
ENERGIZING,
OUT OF THE BOX

DYNAMIC,
INCLUSIVE,
ENGAGING

STYLISH,
EXPRESSIVE,
EMO. INTELLIGENT

LOYAL,
SINCERE,
NURTURING

DISCERNING,
PERCEPTIVE,
CONSIDERATE

ATTENTIVE,
DEDICATED,
EFFICIENT

INVENTIVE,
UNTRADITIONAL,
SELF-PROPELLED

SPIRITED,
MOTIVATING,
COMPELLING

AMBITIOUS,
FOCUSED,
CONFIDENT

PROMINENT,
GENUINE,
SURE-FOOTED

INTENSE,
METHODICAL,
SELF-RELIANT

PROACTIVE,
CAUTIONARY,
STRONG WILLED

ORIGINAL,
ENTERPRISING,
FWD-THINKING

INSIGHTFUL,
DISTINGUISHED,
IN THE KNOW

RESPECTED,
COMPETITIVE,
RESULTS ORIENTED

CLASSIC,
ESTABLISHED,
BEST IN CLASS

SKILLFUL,
RESTRAINED,
POLISHED

DISCIPLINED,
SYSTEMATIC,
INTELLECTUAL

CURIOUS,
ADAPTABLE,
OPEN-MINDED

DEPENDABLE,
TRUSTWORTHY,
APPROACHABLE

STABLE,
DIGNIFIED,
HARDWORKING

SUBTLE,
CAPABLE,
LEVELHEADED

ANALYTICAL,
PROTECTIVE,
PURPOSEFUL

PREPARED,
PRINCIPLED,
CONSCIENTIOUS

NIMBLE,
UNASSUMING,
INDEPENDENT

TACTFUL,
MINDFUL,
SELF-SUFFICIENT

REALISTIC,
INTENTIONAL,
TO THE POINT

ASTUTE,
ELEGANT,
DISCREET

ASSURED,
UNRUFFLED,
OBSERVANT

ON TARGET,
REASONED,
PRAGMATIC

JUDICIOUS,
STRATEGIC,
FINE-TUNED

PRACTICAL,
ORGANIZED,
CONSTRUCTIVE,

DECISIVE,
TIRELESS,
FORTHRIGHT

SKILLED,
DETAILED,
PRODUCTIVE

STEADFAST,
COMPOSED,
STRUCTURED

ACCURATE,
CLEAR-CUT,
METICULOUS